FDR and the Creation of the U.N.

FDR

and the Creation of the U.N.

Townsend Hoopes
and Douglas Brinkley

Yale University Press   New Haven and London

Printed in the United States of America

Library of Congress Cataloging-in-Publication Data
Hoopes, Townsend, 1922–
FDR and the creation of the U.N. / Townsend
Hoopes and Douglas Brinkley.
p.   cm.
Includes bibliographical references and index.
ISBN 0-300-06930-8 (cloth : alk. paper)
1. United Nations—History.   2. United Nations—
United States—History.   3. Roosevelt, Franklin D.
(Franklin Delano), 1882–1945.   4. United States—
Foreign relations—1933–1945.   I. Brinkley,
Douglas.   II. Title.
JX1976.H66   1997   96-35272 CIP
341.23'09—dc20

A catalogue record for this book is available from
the British Library.

The paper in this book meets the guidelines for permanence
and durability of the Committee on Production Guidelines for
*Book Longevity of the Council on Library Resources.

10   9   8   7   6   5   4   3   2   1

To Ann and Tammy

Contents

Preface

The United Nations is the embodiment of the second great effort in this century to organize the international community for the prevention of further global wars. The first such effort brought forth the League of Nations in 1920. But a mere sixteen years later, the League had ceased to exist as a serious factor in world affairs. The League Covenant, largely devised by U.S. President Woodrow Wilson, depended heavily on moral condemnation as a remedy for armed aggression, and further hampered collective action by a rule requiring unanimous agreement of the parties to the dispute. But the League's failure was also attributable to major factors beyond its control, especially the repressive conditions of the Versailles Treaty, which led to Hitler and German revanchism, the feckless policies of Britain and France, and the rigid isolationism of the United States, which refused to join or effectively support the League. These weaknesses and failures were mutually reinforcing, and led directly to the political earthquake of World War II.

The United Nations Charter was forged largely by the initiative and determination of another American President. But because Franklin D. Roosevelt was a disenchanted Wilsonian and a believer in realpolitik, the new organization emerged in 1945 primarily as an extension of the wartime alliance comprising the United States, Great Britain, the Soviet Union, and pre-Communist China. Dominated by these Big Four powers and focused on their determination to use power to reform aggressors and restore a wartorn world, the United Nations was from the outset less attuned to dependence on moral sanctions and more rooted in realities of the balance of power. Notwithstanding the early and fundamental postwar break between the Western democracies and the Communist bloc—that tense forty-five-year power struggle known as the Cold War—the United Nations has proven to be a far more durable, resilient, and useful institution than its predecessor. Despite the weaknesses inherent in any confederation of nation states—each insistent on its sovereign rights—the United Nations has managed to survive for more than fifty years, and has made significant contributions to the political stability, economic development, and physical well-being of mankind.

With the ending of the Cold War, the focus of world attention has shifted away from that consuming superpower confrontation and once more toward the possibilities of realizing a world of greater stability and less international tension through an effective collective security system. Concurrently the United States is engaged in a controversial debate about the future role of the United Nations in world affairs, and specifically about the place of the U.N. in the development and conduct of U.S. foreign policy. It is our impression that much of the discussion lacks historical perspective. Because this book is the first to tell the full story of how the United Nations organization was conceived, planned, argued, revised, and ultimately endorsed by the community of nations, we are hopeful that its specific focus will contribute to the debate. We hope that it will enlighten people from all nations, while reminding Americans of how deeply, and under what circumstances, their own country was involved in the creation of the United Nations, and of the decisive role played by Franklin D. Roosevelt.

We are equally hopeful that a wider and deeper appreciation of the realities involved in the process of bringing this grand experiment into being will lead to the development of more reasoned, more consistent American support for an instrumentality which, despite inherent inefficiencies, still uniquely embodies the highest hopes of humankind.

Acknowledgments

In writing this book, we have drawn heavily on a handful of superb historical narratives related to Franklin Roosevelt's internationalism, especially *Second Chance: The Triumph of Internationalism in American Policy During World War II* by Robert Divine; *Franklin D. Roosevelt and American Foreign Policy, 1923–1945* by Robert Dallek; *Roosevelt: The Soldier of Fortune* by James McGregor Burns; *Secret Affairs* by Irwin Gellman; and *Dumbarton Oaks: The Origins of the United Nations and the Search for Postwar Security* by Robert C. Hilderbrand. Another much consulted source was Ruth B. Russell's encyclopedic *History of the United Nations Charter: The Role of the United States, 1940–1945*.

We are additionally indebted to Messrs. Divine and Dallek, Stephen Ambrose, and Warren Kimball for their willingness to read the manuscript and give us the benefit of their informed judgments. Their valuable insights enriched the text. Stephen Schlesinger generously shared his thoughts on the 1945 San Francisco Conference, which is the subject of his current work in progress. Verne Newton, director of the Franklin D. Roosevelt Library, and his head archivist, John Ferris, made helpful comments on portions of the manuscript and helped us to locate important documents and photographs. Ambassador William vanden Heuvel, president of both the United Nations Association and the Franklin and Eleanor Roosevelt Institute, was a source of strong and warm encouragement throughout.

We are grateful to the research staffs at the Library of Congress, the National Archives, the Harry S. Truman Library, the Woodrow Wilson House, the Eisenhower Center for American Studies at the University of New Orleans, and the Alderman Library at the University of Virginia for helping us to find important primary and secondary documents and a wide range of photographs.

We owe a special thanks to Benjamin Welles, a former *New York Times* foreign correspondent, who graciously allowed us to read and quote from his unpublished biography of his father, Sumner Welles.

Charles Grench, editor-in-chief of Yale University Press, and assistant editor Otto Bohlman were enthusiastic and cooperative supporters throughout the publishing process. Noreen O'Connor did a superb job of copyediting the manuscript, and Joyce Ippolito performed admirably as production editor.

Finally, and closer to home, the warm presence, enthusiasm, and patient forbearance of our respective better halves, Ann Hoopes and Tammy Cimalore, greatly eased the task of bringing this book to life.

1

The Ghost of Woodrow Wilson

As the United States was being drawn inexorably into the maelstrom of World War II, the ghost of Woodrow Wilson was in the mind of every person and institution, public or private, who set out to think about, plan for, or create a new system of world security to ensure peace and stability in the postwar period, when the guns would once again fall silent after the democratic victory. Although by no means assured until perhaps late 1943, victory was a necessary article of faith for all who struggled to preserve civilization against the darkest forces of tyranny in modern history.[1]

Many continued to believe that Wilson's ideals remained a body of profound political wisdom that could still light the true path for humankind, despite the undeniable failure of the League of Nations and the onset once more of bloody global war. This was the implicit conviction in Wendell Willkie's best-selling 1943 book, *One World,* as well as the principal theme of the 1944 film *Wilson,* produced by Darryl F. Zanuck.[2] Also in 1944, Sumner Welles, who had resigned as Under Secretary of State just a year before, wrote that it was time to reaffirm the Wilsonian ideals, which had thrilled his generation "to the depths of our intellectual and emotional being" and whose realization was "well within human capacity."[3]

But many others concluded that Wilson's high principles amounted to a moral code which humans could never live up to, and which thus led the world into dangerous

1

delusions of what was possible. Also in 1944, the eminent editor, scholar, and political columnist Walter Lippmann wrote that Wilson's "supreme spiritual error" lay in "forgetting that we are men and thinking that we are gods. We are not gods. . . . We are mere mortals with limited power and little universal wisdom."[4] To President Roosevelt and the other leaders of World War II fell the hard task of searching anew for some workable solution to the human race's most besetting problem—recurrent, ever more destructive wars.

Wilson's Tragic Rigidity

The Senate's rejection of the League of Nations treaty on March 19, 1920, was a result of many factors, of which perhaps the most basic was the enduring American fear and contempt for Europe's continual intrigues and wars. As most Americans saw it, they had sent their young men to France in 1917 to fight and die for a worthy cause—"to make the world safe for democracy." But they had recoiled in disgust and disbelief at the spectacle of greed displayed by the European victors and embodied in the vengeful Treaty of Versailles. More direct and immediate reasons for the Senate's rejection of the League were the personal bitterness between President Wilson and Senator Henry Cabot Lodge (R-Massachusetts), chairman of the Senate Foreign Relations Committee, and the misplaced loyalty of the Democratic Senators to their party leader in the White House. The primary cause of failure, however, was the absolute rigidity, rooted in moral and intellectual arrogance, of Woodrow Wilson.[5]

Wilson had arrived at Brest on December 13, 1918, to overwhelming acclaim and adulation. Frenzied, cheering crowds welcomed him in every European country. It was said of him that "no such evangel of peace had appeared since Christ preached the Sermon on the Mount . . . that only Augustus nineteen centuries before had such an opportunity to create a new world."[6] In the peace conference at Paris, however, his high-flown idealism met and was forced to accommodate the hard realities of age-old feuds, territorial disputes, and the European victors' utter determination for revenge against the evil Germans who had cost them so much blood and treasure. But if he was forced to swallow the corrosive Versailles Treaty, he believed that all could be redeemed by the Covenant of the League of Nations, which was his creation and which he had sold to the statesmen of Europe.

President Woodrow Wilson in Paris, early 1919. (National
Trust for Historic Preservation, Woodrow Wilson House)

Pale and tired, but confident that he could raise American awareness to
the height of his own vision, he returned home on July 8, 1919, determined
to obtain quick Senate ratification of the League treaty. But his laying of the
political groundwork for Senate approval had been negligent, even offensive.
In 1918, he had asked the American people to give him a Congress dominated
by his own party, but the voters had returned Republican majorities to both
houses. Ignoring this political fact, he had included no Republicans of stature
in the U.S. delegation to Paris, implying that he did not consider the GOP to
be a factor in the peace-making. In Paris, he consulted only with himself,
treating even politicians of his own party with suspicion and thinly disguised
disdain. All of this provoked anger and distrust on Capitol Hill.[7]

On July 10, 1919, Wilson went before the Senate to present the League
treaty. His manner was not ingratiating. To his listeners, he was "the school-

master incarnate raised to unthinkable heights from which he flung down not requests but dictates." He seemed to be saying to the Senators that "as he had redone the world, so now it was their duty to approve his work and then be gone." In the press gallery, a journalist named Henry L. Stoddard thought to himself that "below stood a being utterly suffused with arrogance." In April, Wilson had announced that the European governments had accepted several amendments to the League treaty to accommodate American critics. He considered these appropriate but would go no further. He wanted the treaty ratified as presented, without a single further amendment. To the affronted United States Senate, he seemed to be asking for a rubber stamp.[8]

The changes accepted by the Europeans did not go far enough for the Republicans. The heart of the problem was Article 10, which they read as automatically committing each League member to guarantee the territory and independence of all nations. This was an extreme interpretation, given the unanimity rule in the League Council (which would permit the United States to veto any proposed action), but a distrustful Senate wanted tangible safeguards. Some thoughtful Republicans were seeking a workable compromise. Elihu Root, a distinguished former Secretary of State, proposed that the United States exempt itself from the presumption of an automatic commitment under Article 10. Senator Lodge put forward several additional reservations, the most important of which was to require prior congressional approval for the deployment of American armed forces abroad. This requirement was not inconsistent with the exclusive constitutional power of Congress to declare war, but it chose to ignore similar presidential powers to conduct foreign policy and implement U.S. treaty obligations.

A growing number of devoted internationalists, both in the government and outside it, understood the partisan political realities as well as the constitutional ambiguities and were prepared to support the Lodge reservations. For them, the moral and strategic imperative was for the United States, the most powerful and prestigious democracy, to join the League. They were confident that time and experience would show that a number of the commonly expressed fears were exaggerated. It appeared that a majority of the American people and nearly 80 percent of the Senate supported the central idea of collective security to prevent future wars.[9]

A Failed Crusade and a Cover-Up

Wilson's political advisers persuaded him to confer with a number of Senators during the summer, but these talks only confirmed the political fact that he did not have enough votes to ratify the treaty without further amendments. Frustrated, but obsessive about protecting the purity of his League Covenant, Wilson decided that he must go over the heads of the politicians and "take the issue to the people." In early September he embarked on a grueling railroad campaign through all but four of the states west of the Mississippi. In deciding to undertake this trip, he acted against the advice of his doctors, who were worried that he could not stand the strain of traveling 9,800 miles between the Canadian and Mexican borders in a jarring railway coach, making twenty-six major stops and giving ten rear-platform speeches every day. They worried especially about his ability to withstand the intense late summer dust and heat in places like the Badlands of South Dakota and the Great Salt Desert. One of Wilson's closest political aides, Joseph Tumulty, later wrote, "It needed not the trained eye of a physician to see that the man . . . was on the verge of a nervous breakdown," and he warned the President of the possibly "disastrous consequences" of making the trip.[10] Wilson replied that he could not place his personal safety before his duty. He seemed prepared for martyrdom: "I don't care if I die the next minute after the treaty is ratified," he told a friendly journalist, who predicted that he would break down before he reached the Rockies.[11]

His doctors were proved painfully right. Plagued by excruciating headaches throughout the trip, the President, previously a compelling orator, began slurring his words and losing the thread of his argument. On September 25, after a speech in Pueblo, Colorado, he suffered a mild stroke and was forced to cancel all further plans and return to Washington. Back in the White House, a second, far more serious stroke on October 1 paralyzed his entire left side. For several days he could not speak. His condition raised the urgent question of his capacity to perform his constitutional duties. But his inner circle, dominated by his doctor, Admiral Cary Grayson, and his second wife, Edith Galt Wilson, then organized perhaps the most complete and sustained cover-up in the history of the American presidency. Refusing to disclose the nature of the President's illness or to acknowledge any incapacity, they formed an impenetrable defense of his sickroom and issued vague, reassuring medical bulletins, while all but the most routine and perfunctory business of government ground slowly to a halt.[12]

After six weeks, a slightly recovered Woodrow Wilson received Senator Gilbert Hitchcock (D-Nebraska), the minority leader, on November 18. Hitchcock informed him that a vote on the League treaty was imminent, and defeat unavoidable without compromise. Hitchcock said that all of the prominent men who had been with the President in Paris—Herbert Hoover, Bernard Baruch, Secretary of State Robert Lansing, even his closest political adviser, Colonel Edward Mandell House—were for acceptance of the Lodge reservations. But Wilson's rigidity and political purblindness had been, if anything, intensified by his physical affliction. "I have no moral right to accept any change in a paper I have already signed," he said. Then he dictated a brief letter, taken down in longhand by Edith Wilson and handed to the Senator; it said, "I hope all true friends of the treaty will refuse to support the Lodge reservations." He asked Hitchcock to convey this message to all the Democratic Senators.[13]

The next day, Hitchcock, who lacked any conspicuous qualities of leadership, read the letter to the Democratic caucus, and fatefully they all agreed to follow the wishes of their President. Accordingly, that same afternoon, Democratic votes ensured the defeat of a motion for American entry into the League with the Lodge reservations. The margin of defeat was increased by the votes of a handful of "Irreconcilables," extreme isolationists who were opposed to U.S. participation under any circumstances. A few minutes later, in a following vote, the same extremists joined with Lodge and the other reservationists to defeat a motion calling for U.S. entry without the reservations.[14]

The public outcry at this rejection was surprisingly strong, and the intensity of the continuing national debate on the treaty suggested that the Senate might reconsider the matter. The White House received hundreds of appeals to accept the reservations, but they never reached the President; they were ignored or left unopened by the palace guard, of which Edith Wilson had become the undisputed captain. She was not concerned with public issues, but only with her husband's health. His views were her views and his wishes were her commands.[15]

A Mind Unhinged

The President remained in extremely precarious health, and his actions gave increasing indication of a distinctly unbalanced mind. Lord Grey, who had left Washington after waiting in vain for four months to penetrate Wilson's sickroom and present his credentials as the British Ambassador, wrote a letter to the *London Times* on January 31, 1920, expressing the growing apprehension in Europe that the United States might not come into the League. His letter emphasized the vital importance of American participation and dismissed the reservations as essentially innocuous and unobjectionable. Edith Wilson carried the letter, which was reprinted in the *New York Times* on February 1, to the President's sickroom and came out with a statement he had dictated and she had written down in her childish scrawl: "Had Lord Grey ventured upon any such utterance while he was still at Washington as Ambassador, his government would have been promptly asked to withdraw him."

In February 1920, Wilson suddenly wrote to his Secretary of State who, with the knowledge of the palace guard, and indeed of the press and the general public, had been holding regular Cabinet meetings since October to keep the wheels of government turning at least in routine orbits. In the letter he asked, "Is it as true, as I have been told," that Lansing had been holding these Cabinet meetings? An astonished Lansing replied that of course it was true, and that the meetings were prompted by a general agreement among Cabinet members that, being denied communication with the President, it was "wise for us to confer informally together." Wilson wrote back demanding Lansing's immediate resignation for an unjustified "assumption of Presidential authority." Lansing resigned and released the exchange of letters to the press, which led to the venting of serious questions about the President's mental state and the honesty of the medical bulletins issued by the White House. "It is unthinkable that a sane man would offer any objection to the department heads getting together," said the *Worcester* (Mass.) *Evening Gazette*. A *Los Angeles Times* headline read, "Wilson's Last Mad Act." The "act" was almost certainly triggered by Wilson's remembering that Lansing supported the Lodge reservations.[16]

In a last-ditch effort to save the League treaty from all but certain death, the President's liaison man in Paris, Ray Stannard Baker, returned to Washington, and was finally allowed to see Wilson in early March. He pleaded passionately for the reservations, appealing to the need to put first things first, but his arguments fell on deaf ears: "If I accept them, these Senators will merely offer new ones, even more humiliating. . . . These evil men intend to destroy the League."[17]

The end came on a second and final Senate vote, on March 19, 1920. This time twenty-one Democratic Senators disobeyed the President and voted to accept the Covenant with the Lodge reservations. But the tally fell seven votes short of the two-thirds required to ratify a treaty. If only seven more Democrats had mustered the courage to defy their President's self-destructive stance, the United States would have become a member of the League of Nations.[18]

The Impact

The refusal of the United States to join the League was without question a major cause of the League's weakness from the outset. The added weight of the world's largest democracy would, at the very least, have reassured and lent courage to Britain and France. But it is by no means certain that U.S. participation would have prevented Hitler's coming to power, the progressive erosion of international stability during the 1930s, or the ultimate cataclysm of World War II. Woodrow Wilson's conviction that the mere presence of the United States on the League Council would be a decisive deterrent to future wars rested on the assumption that Congress and public opinion would, owing to the simple fact of U.S. membership, support strong and consistent policies to deter or punish aggression—backed by active diplomacy, economic and political sanctions, and if necessary by overwhelming military force.

That is a very large assumption. It tends to dismiss, or heavily discount, Americans' historic sense of separateness and their enduring instinct to avoid foreign entanglements—an instinct that in 1920 still pervaded hundreds of small towns "where the paving ended at the limits where the trolley made its turn-around . . . and Europe was strange, foreign, different—bad."[19]

It is also an assumption undermined by what then happened in American life: a decisive inward turning, and the successive election of three Republicans—Warren G. Harding in 1920, Calvin Coolidge in 1924, and Herbert Hoover in 1928—whose common denominator was narrow isolationism. There was also Congress's steady refusal—heedless or deliberate—to fund the armed forces above a starvation level. Would Senate ratification have suddenly and decisively transformed the main currents of American life and greatly enlarged the nation's political willingness to take a major part in shaping world events between 1920 and 1940? It is and will remain a question with no certain answer, but the burden of proof is on the supporters of Woodrow Wilson's idealism.

Wilson himself, although his vision of American leadership of the League was shattered, stayed on in the White House through the 1920 election, in which the Republican, Harding, defeated the Democratic nominee, James M. Cox. Still weak and frail, Wilson accompanied Harding to the inauguration in March 1921 and lived as a private citizen in Washington until his death in 1924.

Franklin Roosevelt and the League

As the Democratic vice presidential nominee in 1920, Franklin Roosevelt made more than eight hundred speeches in support of the League of Nations.[20] But in contrast to Wilson, who had emphasized the idealism of the League idea, Roosevelt argued for it in terms of "practical necessity." He told audiences at campaign rallies that if the United States did not join the League, it "would degenerate into a new Holy Alliance" dominated by the European states. Nor did he share Wilson's uncompromising attitude toward the Covenant text, but was open to commonsense amendments if these were needed to make it politically palatable to the U.S. Senate. He repeatedly argued that it was important not to "dissect the document," but to "approve the general plan."[21]

During the following two decades, however, even Roosevelt's qualified enthusiasm for the organization and its relevancy steadily cooled to a point which intimates described as "glacial."[22] He was disgusted by the ways in which France and Britain consistently blocked the League's efforts to respond effectively to aggression and used the League as an instrument of their own myopic, self-destructive policies. But he also came to believe that the organization's inherent structure and its rules of procedure were grossly inadequate to the basic task of safeguarding peace and preventing war.

The Covenant of the League was mainly the creation of Woodrow Wilson and reflected a soaring idealism rooted in the philosophical premise that there could and must be genuine equality in relations among the sovereign nations of the world. It provided for: an Assembly, composed of representatives from all member nations, with each member having one vote; a Council, composed of one permanent representative from the United States, Britain, France, Italy, and Japan (known as the Principal Allied and Associated Powers), plus four nonpermanent members to be elected by the Assembly; and a Permanent Secretariat.[23]

League members were obligated by the Covenant's preamble "not to resort to war" and to conduct "open, just and honorable relations" with all other nations. Great emphasis was placed on the peaceful arbitration of disputes and, after 1924, on the referral of contentious issues to the new Permanent Court of International Justice, located at the Hague. But League members were obligated to preserve "the territorial integrity and political independence" of all nations, whether League members or not, against "external aggression," and it was the duty of the Council to "advise upon the means by which this obligation shall be fulfilled" (this was the controversial Article 10). If negotiation and arbitration failed to resolve an international problem, and a member nation resorted to war in disregard of the Covenant, it would be deemed an act of war against all League members, who would immediately impose financial and trade sanctions. If such sanctions proved insufficient to halt the aggression, it would be the duty of the Council to recommend that member governments contribute effective army, naval, or air forces to carry out "enforcement by common action of international obligations."

This sounded like an impressive armory of collective responses, but a fatal weakness lay in the unanimity rule, which flowed directly from Wilson's belief in the necessity for the sovereign equality of member nations. The Council could therefore respond to situations of external aggression only by unanimous decision (Article 5). Moreover, whatever might be the normal prospect for unanimous agreement to act against aggression, it was fatally compromised by a provision that any member nation whose interests were affected by the matter under discussion was permitted to sit with the Council as a member thereof—and thus to cast a vote (Article 4). This meant that an aggressor nation could sit with the Council and veto proposed sanctions against itself. The Council's only recourse was to expel the aggressor from the League, which happened in the cases of Japan and Italy. As later events proved, the League was paralyzed by the unanimity rule, which could have been changed only by the determined unity and vigor of the major democracies. Because the United States was not a member, and Britain and France were irresolute, the League could not cope with the rise of aggressive dictatorships driven by revenge and quite prepared to flaunt all forms of international law.[24]

In 1923, Franklin Roosevelt, as a private citizen, developed a "Plan to Preserve World Peace" for a competition for the American Peace Award sponsored by the *Saturday Evening Post*. Its most notable feature was the proposal to eliminate the League Covenant's requirement for unanimity in decisions involving sanctions and the use of collective force. "Common sense," he wrote, "cannot defend a procedure by which one or two recalcitrant nations could block the will of the great majority."[25] On the basis of his political instincts and his own direct experience, Roosevelt accordingly approached the problem of securing peace and stability after World War II as a thoroughly disenchanted Wilsonian idealist. He had become an advocate and exponent of realpolitik.[26]

2

A Grim Road to War

The League of Nations had been created after World War I to establish a system of international cooperation and collective security that would spare future generations the curse of war. Although an American President, Woodrow Wilson, had been the League's principal inspiration and architect, by a profound irony of history the United States had refused to participate. Thus denied the weight of American influence and support, the League was also ill-served by its two most powerful European members, Britain and France. Drained of self-confidence and first-rate leadership by the carnage of World War I, these nations had throughout the 1930s pursued policies so myopic and irresolute as to make it appear at times that they were bent upon national suicide. As a consequence of American abstention, European weakness, and fatal defects in its rules and procedures, the League of Nations had conspicuously failed to erect barriers against the designs for world conquest of the German, Japanese, and Italian dictatorships—a rising totalitarian tide that soon became a flood.[1]

Moral Drift and Appeasement

In September 1931, the Japanese army swept through the Chinese province of Manchuria, overrunning the area in a few months and creating the puppet state of Manchukuo. China turned for help to the League of Nations which, after weeks of debate, appointed an investigating committee. A year later, the League adopted the committee's report condemning the Japanese attack but took no further action. Japan withdrew from League membership in March 1933.

In 1935, Italian dictator Benito Mussolini invaded the African kingdom of Abyssinia (modern-day Ethiopia). In reply to Emperor Haile Selassie's plea for help, the League voted to impose economic sanctions, but Britain and France—fearful of driving Mussolini into the arms of Hitler—refused to embargo oil shipments, which were crucial to the Italian war effort. The League had failed a second critical test to organize effective collective security. From that point forward, the League of Nations was never taken seriously as a factor for peace and stability, but became a kind of grim joke in international politics.[2]

Germany had been admitted to the League in 1926, but on coming to power in 1933 Hitler immediately showed his disdain for the organization by withdrawing the nation from membership. In 1936, he took the first daring gamble toward his aim of conquering all of Europe by occupying the Rhineland in direct violation of the Versailles Treaty. It was a dangerous ploy, for Germany was not yet ready for war against the far superior combined military power of Britain and France; moreover, Hitler could not rule out the possibility that the United States would support the democracies. He knew that he would be forced to retreat if challenged. But the crisis revealed the extent to which postwar British governments had recklessly abandoned the cardinal policies by which London had long sustained its influence throughout the world and safeguarded its democracy at home. These policies were, in essence, always to oppose the most aggressive nation on the continent, in order to prevent Europe's domination by any single power, and to control the seas in order to safeguard the British Isles from blockade or invasion. War-weariness and the Great Depression had spawned pacifist movements and weakened national resolve. To maintain their popularity, successive British governments had cut military spending to the bone and deliberately ignored the fact that Germany was rearming.[3]

In the Rhineland crisis of 1936, the London government counseled the French to be patient, although it had given Paris a guarantee against German aggression. The jittery French were deeply shaken by this evidence of British supineness, for it threatened to leave them alone on the Continent, facing a vengeful, resurgent Germany whose population was one-third larger than France's. When Hitler moved into the Rhineland, the French were so lacking in self-confidence that they could not muster the courage to act alone—even to meet a provocation that directly threatened the nation's survival. Thus Hitler won his first high-stakes gamble, and raised tensions that brought the situation closer to the edge of another European war.

In March 1938, Hitler, claiming it the duty of Germany to "protect" fellow Germans who lived in adjacent countries but were being denied their full freedom to be German, combined a threat of unrestrained military force with ethnic propaganda and subversion to secure Austria's bloodless surrender to German occupation and control. Almost immediately, Hitler made similar threats against Czechoslovakia, using the same technique. The Czechs, however, possessed not only a strong, well-equipped army and an impressive fortress defense line, but also a formal guarantee of French military support. Although willing to discuss reasonable compromise, the Czechs were prepared to fight and were counting on the French to fight by their side.

During the summer, however, British Prime Minister Neville Chamberlain, who was in complete control of British policy, made every effort to discourage the French from honoring their solemn commitment and to persuade the Czech government to yield to Hitler. In September, Chamberlain engineered an Anglo-French proposal which accepted Hitler's complete demands for the annexation of western Czechoslovakia, and he informed the Czechs that Britain and France "could take no responsibility" if they rejected the proposal. Totally abandoned, the Prague government capitulated. On his return to London after a final meeting with Hitler in Munich, Chamberlain declared that this arrangement amounted to "peace with honor," and meant for all of Europe "peace in our time." It was in fact a policy of capitulation, which made the word "Munich" forever afterward a universal code for shameful appeasement. The Munich agreement also made World War II a virtual certainty.[4]

In the Rhineland crisis of 1936 and the Czech crisis of 1938, the success of Hitler's violations and aggressions still depended on the timidity and confusion of France and Britain. They possessed a heavy preponderance of military strength (the French could mobilize a hundred divisions), and Hitler's military staff was opposed to any war until German rearmament was further advanced. By 1939, however, and especially by 1940, Germany was armed and ready. Hitler's bluff was bluff no more.

Another ominous development occurred at the end of July 1936, when a violent upheaval in Spain quickly led to vicious civil war between the ideological extremes of Communism and Fascism. The Spanish Civil War—as this bloody struggle became known worldwide—immediately polarized politics in much of Europe. A weak center-left parliamentary regime was supported, then progressively subverted, by a Communist faction that saw an opportunity for Marxist revolution. In Churchill's words, "A perfect reproduction of the Kerensky period in Russia was taking place in Spain," punctuated by political assassinations on a growing scale. After the murder of the leader of the parliamentary Conservatives, the Spanish army, led by General Francisco Franco, raised the standard of revolt and was supported by the Catholic church, the conservatives, and most of the center-moderates. This made Franco the master of several major provinces. Civilized government collapsed, and bitter civil war ensued. Wholesale massacres of the well-to-do were repaid with interest by the forces under Franco.[5]

No one referred the Spanish issue to the diminished League of Nations, but France proposed a policy of strict nonintervention, to which Britain, Italy, and Germany all agreed. This meant that neither side in the civil war could purchase arms in Europe. Britain faithfully adhered to the agreement, but the other powers soon concluded that the ideological stakes were too high for a policy of abstention. Germany and Italy were soon assisting Franco with troops as well as arms, and Russia was heavily engaged on the side of the Spanish Republic. In an ideologically divided French government, the Air Minister secretly delivered planes and equipment to the Republican side, which had the effect of weakening the French air force. The Spanish Civil War thus became a dress rehearsal for the weapons and forces that would engage in the larger war between Nazi Germany and Communist Russia which began in 1941.[6] Churchill remarked in his memoirs that "Germany in particular used her air power to commit such experimental horrors as the bombing of the defenceless little township of Guernica." Such violent aggressions in Spain and elsewhere, driven by extreme political ideologies, were progressively destroying the underpinnings of civilized life all over Europe.[7]

War with Germany

Poland appeared to be the next target of Nazi aggression. In March 1939, Britain and France finally broke the paralytic grip of their appeasement policy by giving that country a military guarantee. Undeterred by this development, and assured of noninterference from the East by his swift conclusion of a nonaggression treaty with the Soviet Union, a confident Hitler sent German forces across the Polish frontier on September 1, seized Danzig, and bombed Warsaw. On that same day, a huge bronze sphere was lowered into place on the terrace of the League of Nations headquarters in Geneva. Beneath it an inscription read: "To the Memory of Woodrow Wilson, President of the United States, Founder of the League of Nations."[8]

Britain and France declared war, and Britain sent an expeditionary force to France. Members of the British Commonwealth—India, Australia, New Zealand, Canada, and the Union of South Africa—promptly joined in declarations of war. None of this provided any practical help to the brave, outgunned Poles. Russia then malevolently administered the coup de grâce by invading Poland from the east on September 17. Eleven days later the victim of double aggression was partitioned between the victors.[9]

By threatening to attack the Baltic states of Estonia, Latvia, and Lithuania, Russia quickly obtained military base rights there, and made similar demands on Finland. When the Finns rejected this ultimatum, the Russians invaded, precipitating what became known as "the winter war." The Finns fought stubbornly and well against far larger forces, and this particular aggression ended, in March 1940, in a humiliating stalemate for the USSR, although it gained some territory in the negotiated settlement. The clash had revealed a Red Army that was clumsy, ill-equipped, and ill-led, in sharp contrast to the barbarous efficiency of the German Wehrmacht. The evident disparity did not escape German notice.

The counterpoint to intense fighting in Eastern and Northern Europe (and to sporadic naval actions in the wide reaches of the Atlantic Ocean) was a strange, protracted lull on the ground in the West. Hostile armies faced each other across the French-German frontier, but the guns were silent for the six months from October to April which journalists called "the phony war." Meanwhile, the remaining smaller countries of Europe were paralyzed by a contagious panic. Afraid even to think of concerted action, they huddled fearfully.[10]

On April 9, 1940, Hitler ended the phony war explosively and without warning. German forces invaded Norway and Denmark and brought both under Nazi control within two weeks. On May 9, German forces attacked the

Netherlands, Belgium, and Luxembourg and swept away all resistance in twenty days. Then it was the turn of France, supposedly one of the great military powers on the Continent. But the static French defenses of steel and concrete known as the Maginot Line were breached and broken in the space of a few days, and the nation formally surrendered to Hitler in the forest at Compiègne on June 22. Meanwhile, the British were engaged in a desperate evacuation of their expeditionary force at Dunkirk, in an effort to preserve the largest segment of their outmoded army for the coming defense of the British Isles.[11]

Winston Churchill had succeeded Neville Chamberlain as Prime Minister in May. In June his Tory government flatly rejected Hitler's offer of a "peace" that was tantamount to surrender. Hitler ordered a total naval blockade and an all-out air bombing campaign designed to cripple and terrorize the British nation—the one remaining obstacle standing between him and mastery of Western Europe. The Battle of Britain—a series of desperate air battles over England which Hitler intended to be the prelude to German invasion—was about to begin.[12]

Evolution of American Opinion

The American response to the growing world tensions and depredations of the 1930s was a deepening sense of unease, accompanied by a fierce determination to stay out of any war in Europe or Asia. Congress passed strict Neutrality Laws, which prohibited the sale of any U.S. arms abroad, without distinction between victim and aggressor. At the same time, public opinion vigorously supported measures to strengthen the defense of the Panama Canal and to counteract the feared penetration of German and Japanese espionage in Latin America. As Assistant Secretary of the Navy before and during World War I, Franklin Roosevelt had shared the Navy's conviction that Japan was America's number one potential antagonist, and during the mid-1930s his international focus was primarily on the Far East. In 1937, Japanese forces invaded China proper—shocking the world by their ruthless rape of Nanking and other cities—and gave evidence of an intent to occupy French Indochina and Thailand and to threaten the rich oil fields of the Dutch East Indies. Hypnotized by the unfolding threat of Hitler in Europe, the French and British governments refused to consider any collective counteraction in Asia, either through the League of Nations or outside it. In Washington, Secretary of State Cordell Hull could muster nothing stronger than "pious remonstrances" that were routinely ignored by Tokyo.[13]

The President was frustrated and restive, convinced that unless Japanese aggression were checked, the security of the United States would be gravely jeopardized. In the summer of 1937, Roosevelt considered imposing a total trade embargo on Japan, enforced by the American and British navies, but dropped it when his ranking admirals told him that it would lead to a war for which the U.S. Navy was not yet prepared. Nor was there any likelihood of British cooperation. Thus with the Japanese threat primarily in mind, but seeking also to arrest the moral drift in Europe, FDR made a forceful speech on October 5, 1937, in which he urged the "decent" members of international society to "quarantine" aggressor nations.[14]

Aware that his only weapons were words, his dual aim was to warn aggressive dictatorships and to challenge the European democracies and American opinion to confront them. The dictators were not impressed, and the European democracies remained irresolute. The domestic American reaction was, however, decidedly hostile, with isolationists and even some Democratic leaders in the Congress charging that the President was preparing to plunge the country into war. Although the speech was an isolated warning of danger in a general pattern of mild official comment on the developing crisis, the reaction showed that Americans in 1937 were far from ready to assume responsibilities in the wider world. As Under Secretary of State Sumner Welles later wrote, the quarantine speech "provoked a new wave of isolationism" and thereby crippled any near-term prospects for a strong interventionist policy.[15]

Despite this evidence of powerful isolationist feeling, however, there were significant countercurrents of domestic opinion. Active internationalists at the League of Nations Association, a citizen lobby group whose members tended the flickering flame of Wilsonian idealism, sought to adapt their convictions to new circumstances. Clark Eichelberger, the energetic executive director, formed the Committee to Defend America by Aiding the Allies and persuaded William Allen White, a Pulitzer Prize-winning newspaper editor from Emporia, Kansas, to serve as chairman. Their first aim was to repeal the Neutrality Laws. Professor James T. Shotwell of Columbia University resigned from the League Association to found the Commission to Study the Organization of Peace. Members of its executive committee included John Foster

Dulles (who would become President Eisenhower's Secretary of State in 1953), Max Lerner, Owen Lattimore, Virginia Gildersleeve, and William Allen White. Beginning in January 1940, this group presented its views in a series of fifteen-minute Sunday evening radio broadcasts entitled "Which Way to Lasting Peace?" and carried by ninety stations on the CBS network. In one broadcast, Eichelberger said, "We are at last aware that the challenge to world peace has become a challenge to civilization itself," and the commission's first formal report stated that international law could be enforced only if "the power of the community" overwhelmingly exceeded the power of any of its members. The report did not spell out how this community power was to be wielded, but it disclaimed any intention to create a world superstate or an international police force.[16]

John Foster Dulles apparently felt that the Shotwell group was too secular, for he formed the Commission to Study the Bases of a Just and Durable Peace, under the auspices of the Federal Council of Churches. In one of many speeches, he declared, "the sovereignty system is no longer consonant with either peace or justice," and said that he was "rather appalled" at the lack of any agreed peace aims "to educate and crystalize public opinion."[17] Yet he too offered no specific remedies. In a long editorial in *Life* magazine entitled "The American Century," publisher Henry Luce noted the "golden opportunity" for world leadership that the United States had passed up in 1919, and called on the American people to help Roosevelt succeed where Wilson had failed. It was now the time, Luce wrote, to accept "our duty and our opportunity as the most powerful and vital nation in the world." But how to do this? Luce could offer only "work and effort . . . trial and error . . . enterprise and adventure."[18]

The uncertain tone and vague content of these declarations by concerned and thoughtful opinionmakers reflected the unprecedented scale of the intellectual and moral challenge, but it reflected also a fundamental ambivalence about international organizations in general, and about the League in particular. Most of these individuals had been ardent League supporters, and they clung to the conviction that Wilson's Covenant had been basically sound and would have fulfilled its grand promises, if America had joined. But they faced a stark fact: the League had failed—failed utterly and terribly—and the most honest and perceptive among them realized that the reasons went deeper than the lack of American participation. They sensed that the next effort to secure world order must involve some curtailment of national sovereignty. But how much? And how to achieve it in a world system of national sovereignties? And how to organize collective force to oppose aggression? They did not know. In a sense, their imaginations were circumscribed by a deep emotional and intellectual commitment to Wilson and thus by an innate feeling that the new solution, whatever it might turn out to be, must start with the master's handiwork.

In a 1939 book called *Union Now,* former *New York Times* journalist Clarence Streit brought to the public debate a plan for postwar organization that attracted attention and enthusiasm by a concreteness that contrasted sharply to the vague groping of most old-line internationalists. The League Covenant, Streit argued, was analogous to the Articles of Confederation under whose loose rules the newly independent American colonies were originally governed. When that compact proved inadequate, it was superseded by a federal union with a central government whose powers were defined in the U.S. Constitution. To succeed, therefore, the League must undergo the same metamorphosis, must become a federal union with a single defense force, a single currency and customs-free economy, and a single postal and communications system. Streit's fundamental criterion for membership was democracy. The founding members would thus be confined to the United States, Britain, the self-governing British Dominions, and the countries of Western Europe, excluding Germany, Italy, Spain, and the Soviet Union. Other nations might in time join the "Great Republic," if they could meet the basic democratic test.[19]

The book was an immediate success, selling out fourteen printings in two years. Streit formed Federal Union Incorporated and soon had sixty chapters throughout the country. A number of distinguished writers, actors, and other public figures, including Robert Sherwood, W. Somerset Maugham, Clare Booth Luce, Thomas Mann, Dorothy Thompson, and Raymond Massey became ardent supporters, attracted by Streit's stress on democracy and the exclusively Nordic/Anglo-Saxon orientation. Old-line Wilsonians were affronted and alarmed, and the monthly journal of the League Association called the idea a perversion of history. One historian complained that Streit's plan would mean "a new order imposed on the world by an Anglo-Saxon federation." That, of course, was precisely its appeal.[20]

A Worldwide Threat

These intellectual efforts to awaken the American people to the grave dangers of their situation and the urgent need for measures to bring into being a less threatening world had a modest, though cumulative effect on public opinion. World events in the latter half of the decade had transformed America's geopolitical situation, creating on the Atlantic flank the probability that Europe's vast resources would be consolidated against America by Nazi Germany, and establishing on the Pacific flank the rising likelihood of attack by an armed and expansionist Japan, which became a full-fledged ally of Germany and Italy by signing the Axis Pact on September 27, 1940. The President and his advisers saw these looming dangers and envisioned the unprecedented national effort required to ward them off, but public perception remained worried, confused, contradictory—and this lag was a powerful obstacle to action.[21]

In the early summer of 1940, the Secretaries of War, Navy, and Treasury urged the President to stop all exports of oil and scrap iron to Japan, and to persuade the Netherlands to destroy its oil wells and refineries in the Dutch East Indies to prevent their falling into Japanese hands. FDR gave serious consideration to this recommendation, but finally rejected it out of an overriding concern for the need to buy more time for the U.S. rearmament effort. He was nevertheless determined to act where action seemed possible, and he now moved with increasing boldness to influence both the European and Asian situations.[22]

Congress was persuaded to amend the Neutrality Laws, which opened the way for the British and French to purchase American arms on a cash-and-carry basis. Congress reaffirmed the Monroe Doctrine in June and declared that the United States would resist any German efforts to seize French or Dutch possessions in the Caribbean. Roosevelt extended the doctrine politically by including both Greenland and Iceland and by declaring a vast oceanic "neutrality zone" in which the U.S. Navy escorted British convoys two-thirds of the way to England and defended them aggressively against attack by German submarines. His orders to shoot on sight any German or Italian warships who intruded into this self-declared defense zone made violent clashes with German submarines inevitable, and there ensued sixteen months of semi-secret, undeclared naval warfare in the cold and treacherous North Atlantic.[23]

By these actions the American people were made increasingly aware of the harsh realities of the situation, and their response showed an understanding of how large the stakes were for American security and the entire structure of Western democracy. The President was artfully stretching the instinctive public support for defense of the hemisphere to cover the more controversial matter of strategic aid to Britain. His actions were tacitly supported, in part because the isolationists could not find a way to separate the two strands of this sinuous policy. There was strong moral support for Britain, but many doubted that it could withstand the German air assault or what seemed the inevitable follow-up invasion.

Dramatic events beyond American shores delivered a far more powerful impact. By late summer 1940, the electrifying German Blitzkrieg conquests of Western Europe, and the growing evidence that Japan was preparing a war to drive all Western interests out of the Far East, had produced a marked shift in American public opinion. There was now a broad awareness that the country could not insulate itself from the impact of military, political, and economic upheavals in the outside world, or from their moral implications. But this led to no new consensus as to what policies were now required to safeguard the national interest. There was an overwhelming desire to see the brutal dictatorships destroyed and buried, but this coexisted with a fierce determination to stay out of war.

In this unprecedented situation, Franklin Roosevelt also took the unprecedented decision to run for a third term in the White House. To the surprise of many, his Republican opponent was a maverick internationalist, Wendell Willkie, who had won out over the traditional GOP isolationists at a wild convention in Philadelphia. An authentic midwestern American, Willkie grew up in Indiana, practiced law in Ohio, and then rose to the presidency of a major utility company in New York. A large, rumpled man with unruly hair and a hoarse voice, he won the nomination with the backing of the Eastern internationalist wing of the GOP, and went on to wage a vigorous campaign that laid stress on the need for America, in the interest of its own survival, to play a major role in shaping the future of an increasingly dangerous world. He did not challenge Roosevelt's conduct of foreign affairs, and after losing the November 5 election by a landslide margin of 449 electoral votes to 82, he did everything in his power to prevent his adopted party from blocking American entry into what he now perceived as a necessary war.[24]

A month after FDR's election to a third term, a 4,000-word message arrived from Churchill. The heart of it was a warning that Britain's liquid assets were being rapidly drained away by the total effort to fend off Hitler: "The moment approaches when we shall no longer be able to pay cash for our shipping and other supplies." The problem posed was how the United States could go on sending war materials to Britain in the face of the cash-and-carry requirement of the Neutrality Laws. Roosevelt's ingenious solution, after a period of creative cerebration while cruising the Caribbean in the U.S.S. *Tuscaloosa,* was the formula that came to be known as Lend-Lease, a means of providing munitions to allies without immediate charge and to be repaid not in dollars, but in kind, after the war. As FDR unveiled it to the press, "Suppose my neighbor's house catches on fire, and I have a length of hose. . . . If I can take my garden hose and connect it up to his hydrant, I may help him put out his fire." This winning homespun analogy was followed on December 29, 1940, by a speech in which he declared that the United States must become "the great arsenal of democracy," a message that sent a thrill of hope across the whole anti-Nazi world, shifted American opinion toward greater support for preparedness (though not war), and assured the passage of Lend-Lease legislation.[25]

Crescendo

The world crisis was now moving toward crescendo. As 1941 opened, the massive German air assault on England continued, and Hitler made unrelenting efforts to extend his grip on the Continent. In March he forced Bulgaria and Yugoslavia to join the Axis—and when the compliant Belgrade government was promptly overthrown by coup d'état, he made war on Yugoslavia, using Italian, Hungarian, and Bulgarian troops alongside his German forces. In April, Italy invaded Greece, which conducted a tenacious defense with the help of British troops, until the introduction of large German forces broke the organized resistance and led to British withdrawal.

In response to the movement of Japanese armies southward toward French Indochina and Thailand, the United States embargoed all iron and steel scrap shipments to Japan in January, but still refrained from closing down the export of oil, which was recognized as a move of utmost strategic sensitivity—and likely to provoke a Japanese military response. German forces in

Africa were advancing through Libya toward Egypt and the supreme prize of the Suez Canal. German submarines were taking a fearful toll of British and American ships carrying vital cargoes to beleaguered England. The United States assumed the defense of Greenland and welcomed the arrival of British troops in Iceland. In June the United States froze all German and Italian funds in American banks and demanded the removal of their consular staffs. The Axis nations retaliated in kind.[26]

On June 22, 1941, Hitler attacked the Soviet Union. That massive German onslaught made immediately worse an already highly fragile situation across the globe. Britain's ability to hold out against German bombers and submarines still hung in the balance. Now German armies were slicing deep into Russia, and Japan stood poised to attack in the Pacific. For the American President, the categorical imperative was to keep both Britain and Russia in the fight. There was no other way to preserve hopeful options for the democratic cause, or to prevent the United States from becoming an island in a totalitarian sea.

Roosevelt immediately sent his closest confidante, Harry Hopkins, to Moscow to ascertain Stalin's material needs, then arranged to meet Churchill secretly in mid-August off the Newfoundland coast. The first message from Hopkins reported that Stalin was confident that his forces could withstand the Nazis, provided the United States could help with his supply problem by the following spring, when it would become acute. Also, Stalin would "welcome" American troops under their own command on any part of the Russian front.[27]

On July 24, a Japanese invasion force arrived at Camranh Bay in Indochina. The President called in the Japanese Ambassador and made a last effort to effect Japanese withdrawal and an agreement to neutralize that territory. Tokyo delayed a reply, but Japanese cable traffic intercepted by U.S. intelligence revealed that there was no intention to withdraw. It was at this point that Roosevelt faced a Hobson's choice: to try to hold off a Far Eastern war in order to buy more time for rearmament, but at the risk of remaining passive while the Japanese warlords extended and consolidated their conquests; or to impose immediate further sanctions against Japan as a warning to stop their expansion, but at the high risk of precipitating a war before U.S. military forces and American public opinion were fully prepared. His preference was to go on buying time, but when decoded Tokyo cable traffic made clear the scale and pace of Japanese military activities, he understood an attack somewhere in the Pacific was coming—and probably soon.[28]

On August 1, the United States froze all Japanese assets and brought all trade, including oil exports, to a halt. The British and Dutch governments took similar action. The die was cast, even though futile negotiations continued in Washington until the very moment of the attack on Pearl Harbor. Cordell Hull, who conducted these final talks with Ambassador Kichisaburo Nomura, and the special envoy, Saburo Kurusu, who arrived in mid-November, seemed unable to grasp that the U.S. prescription for "peace" in Asia was in direct conflict with Japan's well-developed expansionist goals. U.S. policy aimed at restoring Chinese sovereignty on the mainland and obtaining Japanese assurances of respect for existing borders and "noninterference" in the whole of Southeast Asia. But Japan was fundamentally determined to achieve the Greater East Asia Co-Prosperity Sphere, which was Tokyo's chosen vehicle for securing Japanese military, financial, commercial, and cultural dominance of the entire area. In both Europe and the Pacific, events were rapidly eliminating the possibility that the United States could avoid full involvement in a global war.[29]

3

Argentia and the
Atlantic Charter

The first glimmering of what was to become the United Nations appeared at the first meeting between President Franklin Roosevelt and British Prime Minister Winston Churchill in Argentia Bay, off the coast of Newfoundland, in mid-August 1941.[1] Two powerful naval armadas arrived at the secret rendezvous, bearing the leaders of the only consequential democracies which had thus far survived the German, Italian, and Japanese dictatorships' designs for world conquest. Roosevelt and Churchill were meeting to make manifest their common cause, take each other's measure, and assess together a perilous world situation in which they were forced to devise common strategies for meeting the even graver ordeals—visible in outline, unknown in detail—that loomed ahead.

The Four Freedoms

On January 1, 1941, Roosevelt worked late in his small study on the second floor of the White House. Accompanied by his adviser Harry Hopkins, Under Secretary of State Sumner Welles, and his speechwriter, Judge Samuel Rosenman, he was putting the final touches on his State of the Union message, which he would deliver before a joint session of the Congress on January 6. There remained only the question of how to close the speech. After a long silence, the President began slowly dictating what became his famous declaration of hope for "a world founded upon four essential human freedoms"—freedom of speech and expression; freedom of religion; freedom from want; and freedom from fear. These were, he said, not a vision for "a distant millennium," but "a definite basis for a kind of world attainable in our own time and generation."[2]

William Allen White, the famous newspaper editor, declared with remarkable foresight that the President had given the world "a new Magna Carta of democracy." The Four Freedoms, which became the moral cornerstone of the United Nations, marked, White wrote, "the opening of a new era for the world."[3]

Six months later, with these Four Freedoms very much in his mind, FDR conferred with his close associate Welles on the coming meeting with the British Prime Minister in Argentia Bay. Roosevelt told Welles that, because the two English-speaking democracies both stood for principles of freedom and justice, they should seize the opportunity of the meeting to "jointly bind themselves" to establish at the end of the war "a new world order based on those principles . . . that would hold out hope to enslaved peoples."[4] There had been vague discussions of this idea between the British and American staffs, though no prior exchange of views between FDR and Churchill, but the Prime Minister had personally prepared a first draft. What became the Atlantic Charter—a declaration that led, within six months, to the creation of the "United Nations" coalition and that formed the moral-political foundation upon which the new international organization was later built—was not, however, the most pressing matter for either leader as they approached their first face-to-face meeting.[5]

Churchill, whose nation was engaged in a veritable death grapple with the German Luftwaffe in the skies over England and with the relentless killer U-boats in the cold Atlantic, wanted above all to avoid war with Japan. The increasing stridency of Japanese policy made clear however that all Western interests in the Far East were threatened. For Churchill, any hope of preventing Japan from expanding farther to the south—to menace the Malay Peninsula, Singapore, Hong Kong, and the Dutch East Indies—depended on a clear-cut warning by the United States, although he hoped that it would appear to reinforce an identical British statement. Preparing for the Argentia meeting, the Foreign Office had drafted "parallel communications" expressly warning that "Any further encroachment by Japan in the Southwestern Pacific would produce a situation in which the U.S. [and Britain] would be compelled to take countermeasures, even though these might lead to war."6

In an early conversation on shipboard at Argentia with Sumner Welles, Churchill stressed his conviction that anything less than a strong U.S. warning would lead inevitably to a British-Japanese war. In that event, he told Welles, Japan would quickly destroy all British merchant shipping in the Indian Ocean, cut the life-lines between the British Dominions and England, then overrun the British land positions. But Roosevelt, who only ten days before, on August 1, had felt compelled to freeze all Japanese assets in the United States and cut off all exports, including the strategically sensitive oil shipments, felt that further provocation was politically imprudent. He was concerned about both the bitter-end isolationists in the Congress and the galvanized militarists in Tokyo. To Churchill's intense disappointment, therefore, "no mailed fist" was shaken at Japan from Argentia.7

For his part, the President's principal aim in meeting with Churchill was to ensure that Britain would make no territorial deals—secret or otherwise—prior to a general peace conference at the end of the war. Now facing a common foe, Britain and Russia had begun negotiating a military alliance in late June. London reported to Washington that Moscow was seeking only military aid and a pledge of no separate peace with Hitler, but Russian Foreign Minister V. M. Molotov was also hinting at the need for a guarantee of Russia's pre-invasion boundaries—which included its 1939 seizure of eastern Poland and its annexation of the Baltic states, in consequence of Stalin's sordid nonaggression pact with Hitler that same year. Roosevelt believed that any recurrence of such spheres-of-influence politics would produce a new wave of American isolationist recoil, rooted in moral disgust, and that this could fatally undermine prospects for American leadership—either in war or in a postwar effort to secure a lasting peace.8

Lord Halifax, the British Ambassador to Washington, had provided assurances that the Anglo-Soviet pact contained no "secret clauses," and the accord had been duly signed in Moscow on July 12, a month before the Roosevelt-Churchill meeting. But at Argentia, a still suspicious FDR sent Welles across the bay to H.M.S. *Prince of Wales* to reaffirm these assurances with Alexander Cadogan, the Permanent Under Secretary of the Foreign Office. Only then did Roosevelt approve publication of the Atlantic Charter.9

The Two Leaders Meet

The first meeting of these two democratic leaders was a historic moment. Franklin Delano Roosevelt, the only person elected three times to the office of President of the United States, was a man of extraordinary range and complexity. Even his closest associates found him a puzzling mix of contradictory moods and motives, and they never fully penetrated his "heavily forested interior," in Robert Sherwood's phrase. He was hard and he was soft; serious and direct, frivolous and evasive. Acknowledged as the premier "artist" in politics, he could be ruthless, but was often an exemplar of charity in its purest form. He could appear "utterly cynical, worldly, illusionless," but always projected a buoyant optimism which, some thought, was sustained by an old-fashioned religious faith that "was the strongest and most mysterious force in him." Whether the source was his religion or his Dutch genes, it was universally agreed that he possessed remarkable inner strength and determination—a tenacity that had been tested and reinforced by his contracting polio at the age of thirty-nine, in 1921, an ordeal that had rendered him unable to walk.[10]

Winston Spencer Churchill had been a member of the British Cabinet and a world statesman while still a young man in World War I. During the disastrous "locust years" of the 1930s, he had become the nation's Cassandra, telling his myopic parliamentary colleagues and heedless countrymen over and over—with vehemence, eloquence, and hard facts—that Hitler's evil ambition and massive rearmament posed a stark threat to the survival of Britain and of Western civilization. In May 1940, when the catastrophic consequences of Neville Chamberlain's shameful policies could no longer be denied or borne, Churchill was called to Buckingham Palace to become the King's First Minister. In a matter of hours and days, he resurrected the latent courage and tenacity of the British people, made himself the embodiment of those virtues, and demonstrated a remarkable strategic vision. He told the House of Commons that he could offer them nothing "but blood, toil, tears and sweat." Then he hurled thundering words at Hitler: "We shall defend our Island, whatever the cost may be, we shall fight on the beaches, we shall fight on the landing grounds, we shall fight in the fields and in the streets; we shall fight in the hills; we shall never surrender."[11]

As French resistance was collapsing in June 1940, Churchill cabled Roosevelt that the "astonishing swiftness" with which Hitler had conquered

Western Europe meant immediate heavy bombing and probably paratrooper attacks against Britain, followed by a major invasion attempt. If necessary, Churchill said, Britain would fight on alone, and if the Island went down, he and his government would go down with it. On June 20, in a secret session of the House of Commons, Churchill asserted that, if Britain could get through the next three months, it could get through the next three years. And he thought that the best way to bring the United States into the war was to demonstrate that the British nation was utterly determined upon a heroic struggle to preserve its own independence and so prevent Hitler's destruction of Western civilization. The President sent his adviser Harry Hopkins to London to test the categorical stance asserted by Churchill. Did not the British have a plan to move the government to Canada, in extremis? Hopkins discovered that there was no such plan. An impressed Roosevelt then made his most momentous decision of 1940—to back Britain and Churchill to the hilt. He was keenly aware that if Britain were swept away, then "all our traditional concepts of security in the Atlantic would be gone" and America would be living constantly "at the point of a Nazi gun."[12]

Roosevelt stretched his constitutional authority by consummating in September 1940 a destroyer-for-bases deal under which the United States transferred fifty older destroyers to the hard-pressed British Navy in exchange for ninety-nine-year leases on British air and naval bases in the western Atlantic and the Caribbean, including Newfoundland, Bermuda, the Bahamas, and Jamaica. Two months later, after his reelection to a third term, the President wrote to King George VI that there had been "virtually no criticism" of the deal in America, except from "legalists" whom he was determined to ignore.[13] In December he declared an "unlimited national emergency" and asserted that the United States must become the "arsenal of democracy," ready to "extend to the opponents of force the material resources of this nation." He then rushed half a million rifles, 80,000 machine guns, and 900 75-millimeter guns with a million shells to beleaguered England. He also set in motion the comprehensive Lend-Lease program, which became law in March 1941 and which Churchill called "the most unsordid act in the history of any nation." Now as the two men met in early August 1941, the United States, though not yet formally in the war, was morally committed. Britain had weathered the fury of Hitler's assault for a full year.[14]

On the morning of August 9, following the customary naval courtesies,

FDR and Churchill after church services on H.M.S.
Prince of Wales, Argentia Bay, August 10, 1941.
(Courtesy Franklin Roosevelt Library)

the Prime Minister, dressed in his signature blue navy peacoat and matching
naval cap, went aboard the U.S.S. *Augusta* to visit the President, who received
him with full military honors. Roosevelt stood, supported on the arm of his
son Elliott, while the two national anthems were played; then he gave his new
colleague (in Churchill's words) "the warmest of welcomes." Conversations
quickly began between the two principals, and the military chiefs and the two
senior diplomats, Welles and Cadogan, met separately.[15]

As Robert Sherwood later wrote, the two leaders quickly established "an
easy intimacy, a joking informality, and a moratorium on pomposity and
cant—and also a degree of frankness in intercourse which, if not quite complete, was remarkably close to it." At the same time, neither man "ever forgot
for one instant what he was and represented and what the other was and represented. . . . Their relationship was maintained to the end on the highest pro-

fessional level."[16] Both leaders placed a great deal of importance on personal diplomacy, for they believed that it was the best way to avoid misunderstanding—in July alone, fourteen messages had passed between them. The meeting at Argentia Bay reinforced their mutual trust and led to an ever growing exchange of personal communications.[17]

The American Advisers

Harry Hopkins, who had returned through London from his Moscow mission in order to brief Churchill on the talks with Stalin, was invited by the Prime Minister to join him and his entourage on the battleship H.M.S. *Prince of Wales* for the voyage to Argentia Bay. Hopkins was an aide and counselor of immense influence in Roosevelt's inner circle. The son of a harness maker from Sioux City, Iowa, he had been a "studiously unsuave and often intolerant and tactless" New Deal reformer in the early Roosevelt years. He had become both famous and infamous as the powerful director of the Works Project Administration (WPA), the Administration's principal vehicle for lifting the nation out of the Great Depression by creating jobs in a thousand public undertakings from building airports and bridges to subsidizing artists and playwrights. He had served briefly as Secretary of Commerce, but his frail health and unpopularity with Republicans in Congress limited his effectiveness. The President, however, found his perceptiveness and loyalty indispensable; since 1940 he had been FDR's closest adviser and was indeed living in the White House. An expediter rather than a man of vision, he was alert, shrewd, bold, prankish, with an intuitive feel for the precise measures necessary to resolve the immediate problem and meet the President's needs.[18]

Churchill was impressed by Hopkins's keen assessment of people and events and his "harshly objective and salty reporting" (six months later, at a strategy meeting in the White House immediately after Pearl Harbor, he insisted that Hopkins's trenchant analyses be rewarded by the bestowing of a title: "Lord Root of the Matter"). As they cruised toward Newfoundland, the two men canvassed a wide range of issues and examined the phraseology of Churchill's draft of what became the Atlantic Charter.[19]

Sumner Welles was at this meeting in part because his chief, Cordell Hull, had fallen ill again in June. Hull, a former Congressman and Senator from Tennessee, had been Secretary of State since 1933. Roosevelt had chosen him

Harry Hopkins and Sir Alexander Cadogan aboard H.M.S.
Prince of Wales, Argentia Bay, August 10, 1941.
(Courtesy Franklin Roosevelt Library)

not for his qualifications in foreign affairs—he had none—but for his high standing and rapport with Senate leaders and his loyalty to the Democratic Party. Also, it was generally understood that Hull accepted the President's intention to provide the creative leadership in international relations. Now seventy-one, he was in chronic ill health and easily fatigued; he had been a mild diabetic since childhood, but in 1932 had contracted tuberculosis which he took great pains to conceal, recognizing that exposure of the ailment could make him unacceptable for national office. When he made a radio speech, a senior aide sat beside him, ready to take over if his voice gave out. Henry L. Stimson, Hoover's Secretary of State and Hull's immediate predecessor, confided to his diary that Hull was "a tall gentlemanly man, with a pleasant Southern quiet manner, [but] on the whole, I got a rather discouraging impression of his vitality and vigor." By temperament cautious, Hull was also slow in comprehension and action and determined to avoid mistakes and public criticism. In the loose, experimental atmosphere of the New Deal, he jealously guarded his reputation as the one Cabinet officer who had avoided conspicuous blunders. Journalists found his public statements akin to official reaffirmation of the Beatitudes, in which he urged the unruly nations of the world to settle their differences peacefully. One close observer was reminded of a Civil War politician whose speeches—more notable for their length than for their content—seemed like a train of twenty cars from which emerged only a single passenger. Hull's single passenger was always the same—trade agreements. Until Pearl Harbor, he seemed to believe that his self-acknowledged preachments plus free trade were sufficient to halt the triumphal march of dictators. Beneath a courtly Southern manner, he was a hard-bitten Tennessee mountaineer, provincial, insecure, and with an instinct for ruthlessness if crossed.[20]

Sumner Welles was Hull's polar opposite. An Eastern seaboard aristocrat, educated at Groton and Harvard, he was a professional diplomat of exceptional talent and energy—calm, precise, sophisticated, thorough, with "the dignity to be viceroy of India."[21] Harold Ickes, the Secretary of Interior, thought that Welles's dignity edged toward "preternatural solemnity" and remarked, "if he ever smiles, it has not been in my presence." A few others in the Roosevelt entourage did not feel at ease in his presence, but these were minor disparagements. Hull, having no interest in managing the department, left this to Welles, who at forty-nine was a tireless and effective administrator. Foreign ambassadors paid perfunctory calls on Hull, then spent two hours talking serious business with the Under Secretary.[22]

As the crises of the late 1930s mounted, demanding swift assessment and action, the President grew understandably impatient with a Secretary of State whose primary concern, as Robert Sherwood later wrote, was to maintain a record of "no runs—no hits—no errors." Needing fresh ideas and quick action, he turned increasingly to Welles, who was also a close personal friend. The two families had long been intertwined; Welles, ten years younger than FDR, had been a page in his wedding. The President had sent him to Berlin, Rome, Paris, and London in early 1940 in a last-ditch effort to avert all-out war in Western Europe; Welles had handled the destroyers-for-bases deal with the British and chaired the Inter-American Committee to administer the Caribbean possessions of those European nations now subjugated by Hitler.[23]

Welles was emerging in official circles and in the press as the "associate"

Sumner Welles aboard H.M.S. *Prince of Wales,* Argentia Bay,
August 10, 1941. (Courtesy Franklin Roosevelt Library)

Secretary of State. In a speech on July 22, 1941, at the Norwegian Legation in
Washington, he was the first highly placed U.S. official to make public reference to postwar aims, declaring that only an "Association of Nations" could
rebuild a shattered world after Hitler had been "finally and utterly destroyed."
The *New York Times* considered this the "most significant" declaration of
peace aims since the onset of the European war and assumed that Welles
spoke for the President, "whom he sees virtually daily."[24] On August 11, while
the Argentia conference was in progress, *Time* magazine put Welles on its
cover and described him as a "Field Marshall in the war of brains."[25]

Welles's rising prominence and ready access to the Oval Office were serious blows to Hull's prickly pride, which had already been wounded by Roosevelt's decision to choose Henry Wallace instead of Hull as his running mate in the 1940 presidential race. The new affronts fed a bitter and cumulative resentment against his Under Secretary, which was in some measure anger at the President that could not be expressed. Hull's overt differences with Welles were over how—and at what pace—to plan for postwar structures and policies, and how to develop public support for them, a debate which pitted Hull's obsessive caution against Welles's instinct for bold initiative. Welles possessed the broader intellect; Hull had a keener feel for what was politically feasible. They could have made a formidable team, but the older man's bitterness became increasingly personal, and led to a dramatic showdown in the summer of 1943.[26]

Negotiating the Atlantic Charter

On the morning of August 10, 1941, Cadogan handed to Welles the British draft of what became the Atlantic Charter.[27] It was the personal handiwork of the Prime Minister himself, which he later confirmed in his memoirs: "Considering all the tales of my reactionary Old-World outlook, and the pain this is said to have caused the President, I am glad it should be on the record that the substance and spirit of what came to be called The Atlantic Charter was in its first draft a British production cast in my own words."[28]

In his stateroom on the U.S.S. *Augusta,* Welles gave the document his close and immediate study. The first three articles he found "essential in their import and admirable in their clarity," but he balked at the latter half of the third, feeling that the words "concerned to defend the rights of freedom of speech and thought" throughout the world involved a commitment which the U.S. Congress would, at that moment, loudly protest.

He judged the fourth article to be flatly inadequate, an attempt to preserve the system of British trade practices known as "imperial preferences." This system, as embodied in the Ottawa Agreements of 1932, was designed to force every component of the British Empire, covering one-quarter of the world's population, to trade only where the British pound sterling was the recognized currency, and to discriminate against traders outside the system. Governments and peoples everywhere now understood that such practices, including the American protectionist tariffs imposed after World War I, had contributed directly to the severe global Depression of the early 1930s, and to the economic desperation and fury that had spawned Hitler and Mussolini. The elimination of all such practices was a major goal of the Roosevelt Administration. Welles shared Hull's deep conviction that there could be "no assurance of any new and better world order to come" until such "fatal impediments" to free trade were removed.

Welles thought that the fifth article, although it proposed an "effective international organization" to keep the peace, did not adequately express the need for the Anglo-American coalition to lead the world to "a true reduction and limitation of armaments."

On the basis of this analysis, Welles revised the British draft: in article three, he deleted the last sentence; in article four, he expressed the elimination of all trade discrimination as an Anglo-American goal; in article five, he inserted the "hope" that world governments would arrest the "continued expenditures for armament," except for "purely defensive" weapons. Also, reflecting a personal devotion to Wilsonian ideals that did not quite mesh with FDR's preference for realpolitik, Welles expanded the preamble to include more sweeping language. He put his alternative draft before the President early on the morning of August 11.

The two men discussed every word. Roosevelt, following his political instincts, quickly made clear that he wanted to limit the entire document to a declaration of general principles. With that in mind, he eliminated most of Welles's eloquent preamble and even shortened Churchill's original. He strengthened the third article by adding the "hope that self-government may be restored to those from whom it has been forcibly removed." He shortened and generalized the fourth article on trade, but retained the central thrust of Welles's revision by inserting the phrase "without discrimination."

In the fifth article, he struck out the words "effective international organization," which Welles had retained from the British draft. Then he wrote in a new sixth article which asserted that, because future peace would be "impossible" if military forces remained in the hands of "any nation which threatens or may threaten to use force outside its frontiers," the "disarmament of such nations is essential."[29]

The new version of the document, slightly tidied up by Welles and approved by FDR, was the main item for discussion between the principals later that morning. Also gathered informally in the admiral's quarters, which the President was using as his study, were Cadogan, Hopkins, and Welles. Roosevelt was wearing a gray suit with his shirt open at the collar. Churchill was, as throughout the conference, dressed in his personal version of a naval uniform. There were substantive differences on only two points: the trade issue and the question of a postwar system to keep the peace.

The Prime Minister asked if the revised trade language was intended to apply to imperial preferences. Welles replied that of course it was, and went on to elaborate the economic and social havoc wrought by the severe constriction of world trade which was the unavoidable consequence of all discriminatory tariffs and similar practices. The President reinforced Welles, saying that it was very important to offer the German and Italian peoples the promise of a fair and equal economic opportunity after the war.

Churchill replied that, while he personally opposed the Ottawa Agreements and was entirely in favor of free trade, he was without the power to approve the proposed paragraph without first obtaining the concurrence of all the British Dominions. Such consultations, he said, might consume several days or more, and might not in the end produce the desired result. Hopkins then suggested that Welles and Cadogan re-draft the article "to take care of these difficulties," but Welles strongly demurred, saying that any effort to mask a basic disagreement could only eviscerate "a vital principle." The practical difficulty remained, however, and there appeared to be a strong consensus that publication of the Atlantic Charter must coincide with announcement of the conference itself.[30]

Hopkins continued to press the President to yield to practical necessity, and Roosevelt soon did so, acknowledging that time was of the essence. Robert Sherwood later wrote, "Of course Welles was right on principle and Hopkins was wrong," but the compromise served a larger immediate purpose.[31] The final language agreed upon read as follows: "Fourth, they will endeavor, with due respect for their existing obligations, to further the enjoyment by all states, great and small, victor or vanquished, of access, on equal terms, to the trade and to the raw materials of the world which are needed for their economic prosperity."[32]

With regard to the new article on the disarming of aggressors (which Roosevelt had inserted, while deleting any mention of an organization for postwar security), the Prime Minister asked if the President would not agree to support some kind of "effective international organization" as proposed in the original British draft. This question produced a candid reply which revealed FDR as a thoroughly disenchanted Wilsonian, indeed, a hardline advocate of realpolitik. He could not mention any form of international organization at this time, he said, owing to the still formidable strength of isolationist opinion in America. To take any clear-cut position on that issue now would generate suspicion and opposition he thought it prudent to avoid.

This judgment was primarily a question of timing, he said. But leaving current domestic politics aside, he would not favor creating a new League of Nations, or anything like it, until the United States and Great Britain had functioned as a world police force for a number of years after the war and had effectively disarmed aggressor nations and established a stable international situation.[33]

The President's requirement for international stability, which he had often shared privately with Welles, in fact went beyond disarming aggressor nations. It included the view that even peace-loving small nations could play no useful role in the international policing function: in time of war, their armies were worthless against the larger, more modern forces of the major powers; and in peacetime, the cost of such establishments was a crushing burden upon their fragile economies. As the maintenance of these numerous small establishments was therefore a terrible social waste, it would be in the general interest to disarm them after the war, "thereby ridding the world of an unnecessary burden upon humanity, as well as of a danger to international peace." Only the major powers would be in a position to undertake such a task. In these private debates with Welles, the President rather impatiently brushed aside all considerations of the national pride of small countries, or the fact that age-old hatreds between national neighbors (as in the Balkans) created an imperative need for the means of self-defense. Nor did FDR address the formidable task of actually disarming such nations, and then making sure that they stayed disarmed.[34]

The full scope of this Rooseveltian concept was not on the table at Argentia, however. The immediate issue was the statement that assumed the special right of the major powers to identify and then disarm all "potential" aggressors on their own authority.

Churchill replied that he would be less than candid if he did not express his feeling that the President's approach taken in the "disarming" article would stir up a great deal of opposition from "extreme internationalists" and others who were seeking solutions based on the presumed sovereign equality of nations. FDR said that he understood the risk, but that the time had come to be realistic and the language he proposed reflected "complete realism." Welles remained silent, but could not agree that his chief's view reflected political realism. Churchill also doubted the feasibility of the proposal, although he understood the attraction of its pure logic. He ended by remarking that, of course, he fully shared the President's view.[35]

However, following this session, Churchill, Welles, and Hopkins all sought to change the President's mind, especially to persuade him to accept some reference to a new international organization. Hopkins, who may have been the decisive influence, told the President that he was certain that the American people were ready to support a strong organization for world peace—"indeed they would settle for nothing less."[36] The President would not yield to the term "international organization," but finally agreed to language that seemed very close to the same thing—"the establishment of a wider and permanent system of general security." The formidable implications of FDR's notion to disarm all small nations were masked by a statement confining "essential" disarmament to "aggressors or potential aggressors."[37]

Impact on World Opinion

When finally agreed upon, the text of the Atlantic Charter was issued as a press release and was cabled to Stalin for his endorsement, but the fact that the Soviet dictator had been given no advance notice of the Argentia conference deepened his innate suspicion of Anglo-American designs to dominate the postwar world. His endorsement did not come for several weeks, and then arrived with a caveat that was both understandable and ominous. The "practical application" of the Atlantic Charter, Stalin said, "must necessarily adapt itself to the circumstances, needs, and historic peculiarities of particular countries." Four months later, he spoke to British Foreign Secretary Anthony Eden in much blunter terms: "It now looks as if the Charter was directed against the USSR."[38]

Stalin's relatively polite initial observation, that practical application of the Atlantic Charter must change depending on different national circumstances, also applied, if to a lesser degree, to the United States and Britain. Neither society perfectly embodied the high moral principles of the declaration, and the British were the more immediately vulnerable party. The ringing words "They will respect the right of all peoples to choose the form of government under which they will live" brought insistent, embarrassing questions about self-determination from India, Burma, Malaya, and other parts of the British Empire. So acute did the questions become that Churchill was forced to state in Parliament that the Atlantic Charter was directed primarily to the "restoration" of sovereignty to those European nations "now under the Nazi yoke." The progressive evolution of British dependencies in other regions was "quite a separate problem."[39]

The immediate public reaction in Britain was curiously muted, for the people had evidently hoped for some momentous U.S. commitment that would, visibly and immediately, improve the odds for their survival and ultimate triumph. They wanted an American declaration of war. What they got seemed, at first glance, merely a collection of pious words. As one British historian later wrote, "The meeting that is now celebrated as the genesis of a great alliance was regarded in London at the time as a disappointment, close to a flop."[40]

Similarly, to American isolationists, the language of the declaration was only a smokescreen for secret deals, hatched at a secret meeting, and designed to enmesh America in the tangled affairs of Europe.

Yet the words of the Atlantic Charter—and, equally, the large implications of the conference itself—were met with an overwhelming sense of reassurance by the great majority of the American people, and with a surge of new hope throughout the many lands "under the Nazi yoke." The charter was in fact a revolutionary pronouncement for American diplomacy, representing a total break with the narrow isolationist policies of the Harding, Coolidge, and Hoover administrations. It signaled that the United States, not yet formally engaged in a conflict possessing the gravest geopolitical and moral implications, was prepared to place its leadership and its strength on the scales, in cooperation with the one other surviving democracy of consequence, in a supreme effort to bring into being a decent and peaceful postwar world.

The President was heartened, and slightly surprised, by the favorable reception of the Atlantic Charter both at home and abroad, but his mind remained focused primarily on the urgent problem of national defense. Welles wanted him to use the new momentum to begin postwar planning within the

Administration, and to define publicly at least the outlines of a desirable post-war world, but FDR rejected this advice, insisting that it was imperative to concentrate public attention and energy on the overriding need for rearmament and defense. Any attempt to offer vague postwar formulas for public discussion would, he said, only raise the level of controversy and divert the nation's attention from the immediate problem. It was necessary to put first things first. However, he assured Welles, when "the moment became ripe," he would exert American leadership to build the kind of world envisioned in the Atlantic Charter.[41]

4

Postwar Planning Begins

Although it had been visible in fearful outline for nearly a decade, the actual fact of war in Europe came as a major shock to the American nervous system and raised with new urgency the question of what the United States must now do to safeguard its interests in both the short term and the long. But no element within the State Department was charged with long-range planning, and no such planning was being carried on in any part of the government. On November 10, 1939, Pope Pius XII proclaimed the need to establish "a stable international organization" after the war. In a private response of December 23, President Roosevelt voiced his belief that, while no spiritual or civic leader could now define a specific structure for the future, "the time for that will surely come"; meanwhile, the United States would "encourage a closer association between those in every part of the world—those in religion and those in government—who have a common purpose."[1]

A Desultory First Effort

Into this planning vacuum stepped the private Council on Foreign Relations with an offer to study postwar issues secretly and make its deliberations available to the State Department. The council was a Northeastern seaboard phenomenon, an elitist mix of prominent New York bankers

and lawyers with European interests and prominent academics and intellec-
tuals, many of whom had served as advisers to Woodrow Wilson at the Paris
peace conference. The businessmen provided the money, while the scholars
furnished most of the intellectual leadership. The council operated mainly
through off-the-record conferences, study groups, and small dinners confined
to members, who were addressed by foreign or American statesmen. It published *Foreign Affairs*, a scholarly quarterly that had become the leading American journal of its kind. In an age when fewer than one thousand Americans
could claim a journeyman's competence, or even a sustained interest, in foreign affairs, the Council on Foreign Relations was a rare island of influence
and expertise in the body politic.[2]

Secretary of State Cordell Hull accepted the council's offer with alacrity
and, with financial support from the Rockefeller Foundation, the council created four committees to study postwar armaments, economic relations, colonial territories, and cross-border aggression. Norman H. Davis, head of the
American Red Cross and a former Under Secretary of State, was assigned to
coordinate the studies and their presentation to the State Department.[3]

On December 27, 1939, Hull formed a high-level committee, composed
mainly of State Department officials, to consider and use the reports from the
New York group as a basis for developing future U.S. foreign policy; at the
same time he created a new research unit under his principal assistant, Leo
Pasvolsky. Fearing, however, that any disclosure that the U.S. government was
discussing postwar issues would reinforce public misgivings about the League
of Nations and trigger divisive protests from isolationists, he was careful to
disguise the true purpose of the undertaking. In early January 1940, the
department quietly announced creation of an Advisory Committee on Problems of Foreign Relations, which would "survey the basic principles which
should underlie a desirable world order to be evolved after the termination of
the present hostilities." Under Secretary Sumner Welles was appointed chairman. Norman H. Davis and George Rublee, a New York lawyer, became the
only outside members.[4]

The new committee began its work, but the intense pressures of coping
with the ongoing war in Europe soon made it impossible for the already over-
burdened departmental officers to give any appreciable time to problems of an
unknown and distant future. In Welles's later assessment, the proceedings were

"desultory," and the effort soon fell of its own weight. Postwar planning was thus in abeyance for most of 1940 and 1941.[5]

In the late summer of 1941, after his return from the meeting at Argentia, Welles worked within the State Department to organize a more systematic and sustainable postwar planning effort. Hull was amenable. The Atlantic Charter was now a tangible and visible, if disturbingly vague, guide to U.S. foreign policy. By mid-October a directive had been prepared for the President's approval, describing the proposed new effort, including the persons recommended for appointment to a new planning group. However, for the next two months Hull was totally absorbed by tense and fruitless negotiations with the two Japanese envoys which continued until the very moment of the attack on Pearl Harbor. As a result, he did not sign the planning directive until December 22. The President returned it with his approval on December 28.[6]

The Japanese attack on Pearl Harbor on December 7 plunged the nation into war against Japan, and into a maelstrom of global scope four days later when Hitler declared war on the United States. This latter move was, in Dean Acheson's later assessment, "a colossal folly on Hitler's part" and a diplomatic boon for the President, for it was by no means certain that his own move to initiate formal hostilities against Germany would have been supported by Congress, even after the Pearl Harbor attack. Had Hitler withheld formal support for his Tokyo ally, he would have engendered an ambivalent American reaction, which probably would have led to a concentration of American power in the Pacific, thereby greatly improving Hitler's prospects for consolidating German hegemony in Europe. But his strategic mistake resolved all American dilemmas and produced a united determination to fight to the finish a global war against totalitarianism.[7]

The Declaration by United Nations

On January 1, 1942, the Soviet and Chinese ambassadors in Washington joined with Roosevelt and Churchill (who had arrived at the White House in late December) in signing the Declaration by United Nations. The following day, representatives of twenty-two other nations at war with the Axis powers added their signatures to the document, which created a wartime alliance of states who promised to wage war with all their resources and not to sign a sep-

FDR asks Congress for a declaration of war against Japan,
December 8, 1941. (Courtesy Franklin Roosevelt Library)

arate peace. The document also pledged them to accept the principles of the
Atlantic Charter as "a common program of purposes." The President apparently thought up the name "United Nations" and secured the Prime Minister's
approval by bursting into his bedroom at the White House while the doughty
Briton was taking a bath.[8]

The order in which the declaration was signed, first by the four major
powers and subsequently by the other nations, was not inadvertent, but
reflected FDR's ingrained belief in the rightful primacy of the strong, combined with the moral concept of "trusteeship of the powerful" for the well-
being of the less powerful. The President now privately referred to these major
powers as the Four Policemen, and this distinction between great and small
nations quickly became a fundamental element of all U.S. postwar planning.[9]

Meanwhile, the planning effort in the State Department was further delayed by a harsh and bizarre clash between Hull and Welles over the Under Secretary's handling of a mission to Latin America. In mid-January, the President had arranged a meeting of foreign ministers in the hemisphere in Rio de Janeiro, and had sent Welles to obtain an immediate—and, if possible, unanimous—Latin American agreement to break diplomatic relations with the Axis powers. The negotiations seemed to go smoothly until the eleventh hour when Argentina, which had close ties to Germany, balked. So did Chile. This impasse threatened to unravel the entire agreement. After further arduous debate, the Argentine and Chilean governments finally agreed to "recommend" a break to their respective legislatures, and Welles accepted this watered-down commitment in the interest of hemisphere solidarity. This decision, however, infuriated Hull, who had developed a personal antipathy for the Argentine foreign minister. He telephoned Welles in the middle of the night and ordered him to reverse the decision, his voice trembling with fury. Welles told him that any reversal would be a disaster for hemisphere relations, and that he would undertake it only on the direct order of the President. In a three-way conference call the next morning, Roosevelt backed Welles unequivocally. The incident deepened Hull's resentment and distrust of the Under Secretary. Then—six weeks after the nation had been plunged into a war of survival—Hull left for his usual two months of rest and vacation in Florida, leaving Welles in charge of the department.[10]

Idealism Versus Reality in 1942

Welles moved swiftly to implement the planning effort approved by the President, beginning with the appointment of a distinguished planning group. The departmental members included Assistant Secretaries Dean Acheson and Adolf Berle; the economic adviser, Herbert Feis; the legal adviser, Green H. Hackworth; the chief of the Commercial Policy Division, Harry Hawkins; and Hull's special assistant, Leo Pasvolsky. From private life he recruited Norman H. Davis; Isaiah Bowman, a famed geographer who was president of Johns Hopkins University; Myron Taylor, the President's special representative to the Vatican; Hamilton Fish Armstrong, the distinguished editor of *Foreign Affairs;* Anne O'Hare McCormick, a foreign affairs writer for the *New York Times;* and Benjamin V. Cohen, general counsel to the National Power Policy Committee, a private study group.[11]

The impetus for Welles was not only, nor even primarily, the Japanese attack, but what he felt to be the urgent need to deal with as comprehensively and as soon as possible—and certainly before the war's end—the fractious issues of territorial claims, ethnic enclaves, armistice terms, and occupation policies. If these were left for decision at a postwar peace conference, Welles believed there was the gravest danger that the world would experience a repeat of 1919 and the supreme tragedy of Versailles. Woodrow Wilson had assumed that there would be time after the fighting stopped to persuade all members of the Allied coalition to agree to a just and therefore lasting peace, and he was confident that American advocacy and prestige would carry the day. But the end of hostilities had in fact greatly diminished American leverage. Despite Wilson's best efforts to moderate passions, the victorious Allies had quarreled bitterly over the spoils, and, driven by popular demands for vengeance, they had imposed harsh conditions on the vanquished which had sown the seeds of revenge and new war.[12]

The immediate focus of Welles's concern were Russia's territorial claims to eastern Poland and the Baltic states. These had been finessed in the Anglo-Soviet pact signed quickly the previous July, but Stalin was now pressing for the expansion of that pact into a twenty-year military alliance. Messages in late December from British Foreign Secretary Anthony Eden, who was in Moscow, indicated that, unless the United States and Britain met Stalin's demands, there was danger of an "early break" with Russia, carrying with it the threat of an end to Russian military cooperation and perhaps an attempt by Moscow to conclude a separate peace with Nazi Germany.

Eden believed that these particular demands could not be resisted, especially if the Red Army succeeded in withstanding the German assault. But he considered that the United States and Britain, by conceding them in formal negotiations, could obtain agreed-upon restrictions on further Russian claims, in writing. Such agreements would, in his view, be very useful in the event that victory greatly expanded Stalin's territorial ambitions. Eden therefore thought it "prudent to tie the Soviet Government to agreements as early as possible."[13]

Welles shared Eden's view that every effort should be made to reach such early agreements, but he was more optimistic about the chances to modify Russian demands. In his words, "the political influence" of the United States in 1942 was "at its peak." The nation was aroused to an all-out effort. Its moral prestige made it the only true beacon of hope in a darkened world. Rearmament was moving into high gear. American military forces were rapidly attaining a level that would reach 12 million men and women under arms. On the other side, the German assault on Russia had come within a few miles of Moscow, and the Russian war effort was desperately dependent on American Lend-Lease supplies. Welles believed that this was the period of maximum U.S. leverage and that therefore the President should seize the moment to begin negotiating postwar settlements, primarily, but not exclusively, with Moscow. Given Russia's dire circumstances, Welles thought it reasonable to believe that Stalin could be held to territorial agreements that both met Russia's legitimate security requirements and seemed "just and wise" to the rest of the world.[14] Eden, whose preference for an early agreement with the Russians was not shared by Churchill, had in mind a direct bilateral or trilateral deal with Stalin. But Welles, a devoted Wilsonian who was deeply committed to respecting the sovereign equality of small nations, believed that a multilateral approach was essential. As he saw it, the United States faced clearcut alternative courses of action in the winter of 1942. One was to create an "official international planning commission in the hope that the major allies would at that crucial moment in the war be able to work out political and territorial solutions that would be found acceptable at the end of the war." The second was "to refuse resolutely to discuss any political or territorial question until a peace conference assembled." Welles recognized persuasive arguments for both courses, but believed that adoption of the first was the only way to avoid repeating the consequential failure of 1919.[15]

Discussions in the new planning group began on February 12, 1942. Debate was serious and as thorough as the fast pace set by Welles would permit. A consensus was soon reached on the basic elements of a new international organization, and a set of recommendations was made ready for review by higher authority. The proposals blended Wilsonian idealism with the President's known preference for realpolitik. The central proposal was for the prompt creation of a United Nations Authority composed of all twenty-six nations who had signed the Declaration by United Nations in January. This was to be an interim international political body that would seek broad agreement on major postwar issues by means of preliminary negotiations, prior to the end of hostilities. Control would reside in an executive committee (called the Provisional Armistice Administration), composed of the four major pow-

ers (the United States, Britain, Russia, and China) plus five regional representatives (outstanding individuals, rather than national representatives) selected
from Eastern Europe, Western Europe, the Far East, Latin America, and "possibly the Mohammedan peoples." In ways not spelled out, the executive committee would consult with all members of the United Nations Authority to
develop guidance on postwar issues and to provide assurance that the executive committee was acting in the interests of all concerned members.[16]

The Welles group recommended a "security commission" made up of the
Four Policemen, who would provide all of the forces needed for keeping the
peace; it would operate under the general authority of the executive committee. Other "commissions" for unspecified, nonsecurity functions might be
established subsequently. The planning group finished its work on April 4, by
which time some serious differences of view had developed between Welles
and Leo Pasvolsky, who was Hull's man. Pasvolsky, a Russian-born American
who had covered the Versailles peace conference for the *New York Herald-
Tribune,* shared Hull's strong dislike of the broad, somewhat inchoate
"regional" representation on the proposed executive committee, and felt that
Welles was moving too fast. It was evident that this first effort was at most a
blueprint, a hastily drawn outline plan that did not attempt to address a number of very important and controversial questions. Driven by a sense of
urgency, Welles was concentrating on the essentials.[17]

This blueprint was, from one perspective, a farsighted, even wise proposal—the expression of a passionate determination not to repeat the terrible
failure of 1919. Yet it proved too fragile to withstand the harsh realities of
early 1942—or the peculiarities of the American political system, with its
division of authority and its openness to public debate. This was the darkest
hour of the war. The Pacific fleet was shattered. American forces were being
overwhelmed and brutalized in the Philippines and other outposts. Senate
approval for any kind of international organization was out of the question in
the circumstances, yet an attempt to create an immediate United Nations
Authority by executive order would strain relations with the Senate on both
sides of the aisle—probably to the breaking point. It would call down the
wrath of isolationists, and probably disorient a general public already bewil-
dered and battered by the grim catalogue of military defeats. The Joint Chiefs
of Staff were opposed to any controversial negotiations with Russia and other
nations that might complicate or weaken the war effort.

When Hull returned from his annual trip to Florida in early May, he made clear his own view that the planning group proposal was dangerously premature. He strongly favored a new international organization with America in a leading role, but feared devastating attacks from the still powerful isolationists if any effort were launched before overwhelming popular support had been secured. He also had specific objections: the Welles plan did not make clear how, when, and by whose authority U.S. military forces would be employed in postwar peacekeeping; moreover, Hull disliked the notion of individual representatives from "regional organizations" (which in most cases did not exist), indeed from regions which possessed no sense of collective identity. He was polite, but firmly negative: the whole effort needed more thorough study before it would be possible to define the U.S. position on a number of basic issues. Such definition was a precondition to formal negotiations with other nations.[18]

Although the written record is sketchy, it is clear that the President strongly supported Hull's position. Welles evidently sought to get around Hull by going directly to FDR, but the ploy failed. In a terse note found in his private papers, Welles wrote that his proposal was "summarily turned down at the highest level."[19] The reasons for the President's rejection were not obscure: the supreme crisis created by the Pearl Harbor attack, the still open question of whether Britain could ward off invasion, and the grave doubts about the staying power of the Red Army led the U.S. Commander-in-Chief to believe that absolute priority must be given to one task: to focus the attention and energy of the American people on the war effort until victory was won. His political instincts told him that this task would be impossible, if public attention were agitated and diverted by news that the U.S. government was discussing with other nations such questions as the future boundaries of Poland. The President's position here reflected his own instinct—and the nation's— to separate war from politics, in sharp contrast to the European view of war as the pursuit of politics by other means.

FDR's Tenacious Policy of Postponement

An indication of Roosevelt's determination on this matter was his personal involvement in high-risk efforts to deflect and postpone any settlement of Russian territorial demands in Eastern Europe. Just a few days after Pearl Harbor, he had expressed renewed concern about the apparent British readiness to yield to Stalin on the future status of the Baltic republics, and had instructed Hull to warn them against agreeing to any final arrangements, especially against any "secret commitments," which were a particular bête noire of American opinion. Hull's message to London broadly asserted that the three governments, having now bound themselves by the Atlantic Charter, should make no specific postwar agreements until the final peace conference. Churchill, who was in Washington at the time, supported the U.S. position in a cable to Eden, but the problem did not go away. Stalin continued to press his demands, now fortified by his growing conviction that the Atlantic Charter was being used against him.[20]

When the British Ambassador in Moscow, Sir Stafford Cripps, reported that Stalin regarded this issue as an "acid test" of Western good faith, and that failure to recognize Russia's pre-invasion frontiers risked a "complete reversal" of the dictator's attitude toward the war,[21] Roosevelt reacted with indignation and promptly decided to handle the matter personally. In a handwritten note to Welles, he said: "Churchill to tell Cripps most unwise to advocate now any approval of pre-1941 Russian frontiers. In addition, contrary to Atlantic Charter, and feel sure Cripps will not want me call attention to that fact. The matter had best be handled between Stalin and me a bit later on."[22]

The British were upset to learn that the President intended to inject the United States directly into British-Russian negotiations—and at the highest level—but in a meeting in the Oval Office on March 9, 1942, the British Ambassador to Washington, Lord Halifax, was unable to dissuade him. FDR said that he would tell Stalin that "everyone recognized Russia's need for security," but that it was "too dangerous to put anything on paper now." However, Stalin need not worry about the Baltic states, for their future depended on Russian military progress: "If Russia reoccupied them, neither the U.S. nor Britain could, or would, turn her out." This statement did not sit well with the Foreign Office. Eden disliked it, "because I was sure it would fail to satisfy Stalin and because . . . it would give us the worst of all worlds. We would be ungraciously conniving at the inevitable, without getting any return for it."[23]

But Roosevelt's mind was stubbornly set on his position. "Under no conditions," he told the Russian Ambassador, Maxim Litvinov, would he subscribe to definitive boundary agreements "until the war has been won."[24] Then he sent a personal message to Stalin on April 11, proposing a meeting that summer in Fairbanks, Alaska, to consider "a very important military proposal involving the utilization of our armed forces in a manner to relieve your critical Western front."[25] This seemed, and was, an implied offer to accelerate the opening of the second front in Europe in exchange for Stalin's willingness to postpone territorial claims. It was a reckless ploy, for neither U.S. nor British military forces were ready for an assault on Hitler's Fortress Europe, and the British were adamantly opposed. Stalin declined the proposed meeting in Alaska, but was sufficiently attracted by the lure to send his foreign minister, V. M. Molotov, to London and then to Washington. When Molotov asked what the President's position was on the second front, FDR replied that the foreign minister could tell his government that it could expect such an effort "this year." General George C. Marshall, the Army Chief of Staff, who was sitting near the President, was visibly disturbed by the specificity of this response.[26]

Military and political realities precluded a second front in Europe in 1942—and indeed in 1943—but the President's promise, which was set down in a U.S.-Soviet statement issued to the press on June 9, was enough to persuade Stalin to conclude his alliance with Britain stripped of its territorial demands. The dangerous ploy had worked—temporarily. But Stalin would reassert these, and larger, demands at a later time when he was in the catbird seat and U.S. and British leverage was diminished. As things turned out, territorial concessions and acknowledgment of claims, both formal and de facto, to Russia—and Britain—were made before the end of hostilities and before the conclusion of any final peace treaties. They were rendered unavoidable by strategic and military realities. Welles, who had foreseen this development, was led to the conviction that the United States had ended up with the worst of both possible policies.

Roosevelt's fundamental antipathy to political and territorial settlements before the war's end thus made his rejection of Welles's proposal inevitable. That proposal called for an immediate attempt to negotiate such settlements—and in a multilateral forum which would involve a number of small nations for whose claims FDR had understandably little patience at that stage of the war. His rejection was, however, largely a question of timing, for he was not opposed in principle to an international organization; a year later, when victory in the war was foreseeable, he embraced a similar plan.

But his rejection was also a question of style. He preferred to run the show with his fellow major players, unencumbered by gratuitous advice from lesser nations that carried negligible weight on the scales of power and were making little or no contribution to the war effort. His decision was thus very much an expression of his character and personality. He perceived his leadership and his ability as a negotiator (in which he reposed great confidence) as merged with the vast power of the United States. If there was a price to be paid for postponement of settlements, he was sure he could work things out at acceptable cost.[27]

5

The Widening Public Debate

The President's State of the Union address on January 6, 1942—just one month after the attack on Pearl Harbor—was praised by George Orwell on BBC radio as a "complete and uncompromising break . . . with isolationism." Roosevelt said, "the mood of quiet grim resolution which here prevails bodes ill for those who conspired and collaborated to murder world peace. The mood is stronger than any mere desire for revenge. It expresses the will of the American people to make very certain that the world will never so suffer again." He referred to the signing of the Declaration by United Nations just six days before, and defined the primary objective of that act to be "the consolidation of the United Nations' total war effort against our common enemies." His focus was entirely on the war effort.[1]

But if the Administration had decided that public disclosure of postwar plans was dangerously premature, such inhibitions did not apply to the press and the private sector. Throughout 1942, there was a steady procession of proposals for shaping the new world and educating the American people.

The Commission to Study the Organization of Peace, whose president, Columbia professor James T. Shotwell, was an occasional adviser to the State Department planning effort, accepted the need for an "Anglo-American directorate" to run the world in the immediate postwar period. But his group advocated "a conference of all nations, defeated or otherwise . . . for the purpose of formulating the principles and institutions of the world order" as soon as "stability has been sufficiently restored."[2] Several large donors to the League of Nations Association pushed that organization toward a name change by declaring that their money would henceforth go toward the cause of the United Nations. The journalist Edward R. Murrow provided active internationalists with the slogan, "We must plan or perish." The Carnegie Endowment was persuaded to give Shotwell's group $50,000 to establish regional centers for the study of foreign affairs.[3]

On March 5, 1942, the Commission to Study the Bases of a Just and Durable Peace, headed by John Foster Dulles, proposed a far more radical solution. It called specifically for a world government complete with a parliament, an international court, and appropriate operating agencies. The world government would have the power to regulate international trade, settle disputes between member nations, and control all military forces, except those needed to maintain domestic order. The Dulles group realized that such an arrangement could not be effected overnight, but felt that all Christians should focus on it as the essential requirement for lasting peace. There were secular echoes of this religious impulse. By an overwhelming vote, the North Carolina legislature supported a "Federation of the World," and six other states, including New York and New Jersey, passed similar resolutions.[4]

Clarence Streit's proposal for a world federation of democracies, called *Union Now*, had gained wide popular attention before Pearl Harbor. Now it encountered criticism on the grounds that its insistence on the democratic criterion divided the United Nations by excluding Russia and China. Streit responded by dropping the requirement, declaring ambiguously that "this nucleus union should be open to all peoples who are prepared to share the rights and responsibilities of the union."[5]

Such exuberant attempts to move the world toward various visions of postwar utopia generated inevitable correctives. In April, Professor Nicholas Spykman of Yale published *America's Strategy in World Politics*, which insisted that the underlying realities of the international system were not subject to change. "Plans for far-reaching changes in the character of international society are an intellectual by-product of all great wars," he wrote, but they have never altered "the fundamental power patterns." The new postwar order will remain "a world of power politics in which the interest of the United States will continue to demand the preservation of a balance of power in Europe and Asia."[6]

Former President Herbert Hoover published in June a more popular but equally sobering book, in collaboration with Hugh Gibson. Their thesis was that Man could learn to control, but could never abolish, the dynamic forces that make for war and peace. The book advocated a clean separation between the responsibility to crush threats to peace and disarm aggressors and the responsibility to "build up the fabric of international law and steadily guide the movement of nations toward abolition of war." The first task should be handled by a military alliance of great powers; the second task was for a world council that would "focus solely on the peaceful settlement of disputes." There was surprising, if unacknowledged, similarity between the approaches of Herbert Hoover and Franklin Roosevelt.[7]

A more convincing, more sophisticated argument for realpolitik was Walter Lippmann's 1943 best-seller, *U.S. Foreign Policy: Shield of the Republic,* a brilliant essay designed to counter the idealistic One World internationalism of which Wendell Willkie was the leading purveyor. It sold nearly half a million copies. Lippmann, a crusading editor who had helped Woodrow Wilson prepare his peace program, had been disillusioned by the Versailles Treaty and the League of Nations, but retained the conviction that American leadership in world affairs was an absolute prerequisite of stability and peace. He thought that Willkie's thesis was founded on sand and that its corollary—that the United States must undertake to police the world—was a dangerous doctrine. Lippmann argued that all nations must balance their commitments with their resources and should avoid becoming overextended.

Lippmann's formula for peace was not a new League of Nations, but a basic alliance of the United States, Britain, and Russia. No other nations were serious factors in the world power equation. China and France were not great powers. Only Britain and Russia were strong enough to threaten U.S. security, but given America's close ties to Britain, there was no risk from that quarter. The only real danger was a falling out with Russia, but peace and stability required that this be avoided at all costs, for an Anglo-American alliance against Russia would set the stage "inexorably" for a third world war. A strong three-power pact was therefore "the irreducible minimum" for the peace and security of the great powers. And if they were secure, so would be the smaller nations.[8]

The book received strong critical acclaim in establishment and academic circles, with many commentators pointing out that had the democratic alliance of 1918 been maintained, World War II might have been avoided. Hans Kohn, a professor of history at Smith College, praised Lippmann for putting history "to its best use." Wilsonians and other advocates of a new League of Nations were upset by his denigration of small nations and denounced the book as a rehash of "the old alliance and balance of power theory that has failed over and over again." But Lippmann had offered a solid, rational alternative to the fanciful flights of the One Worlders.[9]

Most of these proposals and opinions from the private sector provoked little or no comment from the Administration, which was generally adhering to the President's edict of official silence on postwar speculation. There were, however, a few exceptions to this rule, and some speeches were privately encouraged by FDR as a means of testing or educating public opinion. On May 8, 1942, Vice President Henry Wallace delivered a major address to members of the Free World Association in New York City. He began by defining the war as "a fight between a slave world and a free world," and asserted that ordinary people everywhere were on a march toward freedom that constituted "a long-drawn-out people's revolution." America had failed civilization after World War I because "we did not build a peace treaty on the fundamental doctrine of the people's revolution." Wallace argued that "the American century" proclaimed by Henry Luce was historically mistaken. "I say that the century on which we are entering—the century which will come out of this war—can and must be the century of the common man." It was apparent that Wallace's aim was a kind of New Deal for the world.[10]

The speech was virtually ignored by most of the press, but was rescued from obscurity by the left-wing newspaper *PM* and its editor, Ralph Ingersoll, who gave it notoriety by accusing the establishment papers of deliberate suppression. The speech was then praised by liberal columnists—one going so far as to declare it the Gettysburg Address of World War II. The Carnegie Endowment printed it as a pamphlet, and it was eventually translated into twenty languages. Yet not everyone agreed with its message. One critic, Dwight Macdonald, found it "a great wind of rhetoric blowing along the prevailing trade route of Stalinoid liberalism." The perceptive Washington correspondent of *Paris-Soir* thought that "its mystical character" was its most striking aspect. And he judged that Wallace failed to understand that Hitler was the "common man gone mad." The president of the National Manufacturers Association declared, "I am not making guns or tanks to win a people's revolution. I am making armament to help our boys save America." The consensus was that Wallace had delivered a basically unhelpful speech, but one that nevertheless filled a large official void. In mid-1942, the war was going very badly. Many Americans hungered for an authoritative voice that would reassure them that they were engaged in a noble struggle to bring forth a better world. With the President concentrating on the war, it was left to lesser figures in the Administration to sketch the outlines of the future.[11]

Wallace continued to speak out boldly and frequently, declaring on Woodrow Wilson's birthday that Wilson had not failed: "Now we know that it was the world that failed."[12] If Wallace's thinking was fuzzy, his emergence as the leading Administration spokesman on the postwar world lifted him "spectacularly out of Vice Presidential obscurity," according to *Newsweek*.[13]

Hull Versus Welles

Although rebuffed in his effort to commit the President to the immediate creation of an interim United Nations organization, Welles had by no means given up the fight. Disturbed by the vagueness of the Vice President's "people's revolution" address, he decided to offer a more pragmatic, realistic view of the future. Speaking to war veterans in the amphitheater at Arlington National Cemetery on Memorial Day, he said that the death of 90,000 Americans in World War I had gone unredeemed, owing to the failure of the United States to join the League of Nations. That act of "unenlightened selfishness" had led to World War II, and "we are now reaping the bitter fruit of our own folly and lack of vision." The only remedy was to abandon isolationism once and for all. Moreover, he declared, the young Americans now committed to battle would insist on the creation of "an international police power" after the war and would "demand that the United Nations become the nucleus of a world organization of the future to determine the final terms of a just, an honest, and a durable peace."[14]

Noting the call for an "international police power" and "the nucleus of a world organization," the *New York Times* called this speech "the first official blueprint of the Roosevelt peace policy" and gave it high praise. Other publications followed suit, which so encouraged Welles that he gave essentially the same speech at a United Nations rally in Baltimore on June 17.[15]

Hull was not pleased by the vague ruminations of the Vice President, but

Cordell Hull and Sumner Welles arrive on Capitol Hill
to testify before the Senate Foreign Relations Committee,
June 1939.

the two speeches by Welles moved him to fury. He summoned the Under Secretary to his office and excoriated him for announcing "new policy" without approval. In a stiff exchange, Welles offered to make no further speeches, but Hull insisted that these "splendid" statements should continue, provided they were cleared with him.[16] Welles told Hull that FDR had privately authorized him and others to launch educational "trial balloons," as the President himself had decided not to make any speeches about postwar organization. Hull received this news with skepticism, and later told Assistant Secretary of State Breckinridge Long that Welles was operating on "illusory consent weaseled out of the White House."[17]

Welles continued to make forceful speeches, presumably now with Hull's approval, but the May incident had intensified their feud over postwar planning and divided the State Department into rival cliques. Hull no longer trusted Welles, and even the Under Secretary's friends and admirers did not blame Hull entirely. Assistant Secretary Adolf Berle confided to his diary: "Things are going badly in the Department. The Secretary and Sumner are further apart than ever . . . [and] in this case I am afraid it is so definitely Sumner's fault as not to be arguable. Briefly, he committed the fatal mistake of speaking as though he were the Secretary of State when there is an alive and very active Secretary of State in the immediate vicinity. The Secretary thereupon went to work to clear the decks; and Sumner on his part has been retaliating by getting control of all the Departmental machinery he can. This bodes no good for anybody."[18]

Hull decided to make a speech of his own to restate his personal position on the postwar world and to make clear that Wallace and Welles did not speak for the State Department. Unfortunately, the result was another plodding recital of platitudes, written by a committee of aides whose every sentence was then placed under Hull's own cautious political microscope. The speech was in preparation for five weeks, and was delivered as a radio address on July 23, 1942. With Breckinridge Long sitting beside him to take over if his voice gave out, Hull listed the catalogue of dire events leading up to the war; then he declared that Americans were "forced to fight" because they had ignored "the simple but fundamental fact that the price of peace . . . is the acceptance of international responsibilities." When the fighting is over, "some international agency must be created which can—by force if necessary—keep the peace among nations in the future." There must be "international cooperative action to set up the mechanisms which can thus insure peace." What would such mechanisms look like, and would the wartime United Nations form the nucleus of a permanent postwar organization? Hull did not say.[19]

Conservatives found in the speech a reassuring antidote to Wallace's utopian approach, but many others agreed with the Washington correspondent of *Paris-Soir* that it was merely "insipid." Internationalists nevertheless pointed out that Wallace and Welles had pushed Hull to declare for an "international agency" to keep the peace "by force, if necessary."[20]

Wendell Willkie, the 1940 GOP
presidential candidate, supported FDR's
internationalism. (Courtesy Franklin
Roosevelt Library)

The Republican Party Evolves

After Pearl Harbor, Wendell Willkie dedicated himself to pushing a mulish Republican Party from its deep-seated isolationist position, but he made little headway. Under his prodding, the GOP National Committee was willing, in April 1942, to state the obvious—that after the war "the responsibility of the nation will not be circumscribed within the territorial limits of the United States." Even the leading isolationist, Senator Robert Taft (R-Ohio), could support this harmless concoction. As the 1942 congressional elections approached, Willkie urged all GOP candidates to sign a postwar pledge to "set up institutions of international political and economic cooperation . . . and devise some system of joint international force." None came forward to sign the Willkie pledge. One hundred and fifteen Republicans did sign a weaker manifesto, but forty others balked even at that.[21]

In August, President Roosevelt invited his 1940 opponent to take a trip around the world, with special attention to China and Russia, as a means of dramatizing the common interests of the United Nations. Accordingly, on

August 26, Willkie took off in a converted bomber accompanied by Gardner Cowles, the publisher of *Look* magazine, and Joseph Barnes, a senior writer for the *New York Herald-Tribune*. After 31,000 miles and a great deal of press coverage, Willkie reported to the American people in a radio address on October 26. "We must fight our way through not alone to the destruction of our enemies, but to a new world idea," he declared to an audience estimated at 36 million people. The trip excited the public imagination, and the speech was widely praised, but his ideas did not immediately advance the cause of internationalism. In the November elections, the Republican Party gained forty-four seats in the House and nine in the Senate, and came close to winning control of Congress. A number of die-hard isolationists were re-elected.[22]

The causes of this severe Democratic setback were many and varied. The year 1942 had been full of turmoil and confusion, punctuated by demoralizing military defeats. But the principal cause was probably that millions of men were in military service and millions of civilians had taken defense jobs in new locations, which rendered them ineligible to vote. Only 26 million people voted, a 50 percent decline from 1940. For internationalists who had expected a sweeping victory, the election results were a shock and a painful disappointment. The appearance, however, was more troubling than the reality, for many of the new congressional Republicans were open to policies dictated by compelling world events. And important new GOP governors, like Thomas E. Dewey in New York, Leverett Saltonstall in Massachusetts, Harold Stassen in Minnesota, and Earl Warren in California, were men who wanted the United States to play an active role in the postwar world.[23]

6

Progress in 1943

As 1943 opened, President Roosevelt remained unwilling to reveal any specific views about the organization of a postwar world. To close listeners, however, what he did say indicated that reliance on power remained his primary consideration. On January 1, on the first anniversary of the signing of the Declaration by United Nations, he told a press conference that the most important "war objective" was "maintenance of the peace." When asked how he proposed to achieve that, he ducked the question: "No, no . . . you are talking about details. . . . I am talking about objectives. . . . The issue is the objective."[1] A week later, in his State of the Union message, he developed this theme with less ambiguity. The country should not now get "bogged down in argument over method and details," but should focus on the vital point: to prevent "any attempt to rearm in Germany, in Japan, in Italy, or in any other nation which seeks to violate the Tenth Commandment, 'Thou shalt not covet.'" The League of Nations was "based on magnificent idealism," but "good intentions alone" were not a sufficient future safeguard against "the predatory animals of this world."[2]

Some grasped his meaning. "The Roosevelt Doctrine," wrote *Newsweek*, "is that we must shatter at the source any threat to the peace of the world."[3] That doctrine stood in stark contrast to the lofty visions of democratic cooperation and equality being offered by Wallace, Willkie, and Welles. It amounted to a categorical repudiation of Wilsonian idealism, which remained the prime motivating force of those in the vanguard of the internationalist movement, but many were slow to note the discrepancy.

Percolation in the Congress

As the Seventy-eighth Congress opened on January 6, a spate of resolutions, both Republican and Democratic, were offered to create postwar planning commissions. Freshman Congressman William Fulbright (D-Arkansas) called upon the House Foreign Affairs Committee to "develop a specific plan or system" for the maintenance of international peace. Senator Guy Gillette (D-Indiana) proposed treaty negotiations to establish a "program of purposes and principles" based on the Atlantic Charter. These initiatives presented the Administration with a dilemma: it did not want to oppose them publicly, but it had not yet formulated a firm position of its own, nor negotiated any arrangement with its allies. Moreover, it feared that public hearings would give isolationists a platform from which to revive popular distaste for the British Empire and popular fear of Russian Communism. Hull, who thought that a venting of the ideological differences within the Big Three alliance would seriously disrupt the war effort, urged the relevant legislative chairmen not to hold hearings and to keep the various resolutions from coming to the floor of either house.[4]

A more formidable challenge to the Administration's aim to keep the lid on discussion of postwar issues came from a small group of Senators led by Joseph H. Ball (R-Minnesota). Ball was a tall, rough-hewn man of thirty-eight with a rural background and a Lincolnesque melancholy, who had been a political reporter in St. Paul before the even younger Republican Governor Harold Stassen appointed him to a vacant Senate seat. After Pearl Harbor, Ball decided that it was imperative for the United States to take the lead in forming a new world organization, and he found three like-minded colleagues who were equally determined to prevent the issue from being pushed under the rug. They were Harold Burton (R-Ohio), Carl Hatch (D-New Mexico), and Lister Hill (D-Alabama).

Ball's resolution (cosponsored by the other three and thereafter called "B2-H2") was more specific and far-reaching than anything previously proposed in the Congress. It called for the United Nations coalition to form a permanent international organization during the war, with authority to run

Congressman J. William Fulbright in 1943.
(Reproduced from the J. William Fulbright
Papers, Special Collections Division,
University of Arkansas Libraries)

the war, occupy liberated territory, and handle economic recovery and the peaceful settlement of disputes. The new organization would also create a postwar world police force to suppress "any future attempt at military aggression by any nation."[5]

In early March, Ball took his resolution to Sumner Welles, who was once again Acting Secretary of State while Hull nursed his fragile health on his regular winter sojourn in Florida. Welles gave Ball his enthusiastic endorsement and urged him to introduce the resolution without delay. On March 14, the four sponsoring Senators discussed their proposals with the President, who was accompanied by Welles, Harry Hopkins, and James Byrnes (who had resigned from the Supreme Court in 1942 to become Director of Economic Stabilization). The discussion was cordial, and Roosevelt indicated his agreement in principle, but he urged them to wait, as he feared that their resolution would stir up a hornet's nest of isolationist reaction. The four Senators respectfully disagreed, and Ball introduced the resolution in the Senate the following day.

Asked at his next press conference whether he supported B2-H2, FDR sidestepped by saying that, while the State Department was discussing a range of such matters with the Allies, he preferred to avoid "any specifics" on post-war issues. However, when the *New York Times* then suggested that his response to the Ball proposal had been "cool," he sought to correct this impression, saying that he did favor having the world know that the United States was "ready and willing to help in maintaining future peace," and that "yes, yes," he endorsed the Ball resolution in principle.

Hull reacted to B2-H2 with characteristic anxiety and set about drafting a shorter, milder substitute resolution that he hoped the Senate would pass immediately by an overwhelming majority. Then he sought assurances from Tom Connally (D-Texas), chairman of the Senate Foreign Relations Committee, that he would keep the Ball resolution bottled up. Connally promptly appointed an eight-man subcommittee to study the issue. Publicly Connally promised thorough analysis and quick action; privately he said that the subcommittee would sit on the Ball resolution as long as possible and then report out a broader, more generalized version.[6]

In early 1943, public opinion was moving toward a definite international orientation, and the Ball resolution gave it added impetus. The resolution also galvanized major elements of the internationalist movement by providing a sharper focus and a power lever in the Senate, neither of which these private-citizen groups had hitherto possessed. Their organized efforts began to pressure the Connally subcommittee to hold hearings, but the resentful senior Senator dug in his heels, arguing privately that open discussion would produce "the damndest gut-pulling you ever saw" and disrupt the war effort.[7]

The most provocative element of the Ball resolution was its call for American participation in an international police force, but the breadth and depth of support for this, as indeed for other long-term American responsibilities in the postwar world, was not easy to gauge. A poll of the Senate in April showed only twenty-four in favor of a world police force, thirty-two opposed, and forty uncommitted. At the same time, a Gallup poll indicated that 74 percent of Americans favored such an organization. Professional observers were skeptical of this latter figure, believing that very few Americans really understood the ramifications of that kind of undertaking. It was easy to be for it in the abstract. The *New Yorker* wrote: "Asking a man whether he wants an international police force is like asking him whether he wants the Rockettes."[8]

The Draft Constitution

Notwithstanding his refusal to go public, the President had been holding frequent meetings with Sumner Welles since October 1942 and had authorized him to develop a "draft constitution" for a new international organization.[9] According to Welles, the more hopeful war developments near the end of 1942—the American victory at Midway, the British victory at El Alamein, and the North African landings in November—had given the President time to turn part of his attention to postwar problems. And as he studied "ever more attentively every detail of international organization," Roosevelt concluded that "no lasting peace was possible . . . unless an effective international organization were founded, and founded, if possible, before the conclusion of the war."[10]

One late afternoon in January 1943, Welles secured an uninterrupted two hours with the President for the purpose of presenting the new work of his group. "For once, he was not in a digressive mood. He read very carefully the memoranda and charts that I placed before him."[11] The plan Welles presented was not strikingly different from the one he had recommended the previous April—which both Hull and the President had rejected—but the situation was now different. As in the earlier plan, the world structure would include all "peace-loving" nations, but it would operate through an executive committee to which supreme authority would be delegated. This would be composed of the Big Four (Roosevelt's Four Policemen) plus seven representatives of "regional organizations." The plan recognized implicitly that each of the Big Four was the dominant power in a particular region, and that collectively they covered the world. The Big Four would have permanent status on the executive committee, whereas the regional members would be periodically rotated. The Big Four would be exclusively responsible for maintaining the peace, but the employment of their armed forces would require the affirmative vote of nine members of the executive committee, including at least three of the Big Four. This qualified veto power would, Welles believed, provide "legitimate security" for the major powers, while giving a "fair measure of authority" to the smaller states. It meant that, if faced by the affirmative votes of three major powers and six regional representatives, no major power could block sanctions, including the use of force, even against itself.[12]

The regional organizations would handle local and regional disputes under the broader authority of the executive committee, a division of responsibility that represented Welles's earnest attempt to reconcile "the sovereign equality of all states with the inevitable demand by the major military powers for such freedom of action as might be required."[13] The basically regional orientation of the Welles plan was heavily influenced by his personal experience as head of the Latin American Division of the State Department, but the Pan-American Union (later formalized in the Organization of American States) was the only existing regional arrangement in 1943. FDR appeared to accept the Welles plan in principle, but doubted whether regional groups for the Pacific and the Middle East were feasible, given the lack of experience with self-government in those areas. Also, he did not believe that Stalin would join an all-embracing international organization without the protection of an absolute veto power.[14]

British Views

Winston Churchill, being a true Britisher, took a generally dim view of carefully structured, long-term planning, for he believed that desirable goals were best reached through wise and experienced management of events as they unfolded. In 1942, he told Anthony Eden that "postwar studies" should be assigned "mainly to those on whose hands time hangs heavy"; indeed, that all planners should "not overlook Mrs. Glass' Cookery Book recipe for jugged hare—first catch your hare."[15] Nevertheless, he had pronounced and comprehensive views on how to organize the postwar world.

While American postwar planners were thinking in terms of some synthesis of regional and global organization to replace the League of Nations, the British Prime Minister was thinking of authoritative regional arrangements without a global nexus, and his focus was on Europe. He was dismissive of China and uneasy at the idea of sharing responsibility for the future of Western Europe with the Soviet Union. In a note to Eden of October 12, 1942, Churchill wrote, "I must admit that my thoughts rest primarily in Europe—the revival of the glory of Europe, the parent continent of the modern nations and of civilization." It would be a "measureless disaster if Russian barbarism overlaid the culture and independence" of these ancient states. "We certainly do not want to be shut up with the Russians and the Chinese" in Europe. Moreover, "I cannot regard the Chungking Government as representing a great world Power."[16]

Churchill launched the essence of these ideas in a radio address in March 1943. Expressing the hope that the "three" major powers would collaborate to create some form of "world institution" after victory in the war, he proposed only a Council of Europe and a Council of Asia. While implicitly subordinate to some global umbrella organization, these regional councils, the Prime Minister made clear, should possess broad authority in their areas. He urged every effort "to make the Council of Europe . . . into a really effective league" into which would be woven "all the strongest forces," that is, military units to enforce council decisions and prevent future aggression, a High Court of Justice, and various other mechanisms to coordinate and adjudicate intraregional disputes.[17]

This British proposal for what appeared to be nearly autonomous regional authorities encountered considerable resistance in the White House and the State Department, although apparently for different reasons. The President was miffed by Churchill's omission of China as a major power, for Roosevelt wanted to strengthen that country in every way as a postwar counterweight to Japan; moreover, he believed that, if China were accepted as one of the Big Four, it would show all non-Caucasian peoples that the Western powers were not seeking to continue their domination into the postwar period, including their colonial grip on the world's major resources. In FDR's view, China's elevation to Great Power status would provide a necessary measure of psychological lubrication in the painful, inevitable transition from the colonial system to independence.[18]

On the more basic issue of a central versus a regional concept of postwar organization, however, FDR seemed comfortable, in early 1943, with the somewhat hybrid approach recommended by Welles. The more passionate opposition to a regional concept came from Secretary of State Hull, who believed that it was weak and unworkable. He feared that the existence of regional blocs would undermine the authority of the central organization and could lead to interregional trade wars and even military conflicts; also that isolationists would fix on the notion of several regional organizations to restrict U.S. participation to the Western Hemisphere group.[19] It was Hull's view that the President's apparent acceptance of a regional approach was attributable to Welles's pernicious influence at the White House. In fact, Welles was not a die-hard regionalist, and FDR, while keeping his options open, was moving steadily toward the idea of a strong global organization.[20]

Anthony Eden had come to Washington in the same month for a broad review of the war situation, as well as to discuss postwar strategy. FDR summoned him to the White House for a meeting that included Hull, Welles, Hopkins, and Lord Halifax, the British Ambassador. The President had in hand the "draft constitution" that Welles had presented to him in January, and he had Welles explain the details. According to Hopkins's notes, both the President and Welles "emphatically" opposed Churchill's idea of "independent" regional councils. There might be a place for such bodies, provided they were clearly subordinate to a global organization, but not otherwise.[21] According to Welles, the President also asserted "rather more strongly than I had hoped" his clear preference for realpolitik. The "real decisions . . . all basic decisions affecting world order," he told Eden, would have to be made by the Big Four for a long time.[22]

Eden said diplomatically that Churchill's position was not basically at odds with the President's, and he expressed his own personal preference for a strong global organization. In fact, there were serious differences of view between the Prime Minister and the Foreign Office on the issue of postwar organization. They agreed on the need to revive France as a major counterweight to Germany and Russia and on the rather dismissive assessment of China, but the Foreign Office saw no future for a Europe-based organization unless the United States was a fully committed, long-term participant. Others in British official circles shared the Foreign Office view, which led one historian to remark later that Churchill's ideas on postwar planning "were not of necessity those of the British Government." In its polite, quietly intense debate with the dogged Prime Minister, the Foreign Office was therefore greatly heartened by Washington's reaction to Churchill's radio address.[23]

Churchill was again in Washington in May 1943 for the bilateral Trident Conference to develop further war plans following the Allied victory in North Africa. The meeting lasted two weeks and covered every aspect of the war. The issue of postwar organization was dealt with—informally, but comprehensively—at a luncheon at the British Embassy on May 22. FDR was not present, but the Americans included Vice President Henry Wallace, Secretary of War Henry Stimson, Secretary of the Interior Harold Ickes, Welles, and Senator Connally. The Prime Minister spoke at length, and there ensued a general discussion. It was evident that American criticism of his March radio address had been taken into account, but it was equally clear that he had by no means abandoned the basics of his regional approach.[24]

Churchill said that to reach the overriding objective of preventing future aggression by Germany and Japan would require "an association" of the three major powers, but if the United States wished to add China to this group, he was "perfectly willing that this should be done." This inner group should form a Supreme World Council. Subordinate to this entity would be three regional councils for Europe, the Pacific, and the Western Hemisphere. Disputes within a region should be handled, in the first instance, by the regional council, but "always under the general overriding authority of the World Council." The basic structural idea was "a three-legged stool—the World Council resting on three Regional Councils."[25]

The Prime Minister nevertheless laid greatest emphasis on the regional councils, for he believed the experience of the League of Nations had demonstrated that "only the countries whose interests were directly affected by a dispute . . . could be expected to apply themselves with sufficient vigour to secure a settlement." In his view, "It was wrong to say that the League had failed. It was rather the member states who had failed the League."

The members of the Supreme World Council would sit on the regional councils in which they had a direct interest. He hoped that the United States would be represented on all three. Russia and Britain would sit on the European and Pacific groups, and Canada would "naturally" represent the British Commonwealth in the Western Hemisphere group. Readily available military force would be required to preserve the peace in each region and globally. To meet its obligations to the world organization, each member nation might consider dividing its forces into two contingents—one for territorial defense, the other to put at the disposal of "an international police force." It is notable here that Churchill's view of participation in international policing extended beyond the Four Policemen.

The Prime Minister hoped that several small nations in Europe might form natural confederations—Scandinavia, the Balkans, and "something" along the Danube based on Vienna "to fill the gap caused by the disappearance of the Austro-Hungarian Empire." Bavaria might become a part of this latter group. It was also politically desirable for Prussia to be separated from the rest of Germany. It was essential to re-create a strong France, for the prospect of having no effective democratic buffer between England and Russia was "not attractive."[26]

Six weeks later, on July 14, the arrival of a formal aide-mémoire confirmed these views as the official position of the British Government, indicating that, despite internal resistance, Churchill's views were being imposed on the Foreign Office. The British note dealt only with the creation of a United Nations Commission for Europe. This would be the supreme United Nations authority on the continent and would deal with the full range of military, political, and economic problems inherent in the maintenance of order after hostilities—including the coordination of armistice commissions, occupation policies for several enemy countries, relief and rehabilitation, shipping, inland transportation, telecommunications, and reparations. The commission's authority would also apply to long-range problems well beyond a transitional period.

Membership in the United Nations Commission for Europe would include Britain, the United States, and Russia, as well as all the other European allies. A steering committee comprising the Big Three would operate under the unanimity rule; France might be added to this group "if she recovers her greatness."[27]

A Gathering American Consensus

The arrival of the British aide-mémoire forced the Administration to focus on its own internal conceptual ambiguities and attempt to resolve them. Hull, who had now reasserted personal control of postwar planning, decided that rather than reply directly to the British note, the United States would present counterproposals at the impending Quadrant Conference in Quebec City. This decision imposed a tight deadline of August 17 for clarifying the U.S. position. As it turned out, this was not a task of great difficulty within the State Department, for there was a gathering consensus among senior departmental officials in favor of a central global authority to maintain peace in the postwar period. The real differences were with the British. The State Department objected to the British note on two grounds: its emphatically regional focus and its notion of combining transitional and long-term authority.[28]

The consensus on the American side appeared to include the President, judging from his remarks to Eden in March, which were critical of Churchill's radio address; yet Roosevelt remained unwilling to reveal his full hand. As the war situation became less desperate, he launched one or two of his own trial balloons to test public attitudes, but they were predictably couched in the broadest generalities. The most significant was an April 10 article in the *Saturday Evening Post* by Forrest Davis, based on a long private interview.[29] It studiously avoided mention of any postwar organization. At the same time, it emphasized FDR's basic conviction that the Four Policemen must undergird the peace. The President's great hope, the article stated, was that the universal need for peace would prove to be the "common denominator" that would bring the major powers to form a "genuine association of interest," for this was the sine qua non of postwar stability. Much depended on Stalin, for the Soviet Union would be the only first-rate military power on the continents of Europe and Asia after the war. If the dictator chose cooperation, the foundations of a peaceful society could be laid with confidence; if he chose another course, the Western allies would be "driven back on a balance of power system."

The President was opposed to reviving the League of Nations, owing to "its aura of failure," but retention of some of its "instrumentalities" might be useful. His thoughts on international organization did not, however, go beyond an unspecified mechanism for "swift and easy consultation" that would express the "united will" of all members. He was specific only on the question of military power: here, "A security commission made up of Russia, Britain and the United States might well police the peace of Europe during the transition period," and a similar body "including China" might do the same for Asia. If the major powers could erect that kind of bulwark against future aggression, then the smaller nations, which could not defend themselves in any event, might more easily "be brought to disarmament." However, to avoid alarming those segments of the American people who remained undecided on the question of a global role for the United States, he made the facile assertion that enforcement of peace would not require "international armed forces," nor the stationing of large American forces abroad. Both would be rendered unnecessary by "the preventive use of air power."

On balance, the President and all supporters of a new and effective organization for keeping the peace had reason to be encouraged by political and military developments during the first six months of 1943.

7

Will the Russians Participate?

Despite the British aide-mémoire of July 1943, which differed from the U.S. view on the role of regional organizations, there was general confidence that differences between Washington and London could be resolved. Where Russia stood on postwar organization remained, however, a consequential unknown. Churchill and Roosevelt had been unable to persuade Stalin to attend the Torch Conference in Casablanca in January or the Trident Conference in Washington in May; now Stalin had declined to join them for the impending Quadrant Conference in Quebec City, citing the seriousness of his military situation. Relations between Russia and the West were increasingly strained by differences over the timing of the opening of a second front, by the pace and volume of Lend-Lease assistance, and by Russian territorial claims in Eastern Europe. While the two Western allies were not yet ready to define their own peace objectives in detail, they were agreed on the urgent need to test Russian intentions with regard to Europe specifically and international cooperation generally. The American side supported Churchill's view that the best approach to Stalin was to present postwar plans as "a continuation of our present cooperation, and to do so while the war was still proceeding."[1]

There was also a growing awareness that the smaller members of the United Nations coalition were apprehensive about the intentions and modus operandi of the major powers. The two-tiered approach to wartime consultations (which presented the smaller states with situations of fact created by the three powers who were conducting the war) and the rumors of President Roosevelt's concept of the Four Policemen contributed to their feeling that the future of most of the world was being arbitrarily decided by the United States, Britain, and Russia.[2]

The Staff Charter

Thus facing a three-part problem—the need to resolve differences with the British, to test Russian intentions, and to reassure the smaller nations—the State Department developed two mutually reinforcing plans. The first was a proposed Four Power Agreement committing those nations to a series of war objectives and postwar aims. The second was a proposal to create a "provisional" international organization encompassing all United Nations members and to make it operational while the war was still being waged. The reason for separating the proposals rested on the belief that testing Soviet intentions was both the paramount need and the simpler task, diplomatically; negotiations with the larger group of states would be more complicated and would take longer.

The most important provisions of the Four Power draft pledged the signatories to continue their "united action" both to prosecute the war until the Axis enemies had laid down their arms "on the basis of unconditional surrender," and to provide for "the organization and maintenance of peace and security." It recognized the "necessity" of establishing "a general international organization" based on the principle of sovereign equality and open to "all peace-loving states." Pending the reestablishment of law and order and "the inauguration of a system of general security," the Four Powers would act jointly to maintain the peace. But to put some limits on this broad assumption of authority, the signatories pledged "not to employ their military forces within the territories of other states," except for the purpose of maintaining peace, and "after consultation and agreement."[3]

The second State Department proposal—for the prompt creation of an interim international organization—became known as the Staff Charter. It bore a striking resemblance to the Draft Constitution plan that Roosevelt had discussed with Welles and informally blessed in January 1943. The Draft Constitution in turn had been essentially a refinement of the United Nations

Authority plan that both Hull and FDR had rejected in 1942. But time and events had changed perceptions of what was desirable and feasible.

A major purpose of the Staff Charter plan was to provide machinery for the entire United Nations membership to authorize action on their behalf by the Four Powers, both during the war and for a subsequent transition period. But until the end of this indefinite period, there would be no direct participation by all members. The only operating entities would be a committee composed solely of the Big Four, plus an eleven-man executive council (composed of representatives of the Big Four as permanent members plus seven individuals chosen periodically from five regional groupings). These two entities would deal only with security matters, and decisions authorizing the use of force would require a two-thirds vote in the executive council, including all of the Big Four. This seemed to make clear that no collective enforcement action could be taken without the consent of all of the Big Four, but State Department thinking on the veto retained ambiguities that continued to bedevil and confuse the U.S. presentation of this issue for the next two years. To facilitate the transition from a temporary organization having only military security functions to a permanent and more comprehensive institution, all United Nations members would pledge to plan for "the creation of a permanent organization" that would deal with "the maintenance of peace and the advancement of human welfare."[4]

Hull was not enthusiastic about the Staff Charter, in part because it retained the notion of regional subcouncils and in part because he thought it was too naked an expression of Big Four dominance. One must infer that he accepted it in July 1943 only because no other plan could be readied within the tight deadline set by the Quadrant Conference, scheduled for August 17. Moreover, Hull was moving to assume firmer control of the State Department's planning effort, and had decided to force a showdown that would result in Welles's resignation and departure.[5]

On August 10, Hull and his advisers, including Welles, met with FDR to consider the issues raised by the British aide-mémoire and the State Department's proposed response, as a basis for formulating the U.S. position for the impending conference in Quebec. The President readily agreed to the substance of the Four Power Agreement draft, but wanted it changed from an agreement to a more flexible declaration of intentions. He also endorsed the idea of establishing an interim United Nations organization before the end of hostilities, but felt that the eleven-man executive committee should be assigned social and economic functions, in addition to its primary military security role. Here again, he wanted the proposal to be expressed not as a formal agreement, but as a set of propositions. These reactions rested on his judgment of the domestic political situation. A more informal approach to negotiations with members of the United Nations coalition would, he perceived, facilitate initial "agreements in principle" and postpone the need to submit a treaty document to the Senate, while also providing more time to educate the American people and win public support. Roosevelt endorsed Hull's view that there were "grave dangers" in having the new world organization rest on the foundations of "full-fledged, previously created" regional councils, thus giving evidence that he was now convinced that a strong central organization was imperative for postwar peace.[6]

Welles Is Forced Out

Hull forced Welles's departure in August 1943, aided decisively by an incident in 1940 that was systematically and malevolently exacerbated by William Bullitt, the recent U.S. Ambassador to France. The aging Secretary of State deeply resented the influence of the vigorous Under Secretary and believed that his own control of foreign policy was being usurped. At the same time, he was keenly aware that the strong personal and professional relationship between Welles and the President made it dangerous to make a direct effort to oust his rival. Hull was unwilling to incur the President's wrath. Bullitt, for his own reasons, was willing to do most of the dirty work.

Bullitt, an upper-class Philadelphian with a personal manner that many found insufferable, was personally close to the President and had served as the first U.S. Ambassador to the Soviet Union in 1933; he moved to the Paris Embassy in 1936. When France surrendered to Hitler in 1940, FDR ordered him to remain with the rump French Government after its flight to Vichy, but Bullitt instead rushed to Washington in search of a Cabinet post. This act of disobedience cost him the President's confidence. When Roosevelt asked Welles who might fill the Vichy post, Welles suggested Admiral William D. Leahy, a former Chief of Naval Operations who was then serving as Governor of Puerto Rico. The President liked the idea and acted on it instantly, without even consulting Bullitt, who thought that he had been asked to stay on. Bul-

William Bullitt in Washington, 1942.
(T. McAvoy, *Life*, Courtesy Franklin
Roosevelt Library)

litt's anger erupted in an agitated telephone call to FDR on November 9, 1940, which ended with a presidential apology for having neglected normal etiquette in the matter. "Bill, believe it or not, but I forgot all about it. . . . It's entirely my fault." But the deed was done, and an embittered Bullitt blamed Welles.[7]

The fateful incident involving Welles had occurred on a train in early September 1940. Having affronted Southern conservatives by choosing Henry Wallace as his running mate for the third-term bid, the President sought to placate them by taking the entire Cabinet, by special train, to the funeral of the recently deceased Speaker of the House, William Bankhead, in Jasper, Alabama. After a grueling trip and a long ceremony in ninety-degree heat, the Administration officials immediately reboarded the train for the return to Washington. There was heavy drinking in the club car throughout the evening, and by two A.M. an exhausted Welles was also drunk. Staggering back to his compartment, he rang for coffee. The porter who answered the buzzer was allegedly "offered money for immoral acts," which he politely refused.[8]

The story was immediately disclosed to the Secret Service and also reported to the railroad president, who passed it to a friend and fellow Southerner, "Judge" R. Walton Moore. The "Judge," seventy-eight, happened to be the Assistant Secretary of State for Congressional Liaison and a confidante of Hull, and was still embittered at having lost out to Welles in a fierce competition for the Under Secretaryship in 1934. Moore also revealed the story to the vengeful William Bullitt. Unable to attack the President directly, Bullitt set out to destroy Welles.[9]

On hearing from the Secret Service, the President ordered the FBI to make a discreet investigation and report directly to him. The FBI report confirmed the basic story, and also indicated Welles's apparent involvement in a similar incident two weeks later on the Pennsylvania Railroad when he was en route to a speaking engagement in Cleveland. FDR accepted the report as factual. But he needed Welles badly in 1940, he was no prude, and he excused the behavior on the grounds that Welles had been very drunk on both occasions. The agreed solution was to provide Welles with a bodyguard for future travel.

Bullitt went to see the President in April 1941 to urge that Welles be dismissed as a potential victim of blackmail. FDR heard him out, but said he already knew the story and had made his decision. A frustrated Bullitt then became the determined blackmailer, spreading the story among those Republican Senators and Congressmen who were rabidly anti-Roosevelt. He also conspired with Hull. The rumors persisted for the next two years, but seemed to have no impact on the steady rise of Welles's professional reputation, nor were any further incidents reported. In January 1943, however, Hull told the President that the rumors were spreading, and that the Administration faced an unprecedented scandal unless Welles were dismissed forthwith. FDR rejected this advice, and proceeded to rely even more heavily on Welles.

On July 27, Bullitt once again went to the White House to press the case. This time a violent quarrel erupted during which the President called Bullitt "un-christian" for attempting "to destroy a fellow-being." He needed Welles, he shouted, more than he needed "that old fool." He said to Bullitt, "Get out of here and never come back."[10]

On August 4, a long story in the *New York Times* reported that the State Department was being crippled at a critical point in the war by "conflicting personalities, lack of a cohesive policy, and a resulting impairment of efficiency." The feud between Hull and Welles was "well-known." The article, which was basically a severe criticism of Hull, ended by suggesting that the "sluggishness" of the State Department could be remedied by a major shaking up. Two days later, Arthur Krock, the *Times* Washington bureau chief and a close friend of Hull, wrote a column which acknowledged "the mess" in the department, but placed the blame on Welles—and the President. Roosevelt had given Welles too much authority, he wrote, and Welles had worked steadily behind Hull's back. The State Department would function "smoothly and effectively when the President permits the Secretary to be the real, undisputed head of a loyal staff."[11]

Bullitt's work with FDR's enemies in the Congress now combined with the airing of the Hull-Welles feud in the press to make clear that public exposure of the train incidents was almost inevitable. Hull seized the moment, on August 10, to demand that Roosevelt accept Welles's resignation or his own. Faced with that stark choice, the President understood he would have to keep Hull, for the Secretary's standing with the Senate, especially with the Southern barons in the Democratic leadership, was crucial for ratification of a United Nations treaty. Nevertheless, he resisted the abrupt termination of a distinguished career and the disgrace of a close and highly valued friend.

Stalin had just agreed to a meeting of the Big Four foreign ministers in Moscow in October. FDR told Hull that Welles should resign in order to undertake that mission, and then go on to Chungking for talks with the Chinese. The primary purpose in both capitals would be to secure approval of the proposed Four Power Declaration. On his return, Welles could retire gracefully to private life. Hull agreed to this plan for a dignified exit.

The President summoned Welles the next day, broke the bad news, and urged him to accept the Moscow mission. Welles offered to resign immediately, but FDR refused this, and Welles then agreed to reflect on the proposed assignment in Moscow. He remained as Acting Secretary while Hull went to the Quadrant Conference in Quebec with the President, but on August 22 (while FDR and Hull were still out of town), he abruptly resigned and left for his home in Maine, leaving a disquieted Assistant Secretary Adolf Berle in charge of the department. Welles had just suffered a mild heart attack, and had definitely decided against the Moscow mission. Press stories of August 24 indicated that his resignation was on the President's desk, but there was no official confirmation for several weeks, and the exchange of letters between Roosevelt and Welles was never made public.[12]

By remaining silent and in Maine for several weeks, Welles became the hero of the tangled affair. The liberal press lamented the loss of the State Department's "most far-sighted internationalist," and *Time* regretted the passing of "a known and respected advocate of U.S. cooperation in international affairs"; indeed, the "forced resignation" of Sumner Welles made the murky uncertainties of U.S. foreign policy "even more obscure."[13] By forcing the issue as he did, and especially by lending himself to the unsavory tactics of Bullitt, Hull won a bureaucratic victory, but at considerable political cost to himself and the State Department. Blame for the turmoil and its consequences also attached to the President, whose instinctive mode of operation was to encourage rivalries among his advisers; in this case, he had inadvertently stoked Hull's smoldering frustration by an undisguised preference for relying on Welles in the formulation and execution of major foreign policies.

Hull, of course, had in mind no ready successor to assume the pivotal position of Under Secretary, but after a month of trying to manage his own bureaucracy, the limit of his administrative skills and the extent of his physical impairment were painfully evident. On September 21, director of economic stabilization James Byrnes suggested Edward Stettinius, Jr., the Lend-Lease administrator, for the post, if the President was still undecided. A surprisingly young former chairman of U.S. Steel, Stettinius at forty-three had no diplomatic training or experience but had run the Lend-Lease program efficiently. Byrnes thought that Stettinius's business acumen "splendidly equipped him" to manage the State Department, but many others were shocked by the suggestion. FDR proceeded to appoint Stettinius in a move that made clear his determination to be his own Secretary of State, as the time approached for crucial meetings at the summit to test Russian adherence to Roosevelt's concept of world organization and to take measures that would ensure enduring cooperation between Russia and the West at the end of hostilities.[14]

8

Quebec and Moscow

The primary focus of the first Roosevelt-Churchill meeting in Quebec, overlooking the St. Lawrence River and the majestic Laurentian mountains (Quadrant Conference, August 17–24, 1943) was necessarily on the war. The task highest on the agenda was to approve the plan for the Normandy invasion (Operation Overlord), which was some nine months away. The surrender of Italy appeared imminent. The liberation of North Africa had intensified the problem of how to deal with the rival claimants to official representation of France—General Charles de Gaulle versus General Henri Giraud. The final communiqué accurately characterized the meeting as an "Anglo-American war conference."[1]

The President and the Prime Minister made another attempt to lure the Russian dictator to a tripartite meeting—this time in Alaska—but that, too, met with failure. While refusing to meet in Alaska, Stalin nevertheless complained at always being in the position of a third party, responding to Anglo-American agreements. He did, however, propose a meeting of foreign ministers "in order not to postpone an examination of the questions which interest our countries," and this led to agreement to hold such a meeting in Moscow in October.[2]

Because the principals at Quebec were so intensely occupied with immediate war plans, the discussion of postwar organization proved less conclusive than the State

Quebec Conference, August 17–24, 1943: (*seated*) Anthony Eden, FDR, Princess Anne, Winston Churchill; (*standing*) Lord Athlone (governor-general of Canada), Canadian Prime Minister Mackenzie King, Sir Alexander Cadogan, Churchill aide Brendon Bracken.

Department had hoped; significant progress was nevertheless made. There was quick agreement on the substance of the proposed Four Power Declaration, and a decision was made to send it immediately to Stalin and Chiang Kai-shek, the leader of Nationalist China, for their concurrence. However, the related U.S. proposal to create an interim United Nations organization before the end of hostilities was neither clearly presented nor formally considered. The President did not faithfully adhere to the briefing papers he had approved, but talked around and through the subject, with a pronounced tendency to fall back on personal preferences he had long and deeply held.[3]

FDR's ambiguities on this occasion were almost certainly deliberate, his purpose being to downplay British-American differences and avoid confrontation on the issue of a global versus a regional approach to postwar security. This interpretation of his motives at Quebec is reinforced by his assiduous lobbying of Stalin at the Teheran Conference four months later. Initially Stalin was opposed to any international organization beyond a military alliance of the Big Three; then he found Churchill's regional approach more practical and congenial than a revival of Woodrow Wilson's global vision. But after two private meetings with Roosevelt, Stalin agreed to support the American concept of organization. Churchill knew what was going on, and was profoundly indignant at being excluded and outmaneuvered.[4]

Thus, at Quebec, FDR suggested to Churchill merely the "possibility" of raising with Stalin the idea of a postwar organization to maintain law and order while the world was recovering from the wounds of war. Also, the President seemed to be talking in terms of exclusive Big Four responsibility, as distinct from the State Department plan, which called for sharing such policing responsibility with the other members of the eleven-member executive council. On the development of surrender terms and occupation policies for Germany and Japan, the discussion at Quebec indicated that both Roosevelt and Churchill continued to view such matters as primarily for Anglo-American military decision.[5]

The idea of an interim United Nations organization thus died a quiet death at Quebec. No further mention of it appears anywhere in the official record. This may not have been Roosevelt's intention, but it surely pleased Cordell Hull. The Secretary of State opposed the still prominent regional elements in the plan—inherited from Sumner Welles—and was uncomfortable with the idea of immediately creating an organization of any kind, for that would require entering into negotiations with a large number of nations. Such activities, he felt, would lead inevitably to leaks, and the leaks would confuse and antagonize large segments of American opinion, in particular the U.S. Senate. Like the premature exposure of film, this would ruin the picture. Organizational structure and timing—especially timing—had been at the heart of Hull's professional differences with Welles.

The demise at Quebec of the plan for an interim organization did not, however, arrest the gathering momentum for a permanent organization. Roosevelt and Churchill approved the text of the Four Power Declaration, which called specifically for the establishment of a new international organization and related postwar collective security arrangements.[6]

Growing Domestic Support for World Organization

The late summer of 1943 was also a time of yeasty change in American domestic politics — change that moved the pendulum of public opinion further toward an internationalist orientation. The influential Postwar Advisory Council of the Republican Party, meeting in early September on Mackinac Island in Lake Michigan, adopted a resolution favoring "responsible participation by the United States in postwar cooperative organization among sovereign nations." This was in large part the work of Senator Arthur Vandenberg (R-Michigan), who was earnestly "hunting for the middle ground" between those who "would cheerfully give America away" at one extreme and those who "would attempt a total isolation" at the other. Operating on his home turf, Vandenberg repudiated his isolationist past to join forces with a group of internationalist governors, including Thomas Dewey of New York, Earl Warren of California, and Raymond Baldwin of Connecticut; at the same time, his formulation retained sufficient safeguards to national sovereignty to reassure conservatives and strict constructionists. By asserting the principle of U.S. participation in some form of international organization while the war was in progress, Vandenberg built a strong defense against a repeat of the obstructionist stance taken by the GOP in 1920. He went on to become a major figure in the effort to create the United Nations organization.[7]

When Congress reconvened in mid-September 1943, the House Foreign Affairs Committee voted to seek immediate passage of the resolution introduced several months before by a promising young Arkansas Congressman, William Fulbright. This had been considered inconclusively in June, owing in part to the Administration's lack of enthusiasm, but a Gallup Poll taken over the summer indicated that 78 percent of the American people now supported Fulbright's simple proposal to create "appropriate international machinery with power adequate to prevent future aggression and to maintain lasting peace." The House debate in September revealed strong bipartisan support and reduced the isolationists to desperate arguments (one of these, pointing out that Fulbright had been a Rhodes Scholar at Oxford, charged that his resolution was a naked attempt to surrender the United States to the British Empire). The resolution passed on September 21 by the overwhelming vote of 360 to 29. The *New York Times* called it a display of Congressional unity unsurpassed since the declaration of war on the Axis powers.[8]

Senator Arthur Vandenberg played a major
role in building bipartisan support for the
United Nations. (Courtesy Franklin
Roosevelt Library)

The President, who was persuaded that this action indicated a convincing
public readiness for a firm postwar commitment, sent word that he wanted
the Senate to go on record with a similar resolution before the Moscow Conference took up the proposed Four Power Declaration in October. But expe-
ditious action was hampered by professional jealousy. Senator Tom Connally
(D-Texas), who still wore the black bow tie and stand-up collar of the old-
fashioned Southern orator, was furious at the House for presuming to intrude
upon the Senate's exclusive foreign policy turf. "God damn it," he thundered,
"everybody's running around like a fellow with a tick in his navel, hollering
about postwar resolutions." Considering the young Arkansas Congressman a
"rube freshman," he refused to accept the Fulbright Resolution and set about
developing a new one.[9]

Connally's creation was slightly stronger than Fulbright's, but much
weaker than B2-H2, which his committee had bottled up for twenty-five
weeks. The Connally Resolution urged action on three points: to wage war
until final victory; to cooperate with allies in securing a just peace; and to join
with other free nations in establishing an international authority with the

power to prevent aggression and preserve peace. Supporting "an international authority," it eschewed any reference to an "international organization." To avoid any charge of White House interference, the President decided not to say or do anything. He hoped for a brief debate and a heavily favorable vote, but the Senate procrastinated.[10]

The Moscow Conference

In addition to proposing a foreign ministers' meeting in Moscow (October 19–30), Stalin agreed, after further haggling, to meet Roosevelt and Churchill in the capital of Iran in December. Also, he wanted the Moscow meeting to focus on preparations for Teheran, so that the heads of government could "take definite decisions on urgent questions" when they met. However, when ideas for the Moscow agenda were exchanged, the Soviets proposed only one item—ways and means to hasten the end of the war—and they insisted that this be discussed first. In a word, they wanted concrete assurances on the timing and scale of the opening of the second front against Hitler. It was apparent to Hull and Eden that the Soviets would have to be satisfied on the military issue before anything else could be discussed.

The U.S. delegation was headed by the Secretary of State who, in travelling to Moscow, had flown in an airplane for the first time in his life. He tabled four items, of which the Four Power Declaration was by far the most important. The others were a proposal that Russia join in talks on postwar economic cooperation; preliminary U.S. thoughts on the postwar treatment of Germany; and a suggestion for tripartite consultations on evolving political and economic issues. (This last was a characteristic Hull response to Stalin's July protest that Russia was not consulted on the Anglo-American handling of the Italian surrender.)[11]

The discussion of military plans for the Normandy invasion appeared to satisfy the Russians that a major Anglo-American invasion of Western Europe would take place in 1944. The meeting then turned to the Four Power Declaration. Hull introduced it, emphasizing his view that postwar cooperation was in the selfish interest of all the major powers, and that the proposed declaration was the essential next step. The world, he said, was watching closely to see whether the leading powers would "adopt the path of cooperation . . . in the interest of self-preservation."

Eden warmly supported Hull, and Soviet Foreign Minister V. M. Molotov said that his government also endorsed the principles of cooperation embodied in the draft. He was, however, opposed to the inclusion of China as a signatory, as China was not represented at the meeting. Having anticipated this ploy, Hull announced that China had already approved the draft; accordingly, it would be necessary to obtain Chinese agreement only to any textual modifications made in Moscow. There ensued several stiff exchanges, during which Hull warned of "terrific repercussions" and "all sorts of readjustments by my Government" to maintain stability in the Pacific if China were "dumped on her face" by the Big Three. Molotov apparently drew the intended inference—that Lend-Lease allocations might be increased for China and reduced for Russia if China was not a party to the proposed declaration—for he agreed to leave open the question of China's adherence, while the meeting addressed the text of the draft.

Molotov balked on only two points, but together they revealed a firm Russian intention to prevent smaller states from strengthening themselves through the formation of federations and to avoid a Russian obligation for joint action with the United States and Britain in dealing with the states of Eastern Europe. On the first point, Molotov objected to a clause that required the Big Four to act together in "any occupation of . . . territory of other states held by the enemy." Eden explained that this language would make clear that the Four Powers did not intend to occupy liberated countries. Molotov said that the words could be misconstrued to interfere with essential military operations. He was adamant, and the clause was dropped.

The related Soviet objection was to a requirement for "consultation and agreement" of the signatories before they employed their military forces "within the territories of other states." Hull explained that this was a self-denying pledge to reassure smaller states against unilateral or arbitrary intervention by one or more of the major powers. Molotov asked whether this provision would require Four Power approval, if Russia were, for example, to conclude an agreement of mutual assistance with Czechoslovakia involving Russian military bases on Czech territory. Hull and Eden both expressed the fear that such arrangements might prejudice the development of a comprehensive collective security system and should be discouraged. Molotov argued that, on the contrary, such arrangements might be necessary to protect the Soviet Union against future German aggression. In the end, the requirement for joint "consultation" was kept, but the word "agreement" was eliminated, which further reduced the safeguards against arbitrary Russian action in Eastern Europe.

Further evidence of Russia's intention to deal with Eastern Europe as an exclusive sphere of influence was provided in the desultory discussion of Poland. In early 1943, the Russians had broken relations with the Polish government-in-exile (the London Poles) and created their own Communist substitute (the Lublin Poles). The United States and Britain refused to recognize the latter group, but were without any real leverage to change the Russian position. Moreover, the United States was reluctant to overplay the issue, for it did not want to stir up anti-Soviet protests from the American-Polish community at a critical point in the war, when maximum Big Three unity was needed. At Moscow, Hull did raise the possibility that U.S. and British troops might join with Russian forces in liberating those countries on the borders of the Soviet Union, but this suggestion met with "a very determined show of opposition" by Molotov.[12]

Eden pressed, along the lines of the British aide-mémoire of July 1943, for the creation of regional machinery to deal with such gritty problems as surrender terms, occupation policies, and the determination of what regimes should be installed in France, Yugoslavia, Poland, and elsewhere. He won agreement to the establishment of a European Advisory Commission (EAC), but with a very limited mandate. Hull, for whom an overarching global organization was the first imperative and who saw a threat to this in every regional idea, insisted that such a commission take up only those problems referred to it with the unanimous consent of the Big Three. Molotov had other reasons for wishing to limit the commission's scope. In the end, there was agreement that the initial mandate of the EAC should be surrender terms and control machinery for the enemy states.

With the language of the Four Power Declaration approved, there arose the question of how to coordinate detailed planning for the new international organization, which was the necessary next step. Molotov suggested a Big Three committee to which other allied governments might gradually be added, but Hull was worried that the inclusion of other nations at this early stage "might lead only to rivalries and jealousies." He wanted the planning work confined to the Big Three and wished even their coordination to be "informal." This somewhat cumbersome approach was accepted, which led in effect to separate efforts in three capitals. The U.S. planning effort proved to be the most comprehensive and therefore the most influential in shaping the ultimate organization and procedures of the United Nations.[13]

The Dilatory Senate

Meanwhile, the Senate was bogged down by a combination of Senator Connally's resentment and timidity. Hull was already well into the Moscow Conference when committee hearings on the Connally Resolution finally began on October 19. Senator Claude Pepper (D-Florida) proposed substituting "international organization" for "international authority" and adding a reference to the need for "military force" to keep the peace, but the committee rejected his amendments by a vote of sixteen to five. The Connally Resolution thus went to the Senate floor in its original mild form. Senator Ball and his B2-H2 supporters—who included a tenacious Harry S Truman—decided to wage a floor fight, well aware that they risked splitting an internationalist Senate majority that seemed unwilling to accept a more specific U.S. commitment. They attacked the vague, tepid language of the Connally Resolution and its omission of any reference to an international force to keep the peace. Despite Connally's pleas for prompt action to bolster Hull in Moscow, the debate went on heatedly for ten days (from October 25 to November 5), with the isolationists hugely enjoying the spectacle of the internationalist coalition apparently coming apart at the seams.[14]

The President had urged Connally to act swiftly, in an effort to show Britain and Russia at Moscow that the U.S. Senate supported the creation of a new international organization. Ironically, the Senate effort was saved from failure by prior action at the Moscow Conference. On November 1, Hull and his fellow foreign ministers published the Moscow Declaration, paragraph 4 of which recognized "the necessity of establishing at the earliest practicable date a general international organization, based on the principle of sovereign equality of all peace-loving states . . . for the maintenance of international peace and security."[15]

When Senator Connally rose on the Senate floor to read the Moscow Declaration and to tell his colleagues it offered further reason to pass the resolution before them, Senator Ball pointed out that, in contrast to the fuzzy Connally formulation, the Moscow Declaration called specifically for an international organization. He expressed the hope that the Senate "now will be at least as clear and forthright in its expression as the agreement signed at Moscow." This illumination of the disparity between the two documents led promptly to an agreement to incorporate paragraph 4 of the Moscow Declaration into the Connally Resolution, which then passed by a vote of eighty-five to five. The *New York Times* called the Senate vote "a great triumph" which opens "the portals to a new world," but the agreement reached in Moscow was of intrinsically greater importance.[16]

Hull's Hour of Triumph

The agreement at Moscow produced a reaction of extravagant enthusiasm in the United States, and this made Hull a temporary national hero. Nearly every element of the press hailed the declaration as a major diplomatic triumph. Walter Lippmann praised Hull for cementing the Four Power alliance, saying that this ushered in "the next period of history."[17] Another syndicated columnist, Raymond Moley, wrote that the Secretary of State had achieved "a foreign policy on which all American parties and factions can agree" and that this achievement had "saved rivers of blood and months of war."[18]

There were a few dissenting voices. Sumner Welles, now relieved of office and writing a column for the *New York Herald-Tribune,* objected to what he perceived as the Four Power dictatorship inherent in the declaration and called for the immediate creation of a universal world body. Wendell Willkie made the same point.[19]

But it was Hull's moment of personal triumph. The President and the new Under Secretary of State, Edward Stettinius, Jr., met him at Washington National Airport when he returned from Moscow, and he was invited to address a joint session of Congress on November 18. Buoyed by a standing ovation as he entered the well of the House, he delivered an eloquent twenty-five-minute report on the Moscow meeting. He said that the continued cooperation of the Four Powers "will be the foundation stone upon which the future international organization will be constructed." Sounding idealistic Wilsonian themes in what seemed to be an attempt to answer the Welles and Willkie criticisms, he declared that "there will no longer be need for spheres of influence, for alliances, for balance of power." By "the process of cooperation with other nations likewise intent upon security," he predicted, "we can and will remain masters of our own fate." The speech was hardly free of Hull's favorite platitudes, but the fact of the Moscow Declaration, the supporting Senate vote, and the positive public response gave powerful reinforcement to its central message: that the Senate must not again sabotage arrangements for American participation in a new world organization to keep the peace.[20]

The British reaction was more restrained, reflecting a lesser national taste for high-flown general principles and a stronger focus on practical machinery. Eden reported to the House of Commons that the Moscow Declaration was "the most far-reaching of the decisions to which we came," but he assigned greater importance to the creation of the European Advisory Commission, which would, he hoped, be able to concert allied action "on the many political problems which arise out of the war."[21]

The Russian reaction was to praise the meeting almost exclusively for the agreements it reached to advance military victory. Little or nothing about a new international organization appeared in the controlled press. And in a speech of November 6, Stalin said that the decisions taken were evidence that "our united countries are filled with determination to deal the common enemy blows which will result in final victory over him."[22]

9

Cairo and Teheran

The Moscow Declaration was a major encouragement to prospects for Big Three cooperation in the postwar period, but a follow-on meeting of the heads of government was necessary to confirm commitments made at the second level, and specifically to ensure that Stalin himself accepted the idea of an international organization to keep the peace.[1]

The heads of government meeting had been difficult to arrange, owing to Stalin's continued refusal to leave his home base, and to FDR's constitutional obligation to deal with congressional bills within a ten-day period. In the end Stalin agreed to make the relatively short trip from Russia to Iran, while the U.S. Government went to considerable trouble to create extraordinary transportation and communications arrangements to ensure that the President could carry out his official duties. For his own part, and considering his acute physical handicap, Roosevelt's willingness to undertake an arduous trip of several thousand miles was both a characteristic act of courage and an indication of the supreme importance he attached to a face-to-face meeting with the Soviet dictator. Of the two leaders, the President made by far the greater concessions to make the meeting a reality.[2]

Arrangements for Teheran were not, however, finally sorted out until late October, by which time FDR and Churchill had agreed to a November meeting in Cairo with Chiang Kai-shek to deal with the stalled Anglo-American objectives in the China theater. A separate meeting with Chiang was necessary, for the Russian position was that China must be "absolutely excluded" from the Teheran Conference. Officially, the Russians argued that inclusion of China would compromise their neutrality in the Pacific war, but the State Department and the Foreign Office discerned another reason: Russia perceived itself as an Asian, as well as a European power; accordingly, it did not wish to encourage situations in which China would be presented as the preeminent power in Asia.[3]

While the conference with Stalin was still in doubt, FDR suggested to Churchill that Russia might be invited to send a military observer to take part in the Combined Chiefs of Staff talks with the Chinese. His purpose was probably to enhance Chinese prestige, but he was also anxious to have some firsthand indication of Russian intentions, given the continuing uncertainty that a meeting with Stalin would take place. But Churchill rejected the idea out of hand. He was adamantly opposed to opening "this door" on Anglo-American military discussions to some Russian general who would "simply bay for an earlier second front and block all other discussions." Moreover, it would "probably mean they would want to have observers at all future meetings." In reply, FDR wrote that "it would be a terrible mistake if Uncle J. thought we had ganged up on him on military action." Fortunately, Stalin's agreement to meet at Teheran mooted this particular Anglo-American dispute. Roosevelt, Churchill, and Chiang Kai-shek thus met in Cairo November 22–26, following which the President and the Prime Minister met with Stalin in Teheran between November 28 and December 1.[4]

The China Problem

FDR was determined to do everything possible to make China an effective fighting ally and to underwrite Big Power status for the Chiang government. In January 1943 Roosevelt had persuaded Churchill to join with the United States in abandoning extraterritorial rights in China, an action of significant political importance to Chiang. Now he had succeeded in obtaining British and Russian agreement to China's adherence to the Moscow Declaration. At the Cairo meeting, he sought to strengthen China's military performance and reputation.[5]

But the situation in China was both a political and a military mess.

Chiang Kai-shek was the sinuous, somewhat mystical leader of a corrupt government and a passive army engaged in a dual struggle against Japanese invaders and a native Communist insurgency. The original Allied strategic plan had called for Anglo-Chinese forces coming from the west through Burma and American forces coming from across the Pacific to converge on the Canton–Hong Kong area, fight their way to North China, and from there establish a systematic air bombing campaign against Japan. But this required recapturing North Burma and building a reliable land route to China through formidable terrain and in the face of tenacious Japanese resistance. Such a road was required to provide the considerable supply tonnage necessary to enlarge and modernize the Chinese armies and to build up a major Allied air capability in China. But both the resources and leadership had proved to be seriously inadequate. Near the end of 1943, the larger questions had become how important was Burma as a front on which to engage the enemy? Indeed, how necessary was China as a strategic base for defeating Japan?[6]

Despite the failures and disappointments, FDR was determined to try again. He therefore sought to obtain firm commitments from Britain and China to carry out the agreed strategic plan. As an inducement to Chiang, he offered American equipment for an increased number of Chinese divisions and suggested the possibility of bringing China into a Four Power military planning agency. The British, however, were very cool to this proposal, and it was dropped. Churchill was also decidedly unenthusiastic about the Burma campaign, and insisted on reserving the British position until it was clear what level of resources would be available, after requirements for higher priority operations in Europe and the Pacific were firmly set. For his part, Chiang vacillated so much as to whether he would commit Chinese troops to the campaign, and under what conditions, that FDR and Churchill were "driven absolutely mad" (in the words of Admiral Lord Louis Mountbatten, who was present).[7] When Chiang demanded a simultaneous Anglo-American amphibious operation across the Bay of Bengal to Burma as a condition of committing Chinese troops, FDR gave his assurances, but the British reservations left the matter unresolved. The Cairo communiqué, thus being unable to report firm Allied agreement on any future military operations, expounded on longer range political goals of special interest to China—including the assertion that "all the territories Japan has stolen from the Chinese, such as Manchuria, Formosa and the Pescadores, shall be restored to the Republic of China."[8]

Chiang Kai-shek, FDR, and Churchill at the Cairo Conference, November 25, 1943.
(Courtesy Franklin Roosevelt Library)

The First Big Three Conference

The President and the Prime Minister left Cairo on November 26 and flew
separately to Teheran to meet with Stalin. FDR's aircraft, dubbed "The Sacred
Cow," flew 1,310 miles over the Suez Canal, Jerusalem, Baghdad, the
Euphrates and Tigris rivers, and the Iranian railroad, which by then had
become a vital link in the Lend-Lease supply line to Russia. The U.S. party
was initially quartered in the American Legation, at some distance from the
Russian and British compounds, which were close together. But after Ambassador W. Averell Harriman reported Stalin's concern that there were many
enemy agents in the city and that measures should be taken to avoid "an
unhappy incident" on the road between their separated residences, the President accepted a villa in the Russian compound, where security would be complete. This proved to be a physical convenience as well, but it was accepted

that the servants in the villa were all members of the Soviet secret police, known as the NKVD.[9]

At Teheran, military discussions occupied the greater part of the formal sessions and were centered on the coming Anglo-American invasion of Western Europe, now set for May 1944. At the first general session, Stalin made the welcome announcement that the Soviet Union would enter the war against Japan after the defeat of Germany. He had mentioned this to Harriman nearly a year before, and to Hull in Moscow in October, but now it was official at the highest level. Although it could not be made public, the announcement was very good news to the British and the Americans, especially to U.S. military leaders, who faced the daunting task of planning for what appeared to be the unavoidable invasion of Japan.

Most of the political discussions occurred informally at mealtimes. Though they did not involve commitments, they were significant for what they revealed of the different approaches and priorities of the three principals. In a deliberate effort to demonstrate that he and Churchill did not see eye to eye on every issue and to allay suspicion that the American and British positions were coordinated before discussion with the Russians, FDR held three private meetings with Stalin. (He held no private meetings with Churchill, much to the Prime Minister's chagrin.) At the first of these, he greeted the dictator with the statement, "I am glad to see you. I have tried for a long time to bring this about." Stalin, after suitable expressions of pleasure at meeting the President, accepted the blame for the delay in their getting together, saying that he had been "very occupied because of military matters." They then turned to a discussion of the Russian front, and Stalin gave an assessment of the battlefield situation, which was somewhat more grim than the information available to Western intelligence. The President replied that a main purpose of the Teheran Conference was to discuss measures that would ease the pressure on the Russian front by drawing off thirty or forty German divisions. Stalin agreed that such relief would be most helpful.[10]

There was a general discussion of France's place in the postwar world. Stalin thought that there was something politically "unreal" about de Gaulle, as he had "no communication with the physical France." He expounded at some length on the decadence of the French ruling classes and said that they "must pay for their criminal collaboration with Germany." The President said he felt that "many years of honest labor" would be required to restore France,

Stalin and FDR at the Teheran Conference, November 29, 1943.
(Courtesy Franklin Roosevelt Library)

and that the first requirement for both officials and ordinary Frenchmen was to "become honest citizens." Stalin said France should not get back Indochina, and the President replied he was "100% in agreement" with that. He told Stalin that he had discussed with Chiang Kai-shek the possibility of a trusteeship for Indochina to prepare the people for independence within twenty or thirty years. Later, in a plenary session of the conference, Roosevelt proposed a Four Power (United States, Russia, Britain, China) trusteeship for Vietnam, Laos, and Cambodia, saying that there was a need to begin the transition away from colonialism and toward independence. Stalin promptly endorsed the proposal, but Churchill objected.[11]

Harry Hopkins, who had met with him in 1941, noted that Stalin was now grayer, but also "much dressier," wearing a well-tailored gray uniform with gold epaulets, each bearing a large white star. His habit was to smoke and doodle during the general meetings, and to speak quietly but with emphasis.[12]

FDR's United Nations

At his second private meeting with Stalin, FDR laid out a plan for a postwar United Nations organization which differed in several important ways from the State Department's Staff Charter, and he added a few quite personal embellishments. First, there would be a worldwide assembly comprising all the United Nations; it would have no fixed headquarters, but would meet in various places at stated times to discuss world problems. Next, there would be an executive council composed of the Big Four plus six or seven representatives selected from several regions—two from Europe and one each from Latin America, the Middle East, the Far East, and the British Dominions. This executive council would deal with "all non-military questions," such as food, health, and economics. Finally, there would be a third entity—an enforcement body, composed of the Four Policemen, with authority to deal swiftly with any emergency or threat to the peace. As he had done at Quebec, FDR presented the Four Policemen entity as having exclusive authority to decide on the use of force. Under the State Department plan, however, the enforcement power, while exercisable only by the Four Policemen, was made subject to the guidance, recommendations, and general supervision of the more representative executive council, which in turn was the presumed spokesman for all members of the United Nations. In this discussion with Stalin, the President was reiterating his strong conviction that small nations should not be allowed to complicate the supreme task of keeping the peace.[13]

Stalin made no immediate comment on the concept of the Four Policemen, but asked whether the eleven-person executive council would have the power to bind other nations to its decisions on nonsecurity questions. FDR said that it would only make recommendations, but with the hope that other nations would comply.[14]

Regarding the American plan as a whole, Stalin was not much impressed. First, he echoed Churchill's doubt that China was or could become a world power. But even if it were, he thought that the European states would resent having China as an enforcement authority for themselves. He proposed an alternative set-up—one committee for Europe and another for the Far East. Membership for Europe would be the Big Three and "possibly" France. FDR noted that Stalin's proposal was similar to Churchill's regional approach, but

the President said he doubted that Congress would agree to American participation "in a purely European committee which might be able to compel the
involvement of American troops." This reply seemed both an evasion and a
non sequitur, for it was by no means certain that Congress would agree to a
"global" organization that had the power to "compel" the involvement of U.S.
forces. That had been and remained the key question in all plans for American
participation in an international peacekeeping organization, going back to
1919. There was apparently no discussion of the composition of a Far East
committee.[15]

Churchill, who resented being left out of the private Roosevelt-Stalin
meetings, later wrote that Stalin's instinctive preference for regional committees showed him to be "more prescient and possessed of a truer sense of values
than the President." At the same time, the Prime Minister expressed annoy-
ance that FDR had failed to explain that the British regional approach "contemplated a Supreme United Nations Council, of which the three regional
committees would be the components." It was regrettable that he, Churchill,
had been unable "to correct this erroneous presentation."[16]

Stalin, who appeared quite interested in the Four Policemen concept,
observed that it would appear to require the sending of American troops overseas, but the President replied that he had in mind committing only U.S.
naval and air forces to deal with problems in Europe. The requirement for
ground forces would have to be met by Britain and the Soviet Union. Again,
there was apparently no discussion of collective security responsibilities in the
Far East, quite possibly because FDR wished to avoid having to argue for
China as an effective regional policeman.

The President postulated two possible types of threat. A minor threat
might arise from a revolution or civil war in a small country, or a border dispute between small neighboring states; this could be dealt with by trade
embargoes and similar "quarantine" measures. A major threat might arise
from the aggression of a powerful state; this would require an ultimatum from
the Four Policemen threatening to bomb or invade the aggressor nation. The
discussion apparently avoided any speculation on what would happen if one
of the policemen was the aggressor. FDR's view of this contingency was
nowhere expressed, then or later. Sumner Welles had anticipated it by including in his earlier Draft Constitution plan a two-thirds voting procedure that
limited a major power's use of the veto. FDR had told Welles that he doubted

if Stalin would ever accept any limitation, but there was no discussion of voting procedure at Teheran.[17]

The President did not raise the issue of international organization at any of the formal plenary sessions, but treated the subject as a matter only for confidential discussion with Stalin. At one point he even suggested to the dictator that it was too early to discuss this subject with Churchill, as the Four Policemen concept in particular needed further study. This was obvious dissembling, for Churchill was fully informed of FDR's views, and it is unlikely that Stalin was fooled. But the President was engaged in an assiduous courting of the powerful, enigmatic Bolshevik whose cooperation was absolutely essential to Roosevelt's hopes and plans for future stability and peace.[18]

On the last day of the conference, Stalin informed Roosevelt that, after reflection, he had come to agree that the new international entity be a central, worldwide organization, rather than a series of linked regional groups. He gave no reasons for this change of view, but it is a fair inference that he was reassured by the President's statements that American troops were not expected to play a police role in Europe, and that decisions of the U.N. executive council would not be binding. From Stalin's point of view, these American positions made the proposed organization essentially innocuous, and Russian participation essentially cost-free. Sumner Welles later wrote that it was "well known" that Stalin opposed a genuine international organization based on the principle of sovereign equality and that he favored a straight military alliance with the United States and Britain which would "assume the right to determine the fate of all other peoples." It must have seemed to Stalin that FDR was offering him basically that kind of deal at Teheran, albeit wrapped in democratic trappings. If the President meant what he said about the role of the Four Policemen, then the Soviet Union could see no objection to participating in a universal United Nations organization, for it would enhance Russian prestige while presenting no serious obstacles to considerations of Russian security and ambition.[19]

Defeating and Controlling Germany

Stalin was primarily interested in obtaining definite assurances on the second front and in concerting measures to control Germany after the war. In the general session on November 29, he asked bluntly, "Who will command

Overlord?" When FDR replied that the decisions taken at this conference would affect that appointment, Stalin said that he "could not believe in the reality of the operation" until the commanding officer was named. According to Sherwood, Roosevelt must have been sorely tempted to name General George C. Marshall then and there, but he was still wrestling with the painful choice between keeping Marshall close at hand to guide the strategy of a global war and giving him the supreme combat command that could make him a great historic figure. He finally decided—on December 5, after he had returned to Washington—that Marshall's brilliant leadership of the Joint Chiefs of Staff was paramount. He made the decision against the impassioned opposition of Harry Hopkins and Secretary of War Henry Stimson, against the known preferences of Churchill and Stalin, and against his own pro-claimed inclination to give Marshall the command opportunity he richly deserved. If it was one of the "most difficult and loneliest" decisions he ever made, it was "surely one of the wisest"—validated by "the whole superb direc-tion of the war," as Sherwood later wrote. General Dwight D. Eisenhower, who had distinguished himself by the victories in North Africa and the Mediterranean, was then named to command Overlord.[20]

At Teheran, Stalin repeatedly returned to the subject of Germany, expressing the view that adequate postwar control must include the continu-ous occupation of "strong points," both within and along the German bor-ders, and "strategic bases" throughout the world to support the general struc-ture of peace. The idea of U.N. strategic bases, to contain both Germany and Japan and as part of the general enforcement machinery in the hands of the Four Policemen, was also central to FDR's conception of a postwar collective security system. All three principals were in full agreement that Germany must be prevented from ever again threatening the peace, but after inconclusive dis-cussion of ways and means, they referred this problem to the new European Advisory Commission.[21]

Poland and the Baltic States

The discussion of Poland was, predictably, totally unproductive. Churchill, who understood the geopolitical realities far better than Roosevelt, thought that the only hope of some accommodation lay in accepting whatever the Russians decided were their security requirements in eastern Poland, and then in seeking to arrange territorial compensation for the Poles in eastern Germany. But the London Poles stubbornly rejected the notion of losing any eastern territory, and Stalin was not showing his hand. At dinner on November 29, he deflected Churchill's question about Russia's future territorial interests by saying, "There is no need to speak at the present time about any Soviet desires—but when the time comes, we will speak."[22]

Despite these intractable realities, FDR approached the problem with characteristic Dutch stubbornness. Before leaving Washington, he had told Hull that he planned to appeal to Stalin on grounds of "high morality," in an effort to persuade him that it was in the Soviet interest to hold a second plebiscite in the Baltic states "two or three years after the war." He would also ask the Soviet leader to consider a plebiscite in eastern Poland—one that might fix the new boundary "east" of the Curzon Line.[23] This was surely whistling into the wind, but the President approached the task with the usual high confidence in his own ability as a negotiator. Welles had always thought that FDR put too much faith in the efficacy of plebiscites for solving Europe's tangled territorial disputes, that indeed Roosevelt was "more wedded to the idea that plebiscites are a universal remedy than Woodrow Wilson." Welles found this a serious weakness of the President's approach to diplomacy, especially in dealing with Stalin. Events at Teheran proved him right.[24]

At dinner on the first evening of the conference, FDR raised a question regarding assured international access to the Baltic Sea. The Russian translator apparently erred, for Stalin replied that the Baltic states had voted to join the Soviet Union by an expression of the people's will, and that the matter of reconsidering that vote was not for discussion.

On the last day of the conference, in his second private meeting with Stalin, FDR raised directly the question of a Baltic states plebiscite, but ambiguously mingled it with the issue of Poland—an approach that was a classic example of his combined tenacity and subtle indirection. He could not, he told Stalin, participate in any decision on Polish boundaries, owing to the existence of about 7 million American voters of Polish descent. There were also, he added, numerous American voters of Lithuanian, Latvian, and Estonian extraction whose opinions deserved equal respect. He wanted Stalin to understand the great importance the American people attached to the idea of self-determination. He said that "eventually" American and world opinion would want some expression of the will of the people in the Baltic states.

The Big Three at Teheran: Stalin, FDR, and Churchill, November 29, 1943.
(Courtesy Franklin Roosevelt Library)

Stalin, who must have been mildly mystified by the President's line of reasoning, and by his curious recusal on Poland, answered bluntly that the Baltic republics had enjoyed no autonomy under the last Tsar, and that he saw no reason why the question should be raised at this time. As there would be "full opportunity" for the people's will to be expressed under the Soviet constitution, he could not agree to any form of international control. After this categorical rebuff, FDR did not raise the question of a plebiscite for eastern Poland.[25]

The Significance of Teheran

The immediate import of the Teheran Conference lay in the military decisions that confirmed the momentous plans for Overlord. Also, Stalin's commitment to come into the war against Japan after Germany was defeated added a factor that at the time—before the atomic bomb was a reality—appeared to be of the greatest strategic importance.

But it was the public display of goodwill (as evidenced in the photographic coverage of the meeting) and the promises of future cooperation among arguably the three most powerful men in the world—leaders of countries that were the main repositories of hope for millions who had been crushed by the Axis tyrants—that generated a palpable surge of expectancy across the globe. Sherwood later wrote that in the press dispatches, and even in the "deliberately dry and guarded" official accounts of the meeting, readers could not fail to sense the extraordinary drama: "That here were Titans determining the future course of an entire planet."[26]

What made Teheran more dramatic and led to higher expectations than earlier conferences was the presence of the Soviet Union, now universally acknowledged to be a powerful influence, for good or evil, on the outcome of the war and the shape and character of the postwar world. Until the meeting in Teheran, little was known of Russian intentions, but Stalin's promises there to press the war against Germany in full collaboration with the United States and Britain, and to continue that collaboration by participating in a postwar organization of United Nations to safeguard the peace, were tidings of hope and joy to a still darkened and anguished world. The straightforward tone of the communiqué, less consciously eloquent than the Moscow Declaration, generated a feeling of confidence, even though it made no mention of a United Nations organization. Pledging themselves to work together "in war and in the peace that will follow," the three leaders said, "we are sure that our concord will win an enduring peace."[27]

The President, who gave close personal attention to the text of the communiqué, was the acknowledged author of the final sentences, which read: "We came here with hope and determination. We leave here, friends in fact, in spirit, and in purpose." In the light of later events, this was incautious and costly hyperbole, but there is little doubt it reflected FDR's ebullient confidence at the end of his first encounter with Stalin. He had found the dictator much tougher than he had expected and "at times deliberately discourteous," but he was drawn to the man's lack of hypocrisy. "The President likes Stalin," Harold Ickes recorded after a Cabinet meeting, "because he is open and frank." Asked by a reporter what kind of man Stalin was, FDR replied, "I would call him something like me . . . a realist."[28]

As Sherwood later wrote, "Roosevelt now felt sure that, to use his own term, Stalin was 'getatable,' despite his bludgeoning tactics and his attitude of cynicism." At Teheran, they had reached agreement on momentous undertakings to win the war and consolidate the peace, and FDR was confident that further agreements were within reach.[29]

Returning to Washington in buoyant spirits, he wrote to Welles: "I want to tell you all about Cairo and Teheran. I think that, as a roving ambassador for the first time, I did not pull any boners."[30] Sherwood stated that, "If there was any supreme peak in Roosevelt's career, I believe it might well be fixed at this moment, at the end of the Teheran Conference."[31]

The Prime Minister did not share the President's optimism, although he was pleased by the "friendship and unity of immediate purpose" that had been achieved at Teheran. Moreover, he understood the necessity of putting first things first: "Stalin's promise to enter the war against Japan as soon as Hitler was overthrown and his armies defeated was of the highest importance. The hope of the future lay in the most speedy ending of the war and the establishment of a World Instrument to prevent another war, founded upon the combined strength of the three Great Powers."[32] Intuitively, however, Churchill distrusted Stalin, whom he had characterized to FDR at Quebec as "an unnatural man." Physically exhausted by the strain and complexity of the global struggle, he felt a deep foreboding about the future. "There might be a more bloody war," he confided to Eden; more privately, to his physician, Lord Moran, he added: "Man might destroy man and wipe out civilization . . . we are only specks of dust that have settled in the night on the map of the world . . . [but] I shall not be there. I shall be asleep. I want to sleep for billions of years."[33]

Stalin's reactions to his first meeting with Roosevelt can only be surmised, but he had every reason to be pleased. He had made no firm commitments regarding the political future of Europe, but the Anglo-American forces would soon land in France with more than a million men, and this would form a powerful second front which, unless it failed, would assure the crushing defeat of Germany. In the Pacific area, his pledge to enter the war against Japan improved his leverage for realizing traditional Russian ambitions there, but again without binding him to any firm political commitments. His agreement to participation in a United Nations organization might help to advance both national and ideological prestige, but without placing any serious restrictions on Russian ambitions.

Then, too, perhaps the Soviet dictator shared at least the transient euphoria arising from the cordial atmosphere achieved at Teheran and from the importance of the decisions taken. At any rate, the U.S. Embassy in Moscow was soon reporting an almost "revolutionary change" in the tone of Soviet press stories about America and Britain. The entire propaganda machine was turned to promote public enthusiasm for the "historic decisions" taken at Teheran which would solidify allied unity and bring closer the day of victory and secure peace.[34]

Force and the Christmas Spirit

On the President's return to Washington, leaders of both parties urged him to address a joint session of Congress, but it was indicative of his state of mind that he decided to report to the nation by radio on Christmas Eve, deliberately linking the bright prospects for a United Nations organization with the Christmas spirit. In a worldwide broadcast from his family home at Hyde Park, N.Y., the President paid tribute to Churchill—"this great citizen of the world"—and also offered him "heartfelt prayers," for the Prime Minister had suffered another bout of pneumonia. Of Stalin, the President said, "He is a man who combines a tremendous, relentless determination with a stalwart good humor. I believe he is truly representative of the heart and soul of Russia; and I believe we are going to get along very well with him and the Russian people—very well indeed."

Throughout the speech he sounded the theme of unity, telling his audience that the Big Four nations represented three-quarters of the world population, and that the peace would be secure so long as they stuck together. He assured his listeners that these four major nations would protect the rights of smaller states and would not abuse their power: "The doctrine that the strong shall dominate the weak is the doctrine of our enemies—and we reject it."

Nevertheless, force and the willingness to use it were the keys to lasting peace. For "too many years," Americans had lived on "pious hopes" that aggressor nations would learn the virtues and rewards of peaceful cooperation with their neighbors. Now, he promised, Americans would not repeat that "disastrous policy," but would rely on "overwhelming military power to halt aggression before it could menace the world." He believed that Britain, Russia, and China were "in complete agreement that we must be prepared to keep the peace by force."[35]

The speech did not expressly identify or describe the Four Policemen concept, but the passages on necessary force were a thinly disguised paraphrase. And the paraphrase made clear that the Big Four—primarily or exclusively—would hold and wield the military power to prevent or punish future aggression; the peace would necessarily be based on Big Four primacy, which the President argued would be benign.

This eloquent essay reflected long and deeply held convictions on what was necessary to avoid further devastating war and the further destruction of civilization. Ironically, it ran directly counter to the assumptions of most democratic internationalists—in every country and walk of life—that the new world organization must be based on the principle of sovereign equality and must permit the smaller nations a meaningful role in the ordering of the postwar world. In the euphoria following Teheran, however, only a few grasped the sharp disjunction between the high principles proclaimed in the Moscow Declaration and the stark doctrine of realpolitik that underlay the President's prescription for a secure peace.[36]

10

High Hopes But Inherent Limits

Franklin Roosevelt had conceived the term "United Nations" a few weeks after Pearl Harbor, and sold it to Winston Churchill by bursting in on the Prime Minister's bath at the White House. The term was used to describe the twenty-six nations who signed the United Nations Declaration in Washington on January 1, 1942, a document that bound them together in the effort to wage war against the Axis and work for a just peace. As they prepared for formal talks on international organization in the summer of 1944, Roosevelt and Hull were determined to apply that wartime nomenclature to the new permanent organization. The British were not enthusiastic about this, but were reluctant to make it a major issue. The Russians preferred "International Security Organization," but yielded when it was agreed to name the principal peacekeeping entity the Security Council. They then suggested "World Union" for the organization as a whole, but its implication of a supranational federation made American leaders uncomfortable. Hull had earlier rejected, for the same reason, a State Department proposal to call it "Commonwealth of Nations." Russia and Britain then somewhat grudgingly accepted the strongly held American view.[1]

For purposes of simplicity and understanding, we will from this point forward use the terms that were finally established in the United Nations Charter—United Nations, Security Council, General Assembly, and so on—instead of

the range of similar but sometimes confusing designations that were used in
the progressive refinement of the planning process.

Detailed Planning

The agreements reached at the Moscow and Teheran conferences had for the
first time provided authoritative and reasonably clear guidelines to detailed
planning for a United Nations organization. On December 29, 1943, Hull
sent to the White House an Outline Plan to serve as the basis for negotiating
with Britain, Russia, and China. After agreement among the Big Four, the
approved plan would be presented to all other United Nations members for
their comment and adherence. In a covering memorandum to FDR, Hull said
that American thinking was based on two central assumptions: namely, that
the Big Four would consider themselves "morally bound" not to go to war
with each other or any other nation, and to "maintain adequate forces" and be
willing to use them as required "to prevent or suppress all cases of aggression."
The memorandum also said that the State Department had been unable to
develop "definitive conclusions on a number of crucial questions," which
accordingly needed further discussion and presidential guidance.

The proposed new organization would consist initially of a Security
Council, a General Assembly, an International Court of Justice, and a Secretariat. Agencies for economic and social activities, for trusteeship responsibilities, and for other appropriate purposes could be brought into being "as
needed." The organization's primary functions would be "first, to establish and
maintain peace and security, by force if necessary; and second, to foster cooperative effort among the nations for the progressive improvement of the general welfare."[2]

After a session with Hull and his advisers on February 3, 1944, FDR
approved the Outline Plan as the basis for a more detailed effort. By mid-
April, the State Department had developed and refined something close to a
complete plan. Postwar planning now became an integral function of the
State Department, which viewed a new international entity as the logical place
to deal with the full range of postwar problems—first and foremost security,
but also trade, economic development, monetary stabilization, colonialism,
and human rights.[3]

Two new high-level committees were created, both chaired by Hull, with different but complementary functions. The Policy Committee would concentrate on current aspects of major foreign policy questions, while the Post-War Programs Committee would focus on postwar policies and the international coordination required to put them into effect. There was overlapping membership on these two bodies, and also between them and the Informal Agenda Group, which comprised Hull's inner circle of advisers. Thus a handful of men, including Isaiah Bowman, Myron Taylor, Norman Davis, Stanley Hornbeck, Benjamin Cohen, Green Hackworth, and Leo Pasvolsky, participated in two or three of these planning groups, provided important continuity, and wielded the greatest influence. In addition, the Advisory Committee on Problems of Foreign Relations—an outside citizens group—was revived as a means of giving departmental planners access to a wide spectrum of opinion in American life.[4]

Concurrently, the organizational structure of the State Department as a whole was realigned on the initiative of the new Under Secretary, Edward Stettinius, who had secured a reputation as an efficient administrator of the Lend-Lease program, after serving as chairman of the U.S. Steel Corporation. The son of a J. P. Morgan partner, he was still in his early forties, energetic, and possessed of a flair for public relations. There developed a general Washington tendency to dismiss his ability as a diplomat. Harry S Truman deplored his "movie star face and wavy gray hair." Dean Acheson later remarked that Stettinius had "gone far with comparatively modest equipment." Despite these denigrating assessments, he made valuable contributions to the founding of the United Nations as the leader of the American delegation at San Francisco.[5]

Inherent Limits

The basic problem facing departmental planners after Teheran was how to convert a wartime alliance into a permanent organization to keep the peace by means of Big Four cooperation and the collective use of force. The emphasis on enforcement power was a major departure from the approach taken in the League Covenant, which had relied mainly on moral injunctions and had failed to organize the threat or use of force against aggression. Although Wilsonian purists still resisted it, the view that world peace must be underwritten by real power was now widely accepted as fundamental by governments and public opinion, but this led to somewhat contradictory considerations. The use of force in any particular case would require the consent of the Big Four, who would not put their armed forces at the disposal of the United Nations organization without retaining a controlling voice in their deployment. However, to make this power reality palatable to the whole world as a permanent arrangement, it was believed that the dominant position of the Big Four would have to be at least minimally circumscribed by some larger legal and moral framework. The three key problems were how to organize the agency charged with keeping the peace, how to provide for decision-making within it, and how to ensure the availability of adequate armed force pursuant to its decisions.[6]

As the State Department settled down to the task of developing detailed plans, it was apparent that the range of practical solutions to these problems was very limited, owing to the basic political organization of the globe into nation-states and their tenacious resistance to fundamental change. A departmental draft of March 15, 1944, expressed the fundamental limitation: the new entity would have to be "founded upon the principle of cooperation freely agreed upon among sovereign peace-loving states." A supranational "federal form" of organization was not in the cards, for "nations should retain, and will insist on retaining, a large degree of freedom of action; no international super-government is feasible at this time, even if it were desirable."[7]

Advocates of world government or a supranational federation were passionately opposed to retaining the system of sovereign nation-states, which they accurately pointed out was a condition of political anarchy and a primary cause of war. The brute fact remained that neither the Big Four nor any of the lesser nations was prepared to yield up any significant part of their claim to sovereignty and independence. Even dependent peoples striving to end their colonial status aspired to the same goal of sovereign self-determination. In the midst of World War II, the nation-state was therefore the only political basis for a new international organization acceptable to the great majority of the world's people.

This irremovable condition meant that the new organization would confront the same dilemmas that had faced the League of Nations with regard to keeping the peace: how to prevent or halt aggression without violating the canons of national sovereignty. All members of the League had pledged to settle their disputes without resort to war and to limit their armaments to levels prescribed by the League. But those who had flagrantly breached their pledges

(Hitler, Mussolini, and the Japanese warlords) had withdrawn or been expelled, which had left the League with progressively less political and military power to keep the peace. Renewed pledges to settle disputes peacefully would be required by the new United Nations, but within a continuing global framework of competing nation-states there could be no guarantee that these would be kept. Accordingly, in order to avoid a repetition of the League failures, the new organization would have to hold a preponderance of power and possess the authority and the will to use it to prevent or defeat aggression.[8]

The ability to meet this fundamental requirement depended squarely on the continued unity and cooperation of those who held preponderant power. But each of the Big Four nations had interests and ambitions it considered too important to entrust to a world body; their individual commitments to enforce decisions of the world body were therefore inherently conditional. In the near term, it was reasonable to assume that they would cooperate to defeat, and then restrain or repress, the current enemy states; and if they remained in even tacit agreement, they could also deal readily with aggressions by smaller powers. It was the relations among the Big Four themselves that constituted the fundamental problem of future war or peace. If one of the Four Policemen turned aggressive, then aggression could be halted only by the combined force of the others. But this would require more than a police action—it would be tantamount to major war. And major war would mean failure for the new system of world security.

Nothing in the hundreds of books, articles, monographs, speeches, and other expressions of opinion or other forms of advice solicited from or gratuitously offered by an extraordinary range of official study groups, private organizations, and individuals could get around this central dilemma. If political reality dictated no basic change in a world system of sovereign nation-states, there were only two possible solutions to keeping the peace: the continued unity and cooperation of the Big Four, or an equilibrium maintained by a complex balance of power between and among them. Within this iron framework, these were the only practical alternatives.[9]

Structure

With regard to structuring what ultimately became the Security Council, Hull's personal assistant, Leo Pasvolsky, is generally credited with two proposals that modulated at least the naked appearance of Big Four dominance. One was to merge the Four Policemen (which under FDR's conception were to constitute a separate entity) with the larger (ultimately eleven-nation) Security Council. The other was to assign exclusive jurisdiction for security matters to that council, while assigning the initiative for all nonsecurity matters to the General Assembly, in which all U.N. members would have a vote. The League Covenant had generated confusion by giving jurisdiction in security matters to both the League Council and the League Assembly.[10]

With regard to the size and composition of the Security Council, the planners were clear that the Big Four must be permanent members, but there was continuing debate about the number of temporary or rotating members and how they should be chosen. Some, who feared situations in which the Big Four could be outvoted, wanted a membership of the "four plus an equal number less one" (an arcane formulation designed to ensure that the Big Four remained in the majority). Others, who assumed the Big Four could protect their own interests by means of a veto power on all substantive matters, felt the small nations should substantially outnumber the Big Four on the peace-keeping body. The British Foreign Office strongly supported this latter view, believing that a large number of small nations on the Security Council would be an important safeguard against attempts to shift responsibility for security matters to the General Assembly. In the February 3, 1944, meeting with his advisers, FDR decided that temporary members should be elected annually by the General Assembly. This meant that they would be representatives of nations rather than of regions, and it ended the ambiguity of the American position on that point.[11]

FDR also displayed an intense interest in the physical details of the new organization and continued to believe in a rather loose, decentralized structure. He favored an island—ideally the Azores, but he was willing to settle for Hawaii—as the permanent seat of the Security Council, but thought that the General Assembly should be a movable feast, holding its sessions in different regions of the world from year to year. The World Court should sit at the Hague, as under the League, but various special agencies, like the existing International Labor Organization and the proposed Economic and Social Council should each be located in a different place.[12]

Voting Rules and the Veto

It was understood that voting rules in the Security Council were crucially linked to its size and composition. Here again the problem was how to reconcile power realities with considerations of equity and justice for the world community as a whole. There was agreement that all U.N. members must be bound by decisions of the Security Council—that is, bound to support sanctions against an aggressor. At the same time, it was recognized that the surest way to make the new organization fail would be to require one of the Big Four to participate in an enforcement action it had voted against.

There was no easy escape from this dilemma. After painful debate, the State Department planners proposed that the Big Four veto should not be absolute, but they drew an odd distinction between two kinds of situations: decisions involving "peaceful settlement" of disputes should require a two-thirds affirmative vote, including all of the Big Four; and decisions involving the use of force to suppress aggression should also require a two-thirds affirmative vote, but only three of the Big Four. The latter formulation meant that a permanent member could not use the veto to prevent a Security Council action it opposed, including action against itself. This restriction was later rejected by all of the Big Four, but in the February 3 meeting the departmental advisers somehow failed to convey to the President its supremely far-reaching implications.[13]

Although FDR made himself "quite clear" that there must be Big Four unanimity on "the most crucial matters," the issue of whether the Security Council could take enforcement action on the basis of three of the Big Four votes seems to have been considered only in the context of situations that might peripherally "embarrass" a permanent member. In such situations, FDR proposed that the "embarrassed" party, while remaining bound by the council decision, should have the option to abstain rather than veto, thus not blocking action favored by the two-thirds majority. He thought that this would facilitate Big Four cooperation. But there was apparently no discussion of whether a permanent member should be allowed to vote at all, in a situation where it was party to a dispute and where, presumably, its serious interests were engaged.[14]

This gap in the reasoning process was closed a month later—at the staff level—when a majority of Hull's advisers decided that a permanent member should be required to abstain when "directly involved in a dispute" of any kind. This eliminated the previous ambiguity of the American position but ignored the hard political fact that voting by a party to a dispute was directly connected to the principle of Big Four unanimity. Steeped in the democratic tradition of majority rule and conceptions of justice and fair play, the departmental planners decided to compromise the principle of unanimity, failing to realize that it was far more than a voting formula, that it was in fact the foundation stone—the sine qua non of the United Nations organization—for both international and domestic political reasons.[15]

Hull himself was not persuaded by his advisers. He believed that an absolute veto on military actions and other sanctions was the only way to get the United States into the United Nations organization and keep it there. Yet he did not formally repudiate his planners. Instead, he simply deleted all reference to the new staff view from the briefing papers being prepared for his private consultations with the Senate leadership; this inevitably added to the existing confusion. Hull left the Senators with the distinct impression that U.S. interests would be protected by an essentially blanket veto, but this was contrary to the position proposed by the State Department staff, discussed with the President, and not formally rejected by Hull. This confusion would cause serious mischief in the later negotiations with Britain and Russia.[16]

Available Armed Force

The third major problem was how to organize and employ armed force on behalf of the United Nations organization. There appeared to be three options: to put together an ad hoc assemblage of national forces to meet each threat to peace as it emerged; to create a permanent international force; and/or to establish a system of earmarked or otherwise precommitted national contingents able to act promptly on the decisions of the Security Council.

The first option was rejected out of hand, owing to its repeated failure under League of Nations auspices. The second was carefully explored, but the planners could not get around a fundamental dilemma: if the international force were of nominal size, it would be inadequate to the task, but if it were superior to a combination of major national forces, the question of command and control would pose an irresolvable political problem. Special attention was given to the feasibility of an international air force that would operate from strategically located international bases. The President had often spoken enthusiastically of this idea as a general deterrent to aggression. Close examination revealed, however, that the acquisition, operation, and re-supply of such bases and aircraft would unavoidably give the international organization the attributes of national sovereignty—land, resources, population—and such a foreseeable development was unacceptable to the U.S. Government. Moreover, the Joint Chiefs of Staff believed that international bases would be inefficient and in the long run unsustainable. They preferred strategic bases under national control which could be made available to the international organization. In addition, the increasingly indiscriminate nature of air bombardment (first against Poland and England, currently against Germany and Japan) was creating second thoughts about treating air power as an appropriate instrument of peacekeeping "police" work.[17]

This left the option of a system of national contingents which, by prior bilateral agreement between the U.N. and each member, would be placed at the disposal of the Security Council. This was the only option the Joint Chiefs of Staff were willing to endorse. The President's early notion that the Four Policemen should be solely responsible for keeping the peace, and that all or most other nations should be disarmed, was abandoned as politically and physically impractical, and was replaced by the concept that all member nations should be obligated to provide forces for collective enforcement missions. Although this seemed the only politically acceptable alternative in an organization of nominally equal sovereign nations, it created new anomalies: for example, it created official tension between enforcement and disarmament, and thereby effectively displaced disarmament as a goal. At least theoretically, each member nation must now maintain a level of forces sufficient to meet its international obligations to the Security Council. Recognizing the imperfections, the State Department concluded that this option was nevertheless the best available basis for establishing new international security arrangements.[18]

International Trusteeship

As the war progressed, it became evident that Roosevelt was entirely serious about carrying into effect in the postwar period "the right of all peoples to choose the form of government under which they will live," as declared in the Atlantic Charter. He had upset the British by a number of candid statements (to Turks, Egyptians, and Chinese) in the course of his trip to Cairo and Teheran, to the effect that the French colonial empire should be dismantled; specifically, that Indochina and Dakar (in West Africa) should be placed under international trusteeship and established as strategic bases for U.N. peace-keeping forces. The British Ambassador asked Hull if these statements represented FDR's "final conclusions." Hull passed the question to Roosevelt, who provided categorical confirmation.

Yes, the President wrote to Hull on January 24, his view was that Indochina "should not go back to France," for one hundred years of French colonialism had left its 30 million people "worse off than they were at the beginning." Moreover, "I am wholeheartedly supported in this view by Generalissimo Chiang Kai-shek and Marshal Stalin." The British Foreign Office was opposed to international trusteeships because "they fear the effect it would have on their possessions and those of the Dutch"—meaning the prospect of "future independence." Roosevelt saw "no reason to play in" with the British on this matter. A part of FDR's vehemence here was his personal antipathy to General de Gaulle, reinforced by the growing likelihood that the "arrogant" Frenchman would become the first leader of postwar France and would tenaciously resist any international attempt to dilute French *gloire*.[19]

Although Hull was also dedicated to the principle of self-determination for dependent peoples, he was far less adamant on the colonial question than his chief. In support of the President's position, the State Department developed a "Draft Declaration Regarding Administration of Dependent Territories," a title carefully designed to minimize British irritation. This document sought to establish minimum political, economic, and social standards for the administration of all "non-self-governing" areas, and to provide "regional consultative commissions" to which the administering states would be accountable for the peoples under their jurisdiction. The purpose of the document was to preserve the goal of independence stressed by FDR, while emphasizing both the gradual nature of the process and the obligation of the dependent peoples themselves to earn the right to self-government by "development of political institutions suited to their needs." As departmental thinking evolved on this question, it seemed logical to link such regional commissions with a comprehensive Trusteeship Council administered by the United Nations organization. The aim was to move toward the gradual elimination of all colonies and dependencies by placing them in a transitional status.[20]

Churchill was a categorical defender of British imperialism, but the Foreign Office was willing to accept the idea of regional consultative commissions, provided they were headed by the "parent" state in each case and were purely advisory. At the same time, the British were clearly not prepared to accept a sweeping plan that would place all colonies and dependent territories under United Nations administration. Believing that Roosevelt's position represented a vast oversimplification of the problem, the British insisted on a case-by-case approach, and for fundamentally strategic reasons. Thus, for example, they supported French retention of Indochina, in part because they needed a strong postwar France as a buffer against Russia and Germany, and understood that French cooperation in Europe would be jeopardized by a British policy that sought the destruction of France's overseas possessions.[21]

Moreover, as planning proceeded during the winter and spring of 1944, it became apparent that opposition to a comprehensive system of trusteeships was not confined to the European colonial powers, but extended to the U.S. War and Navy departments. Their primary concern was the Pacific Islands being wrested from the Japanese at a great cost of blood and treasure. Secretary of War Henry Stimson argued that no purpose would be served by "classing such islands with colonial areas containing large populations and considerable economic resources. . . . They are not colonies; they are outposts of great strategic significance, restored to U.S. control by an effort written in blood. . . . They must belong to the United States with absolute power to rule and fortify them."[22] Navy Secretary James Forrestal told Stettinius, "There should be no debate as to who ran the (Japanese) Mandated Islands."[23] And the Joint Chiefs of Staff insisted on "national as distinguished from United Nations jurisdiction" for this strategic real estate.[24]

The expression of these strong views by the most influential wartime segment of the U.S. Government made clear to Hull that an attempt to press for comprehensive international control of trust territories would become badly entangled in domestic politics. After adding this factor to the opposition of European colonial powers and the notable lack of Russian enthusiasm, Hull decided to remove all reference to the issue from the U.S. papers being prepared for the coming Big Four negotiations, but he did so without the President's knowledge.[25]

International Consultations

Immediately following FDR's approval of the Outline Plan in mid-February 1944, the State Department had proposed to Britain and Russia a preliminary exchange of topics for discussion. The British responded promptly, and their papers indicated that, with the notable exception of the colonial issue, the State Department and the Foreign Office were on the same wavelength. There was, however, no Russian response of any kind until April 5, and when it did arrive it was merely a collection of comments on the American and British papers. Defensive in tone, it suggested that the Kremlin had not given much concentrated attention to a postwar international organization, but the response made clear that the Russians wanted to confine the forthcoming conference to matters of military security and enforcement.[26]

The next step, taken on May 30, was a U.S. invitation to Britain, Russia, and China to hold formal Big Four talks on international organization in Washington in early summer. The British and Chinese governments promptly accepted, but once again weeks went by without an answer from Moscow. After several U.S. diplomatic inquiries, the Russians finally replied on July 9. Their view of the conference was still constricted: they wanted to confine the talks to the scope of the proposed new organization, measures to prevent violations of the peace, and plans for combined enforcement action. This ruled out several major areas of American and British concern, including "pacific settlement" of disputes, and the need for specialized agencies in such fields as economic and social development, health, and labor.

The State Department thereupon firmly reiterated the American view that the new organization must be broader in scope and "must necessarily" include procedures for the peaceful settlement of disputes; it urged the Russians to agree to this wider approach. After further cable exchanges, the innate xenophobia of the Russian political system was temporarily overcome, but it was not until July 17 that Hull could announce publicly that the talks would begin soon—he hoped in early August.[27]

Hull now confronted a special procedural problem, arising out of Moscow's categorical opposition to negotiating directly with the Chinese— ostensibly out of a concern that this would compromise Russian neutrality in the Pacific war. In his invitation of May 30, he had "earnestly" urged that the new talks be held on a Four Power basis, but the Russians would not agree. It was accordingly necessary to work out some sort of double negotiations. The British thought that the idea of separate conferences would be cumbersome and preferred to keep Chiang Kai-shek's Embassy informed behind the scenes, but this risked an affront to Chinese dignity. In the end, all parties agreed to two separate consecutive conferences—the first to include the United States, Britain, and Russia; the second, of far less significance, to include the United States, Britain, and China.[28]

11

Domestic Politics in 1944

Although he had set in motion the development of a detailed American plan to create the United Nations organization, President Roosevelt declined to discuss the issue publicly—or, indeed, any other foreign policy question—during the early months of 1944. His silence created a large gap in communications with the press and the public, whose expectations regarding plans for the postwar world had been greatly stimulated by reports on the Moscow and Teheran meetings. This left the field open to his critics.

The war was gathering more positive momentum, with the Red Army driving the Germans from Russian territory and sweeping toward the Balkans, while American and British forces were massing in England for the momentous Channel crossing that would open the long-awaited second front. During the winter and early spring, leading columnists like Walter Lippmann, Dorothy Thompson, and William L. Shirer pressed the Administration to state its intentions regarding Poland, postwar Germany, and the United Nations, but the White House remained silent, leading many to conclude that Roosevelt had made secret deals at Teheran that could not withstand public scrutiny. An editorial in the *Nation* expressed the fear that Roosevelt and Hull were "tiptoeing toward a new world order" that looked suspiciously like a reaffirmation of the status quo, which could only mean "a new cycle of economic disintegration, dictatorship and war."[1]

In a *Saturday Evening Post* article of February, entitled "Your Move, Mr. President," Senator Joseph Ball (R-Minnesota) took FDR to task for not including members of Congress in the American delegations at Moscow and Teheran, and warned that such continued omission could imperil Senate ratification of postwar treaties. In mid-March, twenty-four freshmen Congressmen complained in an open letter to Hull that the United Nations Council approved by the Moscow Declaration did not yet appear to be functioning; indeed, the American people had received no information on foreign policy for several months. Returning from his annual Florida vacation, Hull released a seventeen-point memorandum consisting of excerpts from recent speeches by himself and the President, in an effort to satisfy the "growing interest" in foreign affairs, but the document utterly failed to satisfy the critics. The *New York Times* described it as "Hull's 17-point mumble."[2]

Despite the criticism, FDR seemed determined not to go public until Hull had a firm plan for the new international organization and had gained the general endorsement of the Senate leadership. But the public clamor continued to rise. In a further effort to be responsive, Hull delivered a radio address on April 9 in which he stated that Administration plans for a new world organization were well along, and that he had asked Senator Connally to appoint a bipartisan group of Senators to consult with him. Following these consultations, the United States would exchange views with other nations and would then be in a position to submit the plans "to the democratic processes of discussion." He entered a plea for public patience and stressed the vital importance of continued cooperation among the Big Four.

The speech was widely regarded as Hull's most effective wartime statement. There was special praise for his plan for congressional consultations, which the *New York Times* called "a revolutionary change in American diplomatic practice."[3]

Consultations with the Senate

On April 25, Hull received Connally's bipartisan Committee of Eight in his office, assuring the Senators that the discussion would be informal and would involve no commitment from them. In addition to Connally, the group included three Democrats (Walter George of Georgia, Alben Barkley of Kentucky, Guy Gillette of Iowa), three Republicans (Arthur Vandenberg of

Michigan, Warren Austin of Vermont, Wallace White of Maine), and one Progressive (Robert La Follette of Wisconsin, who was a leading isolationist). Hull stressed the need for postwar cooperation with the Russians and for keeping the issue of a new world organization out of domestic politics. He handed each Senator a copy of the just completed U.S. draft plan and asked them to provide their comments at a subsequent meeting.[4]

Vandenberg, who proved to be the key figure on the committee because he served as a bridge between internationalist and isolationist Republicans, was amazed and delighted that the plan was "so conservative from a nationalist standpoint." As he confided to his diary, "This is anything but a wild-eyed internationalist dream of a world state. . . . It is based virtually on a four-power alliance." Connally and several other Senators were equally pleased and relieved.[5]

At the group's next meeting on May 2, Hull and his advisers were braced for difficult questions relating to the authority to commit American military forces in collective security actions. The Administration believed that it was essential for the President to possess this power without having to consult Congress on each occasion, but the Constitution gave Congress the exclusive power to declare war, and it was this rock on which ratification of the League of Nations treaty had foundered in 1920. In the event, however, the Senators did not even mention this prickly issue, but instead expressed genuine enthusiasm for the draft plan. Vandenberg, backed by La Follette, raised only one serious objection, that "the peace will create a new status quo in the world" which the new international organization will be bound to defend. Accordingly, he could not endorse U.S. participation until he knew that the war would produce a "just peace." He was disturbed by Russia's unilateral assertion of claims to Poland and the Baltic states, and Churchill's "constant reiteration" of his intent to restore the British Empire "intact."[6]

Hull argued that the prompt formation of a new organization would help to ensure a good peace, but this did not satisfy Vandenberg. A large part of the Senator's concern was rooted in domestic politics: 1944 was a presidential election year, and there were in his state of Michigan (and in the other industrial centers of the Middle West) large numbers of voters of Central and Eastern European origin. They and Vandenberg harbored deep suspicions that Roosevelt had already made secret commitments to Stalin which sacrificed the interests of Poland and other Eastern European countries. Nevertheless, Vandenberg readily agreed that planning should go forward, including consultations with Britain, Russia, and China.[7]

Hull left the Senators with the clear impression that U.S. interests would be protected by the veto on all substantive matters, which effectively finessed all of the complicated, internally inconsistent voting formulas still under active consideration in the State Department. This seemed to sit well with the Senators. When Senator Gillette asked, somewhat ingenuously, if the veto power would not lead to dominance of the world body by the Big Four, the others strongly backed Hull when he explained that the veto was necessary not only to ensure British and Russian participation in an untried venture, but also to satisfy American interests and concerns. There was "no possible way" to establish the new organization "except by each of the large nations on the Council retaining the veto power in connection with the use of force or sanctions. . . . Our Government would not remain there a day without retaining its veto power."[8]

The Controversial "Great Design"

Pleased with these consultations, Hull asked the Committee of Eight to join him in drafting a public statement that would endorse the Administration plan. The Senators seemed favorably disposed, but the appearance on May 13 and 20 of a two-part article in the *Saturday Evening Post* by Forrest Davis put a stick in the spokes. Based on interviews with FDR in March and approved in advance by the White House, the first part reflected the President's felt need to answer his winter critics. Entitled "What Really Happened at Teheran," it disclosed that Roosevelt did indeed have a "great design" for peace, and that he had advanced this at Teheran with a "tough-minded determination to enroll the Soviet Union as a sincere and willing collaborator in postwar settlements." Davis made clear that FDR fully recognized the possibility of failure: "Stripped to the bare essentials, we fought in 1917 and are fighting now to prevent the mastery of Europe by one aggressive power. Should Russia as the sole [postwar] European power display tendencies toward world conquest, our vital interest would again be called into account." The President was therefore "gambling for stakes as enormous as any statesman ever played for," but he was "betting that the Soviet Union needs peace and is willing to pay for it by collaborating with the West."

The second part of the article amounted to the first public disclosure of the Four Policemen concept for the enforcement of peace. FDR opposed "a heavily organized, bureaucratic world organization" with its own police force, preferring to rely on the major powers acting together to establish a situation analogous to the "fruitful Pax Britannica" of the nineteenth century in which "the powers able to make war are convinced their self-interest lies in peace."[9]

The *Saturday Evening Post* articles provoked severe criticism from both ends of the political spectrum. Conservatives were appalled at Roosevelt's apparent readiness to pursue a conciliatory policy toward the Soviet Union, some even equating this with the appeasement of Hitler in the 1930s. One critic said, "We thought Woodrow Wilson blundered because of his utter ignorance of European affairs, but he had his feet on the ground compared to Mr. Roosevelt." On the other hand, Sumner Welles, in a widely quoted speech of May 18, attacked his former chief from the Wilsonian perspective: "History does not record any example of a military alliance between great nations which has endured. . . . At best they have given rise only to a temporary and precarious balance of power." Seeing a dangerous trend to imperialism, Welles urged the immediate creation of a United Nations Council which would recognize "the full sovereignty of every independent nation of the world, no matter how small it may be." A *Saturday Evening Post* editorial inveighed against "imperialism and personal politics on the international level."[10]

This public furor deeply divided the Committee of Eight, and thus destroyed the hope that it would give a written endorsement to the Administration plan. A frustrated Hull sent Assistant Secretary of State Breckinridge Long to negotiate with Connally and the others, but his efforts were in vain. The Davis articles had confirmed Vandenberg's hunch that Roosevelt had already made secret commitments to Stalin and Churchill and, as the recognized GOP leader on foreign affairs, he was unwilling to commit his party and its 1944 candidate to any specific program. Supported by sound logic, he also insisted that definitive peace treaties with Germany and Japan should precede establishment of a new world organization. Other Senators of both parties shared his reservations. "They are shying away like a horse from a snake," Long informed Hull after several unproductive negotiating sessions. After receiving no encouragement in a further meeting with the Senators on May 29, Hull showed them a unilateral statement he planned to release later that day, and they raised no objection. This described the talks as "frank and fruitful" and said that the Secretary of State was "definitely encouraged" by the attitude of the Committee of Eight. Further talks were planned, and "the door of non-partisanship will continue to be wide open here at the Department of State."[11]

Concurrently with the invitations to Britain, Russia, and China to hold formal talks in Washington issued the next day, Hull announced that the United States had submitted a detailed plan for world organization for consideration by the other three powers, but he gave no hint of its content. Presumably, this tactic reflected FDR's conviction that, while it was necessary to say something, it was still too early to discuss specifics. But the assumption that the press and the public would be content with a simple announcement on so momentous a subject was a strange and serious miscalculation. There followed two weeks of artful dodging by both Hull and Roosevelt before they realized that it was necessary to release at least a summary of the plan. On June 15, the White House issued a short version that was extremely thin on details. Stating that the maintenance of peace must be "the joint task of all peace-loving nations," it slid over the fact that the Big Four would dominate the Security Council and possess exclusive veto power, and it left unclear how the peacekeeping machinery would work. At the same time, it sought to reassure the American people that "we are not thinking of a superstate with its own police forces and other paraphernalia of coercive power."[12]

Both the substance of the summary and the casual manner of its release shocked advocates of world federation. Eli Culbertson denounced it as an attempt "to resurrect the bullet-ridden League of Nations" and insisted that the country wanted "a true system of collective security . . . supported by an effective international police force." Even moderate internationalists found the plan much too timid, and they noted with deep disappointment that it did not provide for the automatic use of force in a crisis—a lack that had proven to be the Achilles heel of the League. Isolationists, who could hardly protest that the plan gave away U.S. sovereignty, were reduced to complaining that it was un-American to subject the human race to Big Four domination. *Time's* observation was probably accurate: "Most Americans found the program unexceptionable—what there was of it."[13]

Despite the vague and cautious language of the release, the Administration was lucky in its timing, for by mid-June public attention was riveted on the Normandy beachhead, and Americans were not prepared to grapple with the complex abstractions of international organization. The substance of the release established for the Democrats a safe middle position on the international spectrum. It undercut GOP arguments that FDR was conspiratorially silent or had made secret deals with Stalin or was planning to espouse world government. What was unclear was whether these tactical advantages were the consequence of shrewd political calculation or pure luck. FDR had shown himself quite willing to go on holding the public at arm's length. It was Hull who pressed him to release the summary plan, and it was Hull who made sure that it was issued from the White House. But the Secretary of State's primary motive was to remove rumors of a rift between him and FDR on the issue of Big Power dominance versus equality for smaller nations. According to Breckinridge Long, Hull wanted "to tie the President in" to the State Department plan.[14]

These swirling controversies showed how complicated and interwoven were the tasks facing the President and the Administration in mid-1944. The vast war effort, moving forward like a powerful locomotive, gave the public the confidence to focus on America's role in maintaining peace and security after victory. There was a surge of enthusiasm for some large American role in postwar international affairs, but wide differences on how to define that role. Political scientists like James Shotwell and Dexter Perkins argued for a new and stronger League of Nations. Sumner Welles's new book, *The Time for Decision,* supporting similar Wilsonian themes, sold half a million copies. In *U.S. War Aims,* Walter Lippmann argued that no international superstructure could eliminate the inherent power of nationalism; the theologian Reinhold Niebuhr thought that the United Nations was a necessary experiment, but warned that human nature was too perverse to sustain its idealistic premises.[15]

In other activities closely related to ensuring postwar stability, the Treasury Department convened a conference of international financial experts from forty-four countries in Bretton Woods, New Hampshire, in July 1944 in an effort to prevent postwar monetary chaos through the establishment of a new World Bank and an international stabilization fund. The United Nations Relief and Rehabilitation Administration (UNRRA) continued to handle an ever greater volume of relief, refugee, and health problems in a more immediate effort to prevent social chaos in the wake of war. Many historians would later believe that FDR's management of this vast array of complexities, including the successful campaign for a fourth term, was the climactic feat of his presidency.

The Choice of Washington

Why was Washington chosen as the site for the definitive Big Four negotiations to establish the United Nations organization? The decision was strongly influenced by American insistence on quick and easy communication between the U.S. delegation and the White House, a consideration which ruled out more congenial places like Bar Harbor, Maine. The British wanted reliable communications with London and a place where they could consult promptly with the embassies of the Dominions. The Russian Communists apparently had no objection to meeting in the citadel of the capitalist world. Everyone hoped that it would be possible to find some cool oasis where the delegates could escape Washington's infernal summer heat, but air-conditioning was not yet standard in government buildings and private-sector office space was simply not available. As a partial solution, Alger Hiss, a member of the State Department planning group, suggested Dumbarton Oaks, an estate on the flank of Georgetown and Rock Creek Park which had been owned by Robert Woods Bliss, a former U.S. Ambassador to Sweden and Argentina who had bequeathed it to Harvard University as a center for Byzantine studies. Dumbarton Oaks was not air-conditioned, but its spacious pink buildings, leafy trees, lily ponds, and extensive gardens with shaded walks offered some respite from the heat, as well as a dignified setting for the conference.[16]

Second thoughts soon developed about the wisdom of convening a major conference in the middle of wartime Washington. As the opening day approached, the White House and the State Department belatedly realized that this was likely to entail serious disadvantages in press and public relations. Public opinion polls showed that a majority of Americans favored some kind of new international organization, but specific proposals generated heated disagreements. The conference would involve exploratory talks between sovereign nations of the greatest power and prestige. Private give-and-take was essential to the development of mutual understanding and agreement. Too much press attention, too soon, could seriously hamper the work of the delegations and provide stories that could be exploited for partisan political purposes during an American presidential election year.[17]

The Administration wanted to portray the conference as a major step toward peace and postwar stability; at the same time, it wanted to keep the talks confidential until agreement was reached. This was a dilemma not easily

Dumbarton Oaks, view from the lawn. (Edward R. Stettinius, Jr., Papers, Special
Collections Department, Manuscripts Division, University of Virginia Library)

resolved, for Washington's press corps was perhaps the most aggressive and
sophisticated in the world, and the public was anxious for news. Assistant Secretary of State Dean Acheson, for one, had thought it a mistake to hold this
particular conference in the capital, but the momentum of the planning and
the complexity of the arrangements seemed to preclude any serious thought of
a change. In an effort to dilute press and public interest a few days before the
talks were convened in August, the State Department began downplaying
their immediate importance by emphasizing their informal and preliminary
character. They were to be called "the Dumbarton Oaks Conversations," presumably to contrast them with real diplomatic negotiations, and the U.S. delegation would be designated the American Group. This attempted camouflage
fooled no one.[18]

Hull had planned to serve as chairman of the American delegation, and
he expected Britain and Russia to be represented by men of comparable rank.
But British Foreign Secretary Anthony Eden did not want to be tied down to
daily attendance, and Moscow seemed to signal that the talks were of only

moderate importance by naming the new Russian ambassador to Washington, thirty-five-year-old Andrei Gromyko, to head the Russian delegation. Accordingly, the talks were conducted at the "official," or high technical, level, with the three foreign ministers available to review preliminary agreements as they emerged. The British Government named Sir Alexander Cadogan, Permanent Under Secretary of the Foreign Office, as its chief negotiator, and Hull named his Under Secretary, Edward Stettinius.[19]

Cadogan and Stettinius established an easy relationship and worked well together, in part because the issue of trusteeship over colonial territories was the only serious difference in the American and British positions, and because Hull had decided to finesse this at Dumbarton Oaks and deal with it later. A relieved Cadogan reported to London that "the vexed question of territorial trusteeship seems to have been put in cold storage." Stettinius found Cadogan "calm, intelligent . . . quick on the trigger." The British diplomat thought that Stettinius looked "like a dignified and more monumental Charlie Chaplin." Gromyko was an unknown quantity with a stony demeanor, but his personality was less important than the fact that he operated on strict instructions from Moscow and could exercise only very limited discretion.[20]

Hull had hoped that the talks could begin on August 2, but the British delegation decided to travel on the *Queen Mary* rather than fly, which pushed the starting date back to August 14. The Russian delegation left Moscow on August 8 by air, expecting to meet that starting date, but was delayed by fog over Siberia and by a refueling stop in Fairbanks, Alaska. It did not reach Washington until August 20. When the DC-3 bearing the Red Star of the Soviet Union finally landed at Washington's National Airport, both Stettinius and Cadogan were on hand to greet Gromyko with appropriate pomp and ceremony. Stettinius remarked to his British counterpart that the DC-3 was probably a Lend-Lease plane; having been the Lend-Lease administrator, he presumably knew whereof he spoke. The Dumbarton Oaks Conference was finally convened at ten-thirty the next morning.[21]

12

The Dumbarton Oaks Conference I

Secretary of State Cordell Hull delivered the opening address to the assembled delegates and a large group of reporters and photographers on August 21, 1944. British Foreign Under Secretary Sir Alexander Cadogan and Soviet Ambassador Andrei Gromyko also spoke, in an atmosphere of dramatic ceremony and fulsome platitudes. The overstuffed furniture in the tapestried Renaissance-style music room of the Dumbarton Oaks estate had been replaced by a large U-shaped table at which the three delegations were seated. A portrait of the late Polish composer and statesman, Ignacy Jan Paderewski, had been removed in deference to presumed Russian sensibilities. Washington's wilting August heat was so augmented by the klieg lights and flash bulbs used by the hordes of cameramen that it was decided to adjourn to the cooler precincts of the garden for the second round of photographs.[1]

The Press Flap

Trouble began the next day when the press discovered that the conferees had gone into executive session and that reporters were barred from the grounds by military police, thereafter to be dependent on periodic State Department handouts. Their frustration level was raised considerably on August 23, when the *New York Times* published an article by James Reston which appeared to be an authoritative sum-

Opening session of Dumbarton Oaks conversations. Head of table (*left to right*):
Sir Alexander Cadogan, Lord Halifax, Cordell Hull, Andrei Gromyko, and Edward
Stettinius. (Edward R. Stettinius, Jr., Papers, Special Collections Department,
Manuscripts Division, University of Virginia Library)

mary of the position papers tabled by each of the Big Four participants. An
angry Under Secretary of State Stettinius accused the British Embassy of "this
outrageous breach of security," but the ambassador, Lord Halifax, vehemently
denied the charge. In fact, the Chinese delegation, which resented its exclu-
sion from this first phase of the conference, was the origin of the leaks, but
the link was not discovered until long afterward. Specifically, the source was a
young delegate named Joseph Ku who had some years earlier served as an
apprentice reporter at the *New York Times*, where he had known Reston. The
two men renewed their acquaintance at Dumbarton Oaks, and Ku disclosed
that he was in possession of the "complete texts" of the U.S., British, Soviet,
and Chinese proposals. As Reston wryly remarked in his memoirs years later,
Ku was easily persuaded to give the documents to "the only newspaper of
record," which would ensure "their careful and complete publication." Ku

Gromyko, Stettinius, and Cadogan arrive at the White House
to discuss the press leaks. August 24, 1944. (Edward R.
Stettinius, Jr., Papers, Special Collections Department,
Manuscripts Division, University of Virginia Library)

"opened up a big briefcase and handed me the whole prize, neatly translated
into English." Reston continued to turn out stunningly authoritative articles
on the progress and problems of the conference, to the consternation of all
but the Chinese government. The series won him his first Pulitzer Prize.[2]

On August 24, in an effort to put a poultice on this inflammation, Stettinius, Cadogan, and Gromyko met with sixteen members of the State
Department Correspondents Association to plead for understanding of the
tradition that diplomats must confer privately so that they could speak
frankly. But the uproar did not subside. Isolationist newspapers like the
Chicago Tribune accused the State Department of using secrecy to cover a Big
Four plot to rule the world. Congressmen orated to the same effect. Moderate

internationalists, like the columnist Marquis Childs, wrote that a policy of secrecy could only breed confusion and distrust.[3]

In a further effort to satisfy the press and public, on August 29 the three delegation heads held a news conference attended by two hundred reporters. They announced that "general agreement" had been reached on the nature and purposes of a world organization, and they briefly outlined a description of a General Assembly, a Security Council, and a World Court. But "to go beyond" these generalities, Stettinius told the press, and attempt to describe the discussions in detail "would be not only discourteous but improper." Disgruntled reporters complained that conference officials were giving them less information than Reston was publishing every day. The *Detroit Free Press* said in a sardonic editorial that the Stettinius disclosures "could have been written on a postcard a year ago."[4]

The beleaguered American diplomat made a final effort to appease the reporters on September 4, but this, too, turned out badly. Despite his skill at masterminding public relations behind the scenes, Stettinius was a shy and nervous man in the spotlight, a less than first-rate intellect, and essentially devoid of experience in foreign affairs. His attempt to address reporters by their first names was considered patronizing, and he had difficulty answering questions with precision. In fairness, many could not be answered, for they dealt with matters still under discussion and unresolved by the delegations. Writing the effort off as a "gruesome experience," Stettinius assigned his press aide, Michael McDermott, to hold daily meetings with small groups of reporters, but press relations were never smooth at Dumbarton Oaks. Many thought that the American policy of trying to maintain an official posture of confidentiality after the Reston disclosures was a serious mistake, one which threw away an opportunity to educate the American people on the issues involved at the conference. At the same time, the conference faced several explosive issues on which the differences between Russia and the West were so fundamental that exposure could have threatened collapse of the talks.[5]

Organization of the Conference

The American Group of eighteen people, including six from the Army and Navy, was the largest and best prepared of the three delegations. The group was divided into three working sections: one for the establishment and the structure of the organization; one for the peaceful settlement of disputes; and one for security arrangements. Stettinius headed the full delegation and also chaired the security section, but exerted his principal influence through a small steering committee composed of Leo Pasvolsky, director of special research and Hull's principal assistant; James Dunn, director of the Office of European Affairs; and Green Hackworth, legal adviser to the State Department.[6]

The original U.S. scheme was for the three delegations to meet frequently for general consideration of major issues, but both the Russians and the British thought this far too cumbersome and not conducive to frank exchanges. The three delegation heads thereupon formed themselves into a joint steering committee, which conducted the serious business of the conference. In practice, Stettinius worked out an agreed U.S. position within the American steering committee, then carried this into meetings with Cadogan and Gromyko. Inevitably these arrangements meant that not all American delegates were kept equally abreast of events, and the frequency of nuanced changes of position on particular issues sometimes led to misunderstandings and friction within the U.S. delegation. Stettinius worked conscientiously to keep everyone in the loop, but "the heat and pressure sometimes rubbed tempers raw." He prepared a daily summary of events for Hull and the President, and he usually saw the President every day at five o'clock. In early September, when FDR was at the Second Quebec Conference, Stettinius made his reports to adviser Harry Hopkins.[7]

Impact of the War

Both consciously and subconsciously, the delegates at Dumbarton Oaks sought to insulate their deliberations from the daily calamities and frictions of the war. Stettinius refused to entertain press questions on current policy matters, arguing that the talks were concerned with the future, not the present. He was right, but only in a limited bureaucratic sense. Ideally, the discussions at Dumbarton Oaks would be conducted as a Socratic dialogue on the future of humankind, and at times this seemed to be the case. The issues pointed always to the future which, it was assumed almost as an article of faith, would be better and simpler than the present. This hopefulness seemed particularly characteristic of American thinking, as one historian later noted: Roosevelt, Hull, and other American leaders seemed to believe that the prospective

United Nations was "a sort of talisman" which simply by its existence "would possess a powerful virtue to heal disputes among nations."[8]

But it was, of course, impossible to negotiate the structure of the postwar world in a political vacuum, unrelated to the unfolding shape and pace of the war and to growing strains among the Allies caused by events that were forcing the parties to confront decisions of great consequence—decisions that each felt, for different reasons, could no longer be postponed. Therefore, as the war continued to gather its fateful momentum, it exerted an ever greater impact on the Dumbarton talks. Russian forces were driving into territory that had been Poland before the war. British and American forces had crossed the English Channel, had breached Hitler's coastal defenses, and were fighting through France toward the German border. These developments gave particular urgency to the question of what the Allies intended to do with a Germany whose total defeat now seemed possible by the end of 1944—by Christmas, some optimists believed.[9]

But a serious rift between the British and the Americans had opened over policy toward Germany. The first assignment of the European Advisory Commission (created by decision at the Moscow Conference) was to establish a plan for the joint occupation and control of Germany. The tripartite group had reached agreement on surrender terms by the summer of 1944, but bogged down on occupation zones and long-range policy. As to occupation, it was readily agreed that the Russians should take over the eastern zone, but both Britain and the United States wanted to occupy the northwest sector. The British claim was based on the anticipated position of British troops and supply lines at the end of hostilities and on London's postwar plans for coordinating the British and Norwegian navies. The American claim was basically political. Both the President and the Joint Chiefs of Staff wished to avoid involvement in the internal problems of Southern and Central Europe, while concentrating U.S. energies on the elimination of Germany as a future threat to peace. By occupying the northwest sector, U.S. forces could be supported entirely through north German and Dutch ports, which would permit U.S. policy to avoid (in FDR's words) "the problem of reconstituting France, Italy, and the Balkans"—not a "natural task" for the United States.[10]

General Dwight D. Eisenhower had recommended that the Western Allies "occupy their portion of Germany on a unified basis," but the President definitely wanted a separate American zone—and in the northwest sector. In part his reasoning seemed to be that American public opinion would not support a U.S. military occupation of Germany for more than two or three years. The British continued to stand firm on their own claim to the northwest sector, which meant that the matter could not be resolved in the European Advisory Commission, but had to be addressed at the highest level.[11]

On a more basic issue—the long-term goal of U.S. policy toward Germany—the Administration was so badly divided that it could not even agree on instructions to the U.S. representative to the European Advisory Commission, John G. Winant (who was also U.S. Ambassador to London). This meant that the EAC could not consider the matter. The President finally appointed a Cabinet committee (comprising the Secretaries of War, Navy, and Treasury) a month before he was scheduled to meet Churchill at the Second Quebec Conference in September, but the Cabinet officers remained in deadlock. Stimson and Forrestal agreed that Germany must be rigorously occupied and reformed over a period of many years, but they argued that its industrial capacity must be rebuilt because this was a key factor in the economic revival of Western Europe. Treasury Secretary Henry Morgenthau wanted to eliminate every trace of German industry and reduce that nation to a simple agrarian economy.[12]

Roosevelt, who personally wanted a hard-line policy to impress upon the Germans their collective guilt in their nation's barbaric assault on civilization, finally decided that his Treasury Secretary had the better position. The President called him to Quebec where Morgenthau relentlessly pressed upon the Prime Minister his radical plan to "pastoralize" Germany in perpetuity. Churchill was "violently opposed," telling FDR and the others at dinner that he looked upon this scheme as he would look upon the prospect of "chaining himself to a dead German." But he found both the President and Morgenthau—"from whom we had so much to ask"—so insistent that "in the end we agreed to consider it." The quid pro quo was increased Lend-Lease aid for Britain and an agreement to let the British occupy the coveted northwest sector of Germany (which also handed them the hot potato of deindustrializing the Ruhr and the Saar under the Morgenthau Plan). In another ironic reversal, the United States would occupy the southwest zone, which carried the unwanted risk of deeper American involvement in Central and Southern Europe.[13]

The agreement on occupation zones was carried out, but the plan to pastoralize Germany came unstuck. Renewed British opposition, Russian demands for reparations from current German production, and Republican charges (in a presidential election year) that the Morgenthau Plan would lengthen the war by stiffening German resistance combined to force FDR to climb down from an unwise and untenable position. A few days later, the President told Secretary of War Stimson that Morgenthau had "pulled a boner."[14]

Russia: Friend or Foe?

Tensions between Russia and the two Western Allies continued to rise, reaching fever pitch in August 1944 over events in Poland. With the Russian Army on the outskirts of Warsaw and Moscow radio urging an insurrection to speed the liberation, the non-Communist Polish underground staged an uprising, counting on immediate Russian military support. It was soon clear, however, that Stalin would provide none. While a bitter street-to-street battle engulfed the city, the Russian forces remained in place. Roosevelt and Churchill appealed to Stalin for urgent help, but he refused to assume any responsibility for what he termed "a reckless and fearful gamble." American and British cargo aircraft flew numerous missions from Italy to airdrop food and ammunition to the insurgents, but much of the material was captured by the Germans. Stalin refused to allow American and British use of air bases in the Ukraine. The Germans sent in reinforcements, crushed the uprising, and killed a quarter of a million Poles.[15]

Bitter exchanges between FDR and Stalin followed, but these altered nothing. Historian James MacGregor Burns later underlined Stalin's utterly cold calculation in this affair. The Russian dictator, he wrote, "did not propose to liberate Warsaw from the Nazis only to leave it in the hands of bourgeois Poles who were pawns of London and Washington."[16]

By early summer it was also apparent that Russia was conducting an aggressive policy of support for Communist guerrillas in Central and Southern Europe. In private notes to Eden in early May, Churchill defined "the brute issue" as "Are we going to acquiesce in the Communization of the Balkans and perhaps of Italy?" Events were "approaching a showdown with the Russians about their Communist intrigues in Italy, Yugoslavia, and Greece.

Charles E. Bohlen, Leo Pasvolsky, Edward Stettinius, and
Joseph Grew confer at Dumbarton Oaks. (Edward R.
Stettinius, Jr., Papers, Special Collections Department,
Manuscripts Division, University of Virginia Library)

I must say I think their attitude becomes more difficult every day."[17] By September, the Prime Minister was gravely concerned by the further "dangerous spread of Russian influence" in the Balkans, for they might "never get out."[18]

Determined to head off "chaos" and especially to avoid the imposition of a "tyrannical Communist government in Greece," Churchill asked FDR for U.S. aircraft to transport British paratroops to Athens when the Germans left. He also urged an Anglo-American operation across the Adriatic onto the Istrian Peninsula to occupy Trieste and Fiume, and thus get ready to beat the Russians to Vienna. FDR supported plans for these operations at the Second Quebec Conference in September. He also overruled the Joint Chiefs of Staff, who were opposed to U.S. participation in the occupation of Austria. In general, however, the President was very reluctant to make Central and Southern Europe a major focus of U.S. interest and responsibility. This reticence encouraged aggressive Russian behavior.[19]

By the summer of 1944, opinion within the U.S. Government differed widely on the likelihood of postwar Russian cooperation, but the pessimists outnumbered the optimists. Most members of the American Group had already decided that Russia was less a reliable policeman and more an emerging threat to peace in the postwar period. Nevertheless, State Department planners took their lead from the President's determination to enlist the Soviet Union as a basic partner in postwar peacekeeping, which required that plans and policies be based on the hopeful assumption that Russian policy would not be fundamentally hostile or obstructionist. Despite daily difficulties and frictions and an increasing awareness of the chasm between Western and Soviet standards and values, Hull and his colleagues never seriously contemplated, even as a theoretical alternative, the establishment of a postwar United Nations without Russian membership. The most powerful short-term argument for suppressing distrust of Russian behavior was military necessity: military opinion was unanimous that continued Russian cooperation was necessary to win the war against both Germany and Japan. Tension between hope and reality thus characterized American diplomacy at Dumbarton Oaks.[20]

Four Major Issues

Four major issues dominated the work of the conference: the scope of the new organization; the Russian proposal for an international air force; membership; and voting procedures in the Security Council.

Scope of the United Nations

While fully recognizing that security measures to maintain the peace must be the primary concern of the United Nations, the United States was determined that the scope of the new organization must be broader—in particular, that the General Assembly should be vested with authority to create "additional organs" as it deemed necessary. The first U.S. priority was an Economic and Social Council "to promote the fullest and most effective use of the world's economic resources."[21] On August 25, Cadogan expressed British agreement with the U.S. view that the United Nations should have a broad role in world affairs and should specifically include an Economic and Social Council. Gromyko replied in his precise English that the League of Nations had failed in large part because it had spent 77 percent of its time on just such "secondary" problems. It was the Russian view that "the primary and indeed the only task" was maintenance of peace and security. To reinforce this view, the Russian delegation called to the attention of its British and American counterparts a current article in a Leningrad periodical, *Zvezda*, written by the previous Soviet Ambassador to Washington, Maxim Litvinov. This argued the case for confining the U.N. organization to a "directive body" empowered to take "urgent decisions without endless debate." The article drew the conclusion that "It will be much easier to observe the success or failure of an organization for security if it is not burdened with an endless number of superfluous functions."[22] The Russians were willing to consider economic and social problems, but wanted them to be handled by some separate agency outside the United Nations. As the U.N. organization could not guarantee universal prosperity, they argued, it would be discredited if it made promises that could not be kept.[23]

The Americans did not disagree in substance. Stettinius replied that security was the most important U.N. function, but that the United States preferred to handle all international problems generally under "one tent." Pasvolsky added that the United States viewed the Economic and Social Council as an adjunct of the General Assembly, entirely separate from the peacekeeping functions of the Security Council. Accordingly, its activities would not at all impede the ability of the Security Council to react swiftly to aggression. The aim of the U.S. proposal, he said, was simply to achieve more effective coordination. This discussion revealed a serious difference between Russia and the two English-speaking powers on the fundamental purpose of the United Nations organization, but the British and Americans were firmly united on the view that arrangements for economic and social cooperation must be an integral part of it, and the Russians eventually yielded on this issue.[24]

An International Air Force

The Russian proposal for an international air force reflected the basic Russian perception of the Security Council as a continuation of the wartime alliance whose primary function was to use its power to punish aggressor states and others who disobeyed its rules. The Russians were purportedly disappointed by the Anglo-American rejection of an integrated world police force, and their urging of an international air force was viewed as an attempt to salvage at least a part of that concept. The British conceded that the idea possessed technical merit, but felt that it implied something like a world state, which did not yet exist and was widely opposed. Also, like the Joint Chiefs of Staff, they could not resolve the practical problems of composition, maintenance, location, and especially control, without giving to the United Nations organization the attributes of national or supranational sovereignty, which neither they nor the lesser powers were willing to do.[25]

A special difficulty for the American delegation was the inescapable constitutional question—whether the President could order the U.S. component of an international air force into action without Congressional concurrence. During Hull's continuing consultations with the Senate Committee of Eight, Vandenberg thought that Congress might permit the President to deploy armed forces within the Western Hemisphere without specific prior approval, but "if it takes another world-wide war to deal with him [an aggressor], I do not see how we can escape the necessity for Congressional consent."[26] In view of these difficulties, the Americans proposed that U.N. members with the requisite capability each provide a national contingent of air power as part of its general commitment to furnish armed forces, facilities, and other assistance under a bilateral agreement with the U.N. organization. Gromyko continued to argue that the Russian proposal promised swifter reaction, but hinted that a compromise solution to this issue might be found.[27]

Membership

The Soviets came to Dumbarton Oaks with the view that "founder members" of the new organization should be confined to the twenty-six nations who signed the Declaration by United Nations on January 1, 1942. They were willing to countenance the eventual admission of other "peace-loving" states, if recommended by the General Assembly and approved by the Security Council. The United States wanted the initial membership also to include a number of pro-Allied nations who had not signed the declaration but had cooperated with the war effort—especially Egypt, Iceland, and the South American republics (except Argentina, which retained a stance of pro-German neutrality). The ultimate American goal was an essentially universal organization.[28]

The State Department originally shared the Russian procedural approach, making admission to membership subject to approval by the Security Council, but later decided that all authority on this question should reside in the General Assembly—on the principle that all nations should be entitled to an equal vote on membership. As a practical matter, this American shift to magnanimity was essentially cost-free, for it was understood that the United States and Britain would command comfortable majorities of friends and clients in the General Assembly for the foreseeable future. British analysis followed a similar path and fully supported the U.S. position, in part because it appeared that some of the Dominions might not be admitted under the Russian plan.

From the Russian point of view, the twin questions of establishing criteria and procedures for U.N. membership were directly linked to the issue of voting in the Security Council. The Soviets were acutely aware of being an ideological and political minority in any new world organization, and thus of being perpetually outnumbered—and in danger of being perpetually outvoted. An absolute veto could protect their position in the Security Council, but the best they could hope for in the General Assembly was to whittle down the inherent capitalist majority by narrowly defining the criteria for membership and by "blackballing" questionable applicants via their veto in the Security Council. Retention of an absolute veto power was thus central to Russian considerations.

This mind-set led Moscow to embrace the appealing possibility of including all sixteen Soviet republics among the initial members of the United Nations, as a means of reducing the Russian sense of isolation in the General Assembly. Gromyko introduced this proposal at Dumbarton Oaks in the context of a lengthy debate in the joint steering committee on August 28. It burst upon the British and Americans like a bombshell and rendered the membership issue beyond the possibility of agreement at the conference.[29]

Voting Procedures in the Security Council

Owing to continuing differences within the American delegation and the State Department, the initial U.S. proposals presented at Dumbarton Oaks did not take a position on a crucial element of the voting procedures in the Security Council. As the U.S. document stated, "Provisions will need to be worked out with respect to the voting procedure in the event of a dispute in which one or more of the members having continuing tenure are directly involved."

A majority of State Department planners believed that fair play in a democratic world organization required that the veto not be used by a permanent member who was party to a dispute, but others thought that this was simply an intellectual evasion of power realities which, if insisted upon, could kill the new organization before it was formed. The latter group was strengthened by Hull's treatment of this issue in his senatorial consultations, where he

Stettinius addressing the delegates at Dumbarton Oaks. (Edward R. Stettinius, Jr.,
Papers, Special Collections Department, Manuscripts Division, University of
Virginia Library)

left the impression that the United States and the other Great Powers would
have a blanket veto. The central dilemma remained: a broad veto power could
paralyze the new organization just as the requirement for unanimity had paralyzed the League; yet without the self-protection provided by the veto, Russia and very probably the United States would be unwilling to participate.[30]

The original British proposals argued that, unless large and small states
were placed "on a equal footing" when they were parties to a dispute, it would
be extremely difficult to obtain general acceptance of an organization that
gave extensive veto power to the Big Four. The Russians suggested that some
"special procedure" should be devised to deal with this particular situation,
but they made it clear that this should not impair the unconditional right of
each permanent member to use the veto. In a meeting of the joint steering
committee on August 28, the United States said it had concluded, after extensive study, that a "special procedure" was not feasible and that it now sup-

ported the British position. That is, the United States "should put itself on the same plane" as all other nations, meaning that it should deny itself the veto when it was party to a dispute.[31]

This proposal caught the Russians by surprise, and seemed to them to strike at the heart of the concept of Big Four unity. Gromyko immediately protested that it violated the basic principle underlying the creation of the United Nations and could therefore lead to "actual disagreement." He then dropped his own bombshell (mentioned above) by announcing that Russia wanted all sixteen Soviet republics enrolled as charter members of the United Nations organization. This pronouncement, which in turn left Stettinius and Cadogan "breathless," has been taken by some historians as an extemporaneous reaction to the surprise American shift on the veto question. The contrary evidence is much stronger—that it was in fact a carefully considered demand, motivated by the Russian fear of isolation in a predominantly capitalist organization.[32]

The President was deeply shocked when Stettinius reported this new development: "My God," he responded, and then instructed the Under Secretary to tell Gromyko "privately, personally, and immediately" that this "might ruin" any chance for U.S. participation in the United Nations. He was categorically opposed to the idea, feeling that it was as nonsensical as demanding forty-eight votes for the United States. His immediate concern, however, was to keep it from leaking—especially to domestic critics of world organization and those who opposed cooperation with the Russians. Henceforward, this issue was referred to only as the "X matter," and the few highly secret documents pertaining to it were locked in Stettinius's office safe.[33]

On August 31, FDR cabled Stalin, urging him to reconsider this demand and suggesting that the issue be left for consideration by the General Assembly after it was fully functioning. To raise it now "would very definitely imperil the whole project." Stalin's reply a week later was not reassuring: "I attach exceptional importance to the statement of the Soviet delegation on this question." Explaining that recent changes in the Soviet Constitution had granted autonomy in foreign affairs to all Soviet republics, he argued that several of these possessed larger populations and greater "political importance" than a number of the nations already proposed for U.N. membership. He hoped for an opportunity to explain to FDR the great weight which the Soviet government attached to this question.[34]

13

The Dumbarton Oaks Conference II

When Stettinius reported to Gromyko the President's categorical opposition to giving the Soviets sixteen additional
seats in the General Assembly, the Russian diplomat seemed
unperturbed, saying that there was no urgency to that particular proposal. He was far more concerned about the
American position on the veto. The Russians, Gromyko
argued, had already shown a willingness to support a U.N.
organization that was broader than a military alliance, and
they were constructively seeking a compromise on the issue
of an international air force. Meanwhile, the British and the
Americans were conceding nothing; indeed, they appeared
determined to undermine Russian security interests in
Poland, as indicated by their continued sponsorship of the
London Poles and their logistical support for "anti-Russian
elements" during the Warsaw uprising. Now, Gromyko
complained, they wanted to tamper with the veto, which
was the bedrock of Big Four unity. Did they want an organization stacked against Russia because it was a Communist
nation? As Stettinius observed him, the youngish Russian
official seemed on the verge of despair.[1]

The root problem was of course the chasm separating
Russian Communist and Western democratic political values. The West believed in majority rule and the protection
of minority rights. The British and the Americans believed
that liberated nations should have a free choice as to their
political future. But the Russians saw free choice as leading

to a rejection of Communism and thus to unfriendly governments in Eastern Europe that would undermine Russian security. The West believed in justice in the settlement of disputes, but the Russians disdained the notion of "pseudo-equality" between Great Powers and lesser nations and were determined to safeguard Russian interests, unilaterally if necessary. Litvinov tried to explain this to Ambassador Harriman in Moscow, saying that it was "unreasonable" to give equal weight to the interests of 30 million Poles and 180 million Russians. Where these interests were in conflict, "the Poles would have to give way."[2]

By early September 1944, it was apparent to the American delegation that all other matters in dispute could be settled, provided only that some solution to the veto issue could be found. But this was firmly deadlocked, and it was fundamental. In a general review of the negotiations on September 6, Roosevelt, Hull, and Stettinius agreed that this was the hinge issue on which success or failure of the conference swung. They also agreed that it was desirable to wind up the Russian phase of the talks and move on to the Chinese phase. Stettinius wanted to schedule a full-scale United Nations Conference in the latter part of October, but the more sagacious Roosevelt believed that it would be politically necessary to wait at least until after the election. Their discussion was colored by excessive optimism concerning the war in Europe. According to "the best military advice" reaching him, FDR told his colleagues, Germany might be defeated within "five or six weeks." This was a prediction that failed to anticipate Hitler's desperate winter counteroffensive, the Battle of the Bulge, which possessed sufficient force and fury to deny the Allies their victory for an additional eight months.[3]

The Irremovable Veto

On September 7, worried but determined, Stettinius decided that "bold action"—in the form of a direct talk between FDR and Gromyko—was needed to break the deadlock on the veto and thus bring the conference to a successful close. FDR was willing, but he was leaving the following day for the Second Quebec Conference with Churchill. Stettinius escorted the Russian to the presidential bedroom at nine-thirty A.M. on September 8. After a general exchange about the encouraging military progress in Europe, the President broached the topic of voting procedures in the Security Council, exerting the

Cadogan, Stettinius, and Gromyko confer in the library at
Dumbarton Oaks. (Edward R. Stettinius, Jr., Papers, Special
Collections Department, Manuscripts Division, University
of Virginia Library)

full power of his charm to persuade Gromyko that the Russian idea ran
counter to American custom and would create great difficulties in the Senate.
According to Stettinius, he "told a beautiful story, tracing this . . . American
concept of fair play back to the days of our founding fathers." He cited the
example of husbands and wives, who could present their complaints to a
court, but were not allowed a voice in determining their own cases. Gromyko
"accepted the remarks gracefully" but said merely that he would report the
conversation to Moscow.[4]

The President also cabled Stalin asking for his intervention to break the
deadlock: "We and the British both feel strongly that in decisions of the
Council, parties to a dispute should not vote if one of the parties is a permanent member of the Council. I know public opinion in the United States
would never understand or support a plan . . . which violated that principle."
But Stalin would not give ground. In a cable delivered to the President in
Quebec a week later, the dictator said, in a rather injured tone, that he
thought that the requirement for unanimous Big Four approval of all decisions in a new world organization had been firmly settled at Teheran. In any
event, it was an imperative principle for dealing with future aggressions.

Among the Big Four, "there is no room for mutual suspicions," but the existence of "certain absurd prejudices" against the Soviet Union held by some nations made an absolute veto necessary for self-protection.[5]

The Russian Perspective

Behind this message lay Stalin's genuine alarm at the evidence that the Western powers were drifting away from the exclusive alliance concept of the Four Policemen and toward support for the equal rights of smaller nations. Worse than that, they were abandoning the regionalism inherent in the Four Policemen idea that would assign primary authority for each major region to one of the Policemen. To Stalin, Big Four unity meant mutual respect for the spheres of interest of each, which meant Anglo-American support for Russian hegemony in Eastern Europe.[6]

But now the British and Americans were adopting a "universalistic" approach, showing a worrisome interest in the affairs of nations on Russia's borders, including a readiness to air-drop military supplies to the anti-Communist Poles. This raised the possibility, in a mind conditioned to xenophobia by experience and ideology, that the two English-speaking powers intended to use the United Nations organization against the Soviet Union. Crystallization of such an intention would force Stalin to concentrate on the task of ensuring "friendly governments" on his borders, at the risk of having to abandon his genuine desire to play a cooperative role in postwar international affairs. He wanted to avoid that hard choice, for he understood that cooperation in the war and the far-reaching agreements obtained at Teheran and Dumbarton Oaks had already proved quite valuable: they had enhanced Soviet prestige and illuminated Soviet power. Moreover, new opportunities to advance Moscow's interests were discernible in Roosevelt's plan for international trusteeships which, even though downplayed at Dumbarton Oaks, was bound to sow discord in the capitalist-colonialist camp. The U.N. plans for a collective security system opened up the possibility of distributing worldwide military bases, some of which would surely be placed under Russian control. All this was positive. If, however, the British and Americans did not give way on the veto issue, there could be no Russian cooperation and therefore no United Nations organization. Stalin's priorities were quite clear.[7]

Stettinius, who had thought that the President's talk with Gromyko would lead to a solution ("I am sure we are softening them"), was taken aback on September 13 when Gromyko told him that the Russian position remained "unchanged." He told the Russian that this was a "great blow" to hopes for an organization that all nations could support, and that the U.S. Government "simply cannot understand" the Russian attitude. Unless it were modified, he doubted whether any agreed-upon document could be published at the end of the conference. Cadogan supported Stettinius, but Gromyko was obdurate. There was no possibility of change, he said bluntly. Complete Big Four unity was fundamental. Moreover, the Big Four veto power was already taken for granted by the smaller nations. He doubted if any of them was actually concerned about voting rights, for "they are chiefly interested in peace and an effective organization designed to preserve peace." Stettinius replied incautiously that the U.S. position on the veto "is unalterable, regardless of future developments."[8]

The Failed Compromise

The more cautious Hull, whose personal position on the veto was always pragmatic, now thought that the American delegation should review the entire range of voting procedures with the British and the Russian delegations. Stettinius disagreed, but Hull prevailed. When the suggestion proved acceptable to Gromyko and Cadogan, an ad hoc Formulations Committee, consisting of Leo Pasvolsky for the United States, Gladwyn Jebb for Britain, and Arkadei Sobelov for Russia met for several hours on the afternoon of September 13 and arrived at "an informal compromise solution": a permanent member of the Council would have an unqualified veto over any matter involving the use of force, even if it were party to the dispute, but would have no veto if it were party to a dispute that came under the heading of "pacific settlement." The Russian delegation viewed this compromise as a major concession on its part, and Gromyko was not confident that it would be approved by Moscow.[9] (This proposal was a precise opposite of the position contained in the internal U.S. draft plan which FDR had approved in December 1943. That earlier plan required Big Four unanimity on matters of "peaceful settlement," but only three of the Big Four votes on matters involving the use of force; it was silent on the pivotal question of whether a vote was permitted by a party to a dispute.)

The proposed compromise was cabled to Stalin, and Cadogan carried it the next day to Quebec, where Roosevelt and Churchill were meeting on military matters.[10] Once there, however, the Foreign Office official experienced great difficulty in getting the two Western leaders to focus on the issue, although he "repeatedly tried to pin them down" to a careful consideration of the points in dispute; they were preoccupied with the war in Europe and "always wandered away." The following day, however, the President and the Prime Minister cabled their joint rejection of the staff compromise. Churchill's decision reflected consultation with the British War Cabinet, which was rapidly coming to the view that Russia was less a policeman and more a threat to the peace and which saw the veto issue as a necessary test of will regarding the postwar distribution of power in Europe. FDR's rejection appears to have been based on the opposite consideration—namely, that because Stalin was almost certain to reject the compromise, no purpose was served by inviting another confrontation at this juncture.

FDR urged the American delegation to "keep on trying," but decided that, if no agreement proved possible, then the veto issue should be included in a "general statement" of various matters not resolved at Dumbarton Oaks, to be carried over for consideration by a more broadly based United Nations Conference.[11]

Stettinius was profoundly discouraged by the reply from Quebec, but Cadogan was "completely deflated" and now regarded any further attempts to reach agreement at Dumbarton Oaks as quite futile. Desperate to leave the heat and frustration of the conference, he cabled London that he was wasting his time in Washington and asked permission to go home, leaving Gladwyn Jebb in charge.[12] For his part, Hull angrily resented the offhand manner of the rejection at Quebec and thought that the two leaders had allowed themselves to become too preoccupied with immediate military problems, to the detriment of more important long-term considerations. However, blaming Roosevelt and Churchill for the impasse was diminished the next day by word that Stalin also opposed the compromise. This rejection strengthened the growing conviction in both the American and British delegations that Russian intransigence on the veto was directly related to Stalin's determination to control Eastern Europe on his own conditions, and that he would brook no interference from the Anglo-American powers either directly or by means of a United Nations procedure in which Russia could be outvoted.[13]

The Prospect of Failure

Rejection of the compromise by all Big Three heads of government also rekindled a heated debate within the State Department which had never really cooled. Assistant Secretary Breckinridge Long led a group that argued for accepting the Russians' absolute position on the veto. It was unrealistic to believe, he said, that any international organization could work without the complete solidarity of the Big Four.

Admiral Arthur Hepburn, speaking for the military delegates, agreed, saying, "It seems to me that realities are being thoroughly fogged by theory," for collective security can be effective "only if the three great powers hang together." General Stanley Embick stressed the vital importance that the Joint Chiefs of Staff placed on Russian entrance into the Japanese war, and warned that "a break on this matter with Russia" was likely to affect that question. The military advisers put forward for consideration three complicated alternatives and recommended that, if Russia refused them, then the United States should adopt Russia's absolute position on the veto. Long supported the military recommendations, even claiming that they would return the U.S. position to what was "stated in every paper on the subject for more than two years prior to the Dumbarton Oaks Conference."[14]

Stettinius thought that "the admirals and generals and some of our political advisors have lost their grip . . . are not thinking straight about this thing . . . [and have become] a little bit hysterical."[15] He and others in the delegation were convinced that Stalin would decide whether to enter the Pacific war based on his perception of Russian national interests—not out of friendship for the United States. This view was supported by State Department experts, who told him that the Latin American countries would resist "an unqualified veto" on the grounds that it would lead to a resurgence of Yankee imperialism.[16] Hull rejected the military recommendations and was irritated by Long's "completely erroneous" assertion that the department had originally supported an absolute veto, insisting that "the Secretary of State had never made up his mind" on this question.

Long's assertion was not completely accurate, but neither was it completely erroneous. Thinking on the veto in the State Department and the White House had been, from the very first postwar planning efforts, characterized by moral and philosophical ambiguity because it was torn by the rival claims of Wilsonian idealism and realpolitik, by an earnest hope that the Russians would prove to be genuine partners in a process of democratic give-and-take and the increasingly conclusive evidence that this was a quite false hope. But in 1944, even the pessimists were unready to confront the possibility of a fundamental break with Moscow. The compelling inhibitions were military necessity and the heavy investment of U.S. political capital in the success of the United Nations.[17]

But rejection of the compromise formula by all Big Three heads of state left the veto issue—and the X matter—solidly encased in ice, with no possibility of a thaw at Dumbarton Oaks, and left the conference staring failure in the face. The compelling question was what to do next. The public was getting restive, in America and throughout the world. The three heads of delegation shared the view that they could not simply terminate the conference with a statement that agreement had proved impossible. As Stettinius put it, "civilization as we know it and the entire future of the world" depended on the ultimate success of these efforts. But it was also clear that the Russians would not agree to submit the voting issue and the X matter to a general conference of United Nations. A palpable gloom engulfed the conference delegates.[18]

The President thereupon decided, on about September 17, that these two matters would have to be handled directly with Churchill and Stalin at a later meeting. He agreed with Hull and Stettinius that the talks should now be brought to a close in a manner that emphasized accomplishments and downplayed unresolved issues. The British quickly accepted this strategy, but Gromyko did not receive his instructions from Moscow until September 27. When they came, they were stiff. While agreeing to end the current talks and to put the best face on their results, Gromyko stated that Russian participation in "a general United Nations conference on world security" was contingent on acceptance of the Soviet proposals "as to voting in the Council and the X matter." Moreover, on the voting question, the Soviet government "wished to reaffirm that . . . the principle of unanimity of the four great powers must be carried out unconditionally."[19]

Asked at his press conference on September 22 why the Dumbarton talks were taking so long and moving so slowly, without any indication of clear-cut achievement, the President replied that the delegates had agreed on 90 percent of the issues confronting them. He added, "Well, that is what we used to call

Chinese Foreign Minister Wellington Koo, Stettinius, and
Cadogan at Dumbarton Oaks. (Edward R. Stettinius, Jr.,
Papers, Special Collections Department, Manuscripts
Division, University of Virginia Library)

in the old days a darn good batting average."[20] No one asked him what could
be done with 90 percent of a world organization.

The Russians departed Dumbarton Oaks on September 28, and the
British and American diplomats began discussions with the Chinese who had
been waiting in the wings since mid-August. This phase of the conference went
swiftly, in part because China's foreign minister, Wellington Koo, had been
briefed every day by Assistant Secretary of State Joseph Grew, but in larger part
because the Chinese understood that the British and Americans were unwilling
to accept any changes that could jeopardize their fragile agreements with the
Russians. The Chinese were accordingly resigned to accepting the agreements
reached by the Big Three. As Koo explained to his friend Breckinridge Long,
he "had no disposition to quibble about any details; . . . the important thing
was to agree to something." Moreover, Koo adopted the generous view that any
serious U.S. proposals "would be fair and without selfish interest."[21]

The Conference Ends

The Dumbarton Oaks Conference closed on October 7, with the issuance of
a joint Four Power statement entitled "Proposals for the Establishment of a

General International Organization." The President expressed his pleasure "that so much could have been accomplished on so difficult a subject in so short a time," and added, "the task of planning the great design of security and peace has been well begun."[22] The American people adopted a positive, if somewhat wait-and-see response. British historian Charles K. Webster, who was a member of the British delegation, was not surprised by the incomplete results of the talks. As he remarked to the American Group on September 18, the conference had tried to go too far, too fast, "attempting to settle in three weeks a problem that had gone unresolved over centuries of human history."[23] But this begged the question whether there was, in the swift-moving interdependent world of 1944, a practical alternative.

The published proposals contained few surprises. They called for a United Nations organization; a General Assembly of all member nations; a Security Council of five permanent members (including France) and six nonpermanent members elected by the General Assembly; an Economic and Social Council; and an International Court of Justice. There would also be a Military Staff Committee composed of officers from the five permanent member states which would direct the forces to be made available by all member states for collective U.N. action against aggression. Such forces would be provided in accordance with special agreements between each member state and the Security Council.[24]

What the joint statement could not disguise was the glaring absence of any agreed procedures for voting in the Security Council—a fundamental omission which cast doubt on the entire enterprise. The statement did not disclose who would decide whether and when aggression had taken place, who would vote to impose sanctions, including the use of force, or who would provide the armed forces. It was equally significant that the United States had still not resolved the inescapable constitutional question of control over the employment of American troops for U.N. duty. Keenly aware that Congressional insistence on prior approval to deploy American forces had been at the heart of the Lodge reservation on Article 10 of the League Covenant in 1919, Hull had maneuvered to separate this issue from the question of Senate approval of U.S. entry into the new world organization. But could the two issues remain separated under closer Senate scrutiny?

It was thus apparent that the agreements reached at Dumbarton Oaks were extremely fragile. Domestically, American society had yet to confront the basic issues on which the League of Nations had foundered. Internationally, the growing evidence of distrust and irreconcilable ideological differences between Soviet Russia and the West cast a dark shadow over the possibility of future cooperation.[25]

14

The 1944 Election

President Roosevelt had concluded at the end of 1943, soon after his return from Teheran, that he would need a fourth term to complete the great tasks of winning the war and forging an enduring peace, but he seemed genuinely conflicted by the prospect. He was sixty-two and terribly worn down by eleven years in the Oval Office, and the prospect of retiring to the spacious tranquility of Hyde Park was deeply appealing. Moreover, a physical examination in the spring of 1944, triggered by his chronic bouts of flu and bronchitis, shocked his doctors. He was suffering from hypertension and an enlarged heart, and there was evidence of progressive cardiac failure. "I just hate to run again," he told Admiral William D. Leahy, and expressed the hope that events might play out in a way that would obviate the need for him to be a candidate.[1]

Nevertheless he began making confidential campaign plans early in 1944, while deflecting all public speculation as to his intentions. He seems to have accepted at face value his doctors' cautious advice that digitalis, weight reduction, fewer cigarettes, and more rest could sustain him through a fourth term, provided he reduced his workload. But was there any possibility of meeting that final all-important proviso?[2]

Opinion polls taken at the end of 1943 showed that, with ultimate victory now apparently assured, the principal concern of most Americans had become economic insecurity after the war. Eighty percent feared a lower standard of living and even economic hardship; only 11 percent were primarily worried about the threat of another war. In his State of the Union message of January 11, Roosevelt took account of this pervasive public anxiety, while continuing to press the theme of unremitting sacrifice to win the war as the fundamental first order of the nation's business. He asked Congress for a national service law to prevent strikes and impose an obligation of service on every able-bodied adult. But he also promised, once the fighting was over, a major effort to achieve "a second Bill of Rights under which a new basis of economic security and prosperity can be established for all—regardless of station or race or creed." The goal would be "an American standard of living higher than any before known."[3] Without question, this was an expression of his deepest aspirations for postwar America. Historian James MacGregor Burns later called it "the most radical speech of his life."[4]

Although nearly everyone from politicians and journalists to the man in the street was certain that he intended to run for a fourth term, the President remained coy until a week before the Democratic Convention in Chicago in mid-July. At his press conference on July 11, he read a letter from the national committee chairman, Robert Hannegan, informing him that a majority of the delegates favored his renomination and urging him to become a candidate. FDR then told the reporters that, while he would prefer to retire to private life, the unfinished tasks of war and peace had convinced him that he must bow to the will of his party and the American people.[5]

Attention shifted immediately to the vice presidency, and the party regulars made clear their desire to find a substitute for Henry Wallace. Believing that the election would be close, they felt that the underlying public concern that Roosevelt might not survive a full fourth term would cast his running mate as a possible, perhaps probable, successor in the minds of voters. Wallace had the support of tried-and-true New Deal liberals, including blacks, members of labor unions, and Eleanor Roosevelt, but he would alienate Southern conservatives and attract few moderates or independents. The party leaders calculated that, in a close race, a "Solid South" was essential to a Democratic victory. Roosevelt was fond of Wallace but prepared, as always, to make pragmatic adjustments. After some sophisticated maneuvering, he gave a handwritten note to Hannegan on which he had scribbled two acceptable names: Supreme Court Justice William O. Douglas and Senator Harry S Truman.

There is some evidence that when Hannegan had the notes typed up, he reversed the order of the names.[6] The party bosses chose Truman. The President's oldest son, James, was later quoted as saying that his father "didn't give a damn whether the convention chose Douglas or Byrnes or Truman."[7]

Taking the U.N. Out of Politics

Wendell Willkie, the GOP candidate in 1940, was out of favor with his party four years later, having proved too explicit an advocate of a U.N. organization and an international police force. After suffering a decisive defeat in the Wisconsin presidential primary, he was not even invited to address the Republican convention. Nevertheless, he enjoyed the enthusiastic support of independents throughout the country who were thought to constitute as much as 20 percent of the vote, and he was determined "not to sit by while the peace process is wrecked again as it was in the 1920s." In a series of magazine articles, he urged his fellow Republicans to create immediately a United Nations Council and to help establish "an effective international organization for the good of all." He warned especially against "hoarding" American sovereignty which he regarded as incompatible with effective international cooperation.[8]

The *New Republic* thought that GOP acceptance of these suggestions had about the same chance as "the Sermon on the Mount has of being endorsed by the Gestapo"—a prediction that was essentially accurate. The GOP convention drafted a foreign policy position that fell short of a firm commitment to U.S. participation in an international organization, and Governor Thomas Dewey of New York, who was nominated on the first ballot, chose to say only that "America will participate with other sovereign nations in a cooperative effort to prevent future wars."[9]

The President was convinced that the GOP intended to make international organization a major campaign issue, and specifically to attack the Administration for a presumed willingness to surrender U.S. sovereignty. On August 16, Dewey did attack, but from a different and unexpected quarter. Having read newspaper accounts of the American plan submitted to the Dumbarton Oaks Conference, he argued that it reflected "the rankest form of imperialism," for it "would subject the nations of the world, great and small, permanently to the coercive power of the four nations holding this conference." This appeal to liberal internationalists—and American voters with

roots in Eastern Europe—garnered headlines and won praise even from
journalists who failed to remember that less than a year before Dewey had
called for an Anglo-American alliance as the core of U.S. foreign policy and
security.[10]

In an impassioned rebuttal, Secretary of State Hull called the charges
"utterly and completely unfounded"; he then invited Dewey to confer with
him at the State Department in order to clarify the matter in "a nonpartisan
spirit." The President was privately irritated by Hull's spontaneous invitation,
but the Secretary of State was deeply worried about the domestic political
impact of seeming to dismiss the interests of smaller nations. After some
reflection, including a conference with Willkie, Dewey decided to send his key
adviser, John Foster Dulles, to talk with Hull. After two days of discussion of
the American plan, Dulles told Hull that he was no longer concerned about
the fate of small nations, and the two men signed a formal agreement to keep
the issue of international organization out of the presidential campaign. The
agreement was narrow in scope: Dewey would remain free to attack the
Administration on all other points of foreign policy.[11] But Dulles was right
when he noted that this agreement was "something unique in American politics"; never before had spokesmen for two presidential candidates met to
remove a major issue from the political campaign.[12]

Dewey campaigned effectively against the "tired old men" in the Administration, a line of attack which served to focus the growing public concern
about Roosevelt's health. A newspaper picture taken in San Diego showed
FDR spent and exhausted, head bowed and mouth agape. In an effort to
counteract that damaging image, the President decided to address the nation
on August 9 from the deck of the destroyer U.S.S. *Baltimore*, while standing
in his heavy iron leg braces, but the result was a rare fumbling performance
that deepened public doubts that he was fit to lead the nation for another four
years.[13] But Dewey, too, had his vulnerabilities. He suffered from a wide perception that he was "an ersatz internationalist" without the force or conviction
to control the hardcore isolationists in the Republican Party. And though
demonstrably competent and energetic, he was seen as rather humorless and
colorless, a little man with a "bottle mustache" and mechanical smile who
reminded the actress Ethel Barrymore of "the bridegroom on the wedding
cake."[14] On September 23, Roosevelt bounded back with a masterful speech
to the Teamsters Union, taunting the GOP with clever sarcasm and ridicule

and appearing energized and in complete command. "Well, here we are together again—after four years—and what years they have been! You know, I am actually four years older, which is a fact that seems to annoy some people."[15]

The Policeman and the Town Hall Meeting

It was evident that the election was going to be close, and seemed likely to turn on the terms of U.S. participation in a new international organization. Willkie, who saw an opportunity to be the swing factor, attacked both party platforms for "their insistence on preserving American sovereignty" and urged all independents to vote for the man who took the most advanced position on the authority of the new world body—which for him meant the man who came closest to supporting an international police force.[16] However, Willkie had suffered several heart attacks during the summer and was hospitalized in late September. Although he seemed briefly to recover, the fifty-two-year-old author of *One World* died in a New York hospital on October 8 before he had publicly endorsed either candidate. Like Sumner Welles and Henry Wallace, Wendell Willkie had risked much and lost his position of leadership through his bold efforts to break the isolationist tradition and commit the United States to a much larger role in world affairs. All three men had been instrumental in bringing the issue of internationalism into the American political mainstream, and all three had suffered the slings and arrows reserved for militant reformers.[17]

Against considerable opposition from within his own party, including a public protest by a cosponsor of the B2-H2 resolution, Republican Senator Joseph Ball immediately picked up Willkie's fallen banner by posing three public questions to the candidates. The first two related to entering a United Nations organization before the end of the war and avoiding crippling reservations. They were not difficult to answer, but the third question went to the heart of the degree to which congressional approval should be required for the employment of American armed forces. Should the vote of the U.S. representative on the Security Council "commit an agreed quota" of U.S. military forces "without requiring further congressional approval"?[18]

Dewey answered on October 18, in the course of a major speech to the *New York Herald-Tribune* Forum. He said that the United Nations "must be enabled through the use of force, when necessary, to prevent or repel military aggression," but refused to say who could authorize the commitment of American armed forces or under what circumstances. Roosevelt deftly exploited this opening three days later during a major speech at the Waldorf-Astoria. Asserting that the U.N. Security Council must have the authority to act quickly and decisively, he thought it "foolish" if a policeman, upon spotting an intruder, was required to call a town meeting before he could arrest the criminal.[19]

On October 23, Ball announced that Roosevelt had given the responsible answer and that he would support him for re-election against the candidate of his own party. Republican leaders denounced Ball's apostasy as "a grievous mistake" and a "great disservice to the nation" and threatened to expel him from the party. But the episode had a large political impact. The *New York Times,* which had opposed FDR's third-term bid in 1940, now endorsed the President, albeit with "deep reluctance," owing to his clear commitment to a strong United Nations.[20] Walter Lippmann, who had also opposed Roosevelt in 1940, concluded that Dewey had too much to learn to "be trusted now with responsibility for foreign affairs." Advocates of responsible American internationalism generally came to the same conclusion. One strong dissenter, the GOP activist Robert Moses, pointed out that Roosevelt's response to Ball's question had broken the Hull-Dulles agreement to keep international organization out of the campaign. He was technically correct.[21]

A Victory for Internationalism

On November 7, Roosevelt was re-elected by an overwhelming margin in the electoral college, but by only 3 million popular votes. This was the tightest popular vote since Wilson's slender victory in 1916, and the margin undoubtedly reflected wide concern about the President's health, as well as philosophical misgivings about the perpetuation of individual power. The "Solid South" carried him in. Without question, the election was a clear-cut mandate for American participation in the United Nations and for a large American role in the postwar world. The Democrats picked up thirty seats in the House and retained a healthy margin in the Senate. Internationalists like William Fulbright (D-Arkansas), Wayne Morse (D-Oregon), and Leverett Saltonstall (R-Massachusetts) entered the Senate, while bitter-end isolationists like Senator Gerald Nye (R-South Dakota) and Congressman Hamilton Fish (R-New

Return to Washington, D.C., from Hyde Park, N.Y.,
November 10, 1944, after winning a fourth term (*left to right*): FDR, Harry S Truman, and Henry Wallace.

York) were defeated. Almost without exception, isolationist incumbents, whether Republican or Democrat, were turned out of office.[22]

There was general rejoicing among internationalists of both parties. Sumner Welles praised the American people for their wisdom at the polls and for their ability to learn from "the experience of a great tragedy" in 1920.[23] The *New Republic* urged that Henry Wallace be named Secretary of State as "the best qualified man in the country" for the job.[24] Senator Arthur Vandenberg, now emerging as the main bridge between the Administration and the GOP on foreign affairs, praised Hull for his scrupulously bipartisan approach to postwar problems. John Foster Dulles, another serious believer in the need for bipartisan cooperation, wrote to the President asserting that the election had demonstrated a solid vote of confidence for the Administration's plan to create the United Nations. He added, "I wish you strength and wisdom in this great task, and assure you of my continuing support, without regard to party, of constructive efforts along this line."[25]

15

An Unsettling Winter

Cordell Hull went to the White House on October 1, 1944, to submit his resignation after twelve years as Secretary of State. He had been so skillful at hiding his infirmities that few were aware he was on the edge of collapse. FDR was surprised, and Thomas Dewey publicly pledged that, if elected, he would offer Hull a diplomatic post. But Hull's diabetes had now reached an advanced stage, and his tuberculosis had spread to both lungs. Moreover, his precarious physical condition was aggravated by long nurtured frustration and bitterness. He was tired of being bypassed and overridden, tired of being ignored in private but called upon to provide public support. Now further anxiety was triggered by the fear that FDR was planning to replace him with Sumner Welles.[1]

Recognizing that Hull's presence was invaluable to the electoral campaign, the President persuaded him to hold off resigning until the election, and Hull agreed. Three days later his doctors ordered him to bed and soon thereafter moved him to the Bethesda Naval Hospital, where he remained for seven months. His resignation was announced on November 27, with an exchange of flowery letters that inevitably strained the truth: Hull referred to "uniformly and invariably agreeable" personal relations with the President, cited achievements in foreign affairs that "have been brought to partial or full completion," and expressed regret that he could no longer work to make the United Nations organization a living reality. The President replied that he would "continue to pray that you as the Father of the United Nations may preside over its first session," for it was Hull who "has done the most to make this great plan for peace an effective fact."[2]

Most insiders believed the President had ignored Hull because he had little respect for his judgment, and kept him in office only because of Hull's national prestige; further, that "Father of the United Nations" was an accolade that greatly exaggerated the Tennessean's undeniable contribution.[3] Writing some years later, Dean Acheson judged that the State Department's isolation and lack of participation in major wartime decisions were attributable to Hull's refusal or inability to assert his Cabinet authority: "detached from the practicalities of current problems and power relationships," Hull and the department became absorbed in the "platonic planning of a utopia, in a sort of mechanistic idealism."[4]

The New Team at State

Following Hull's resignation, the President immediately promoted Stettinius to the vacated Cabinet post, ending rumors that Sumner Welles, James Byrnes, or Henry Wallace were in line for the job, and confirming the view of close observers that he intended to retain full control of foreign policy. The limited attainments of Edward Stettinius—a genial personality and an unsubtle mind—were widely recognized, but he was in fact well suited for the task of selling the United Nations to the American people. A born salesman, he understood the importance of generating public support, and his business background was reassuring to Republicans in the Congress and thus helpful in sustaining a bipartisan approach to international organization.[5]

Stettinius quickly surprised official Washington by proposing a clean sweep of the State Department hierarchy. Except for Dean Acheson, who would be retained as the Assistant Secretary for liaison with Congress, there would be an entirely new team. Joseph Grew would become Under Secretary, and there would be five new Assistant Secretaries: Will Clayton, James Dunn, Nelson Rockefeller, Julius Holmes, and Archibald MacLeish. Except for MacLeish, who was a former Librarian of Congress and a Pulitzer prize-winning poet, the new group was business-oriented and generally conservative, a fact that alarmed liberals. One sarcastic observer called them "a bevy of tycoons surrounding a poet,"

The new team at the State Department (*left to right*): Will
Clayton, Dean Acheson, Joseph Grew, Edward Stettinius,
Archibald MacLeish, Nelson Rockefeller, and James Dunn.
(Edward R. Stettinius, Jr., Papers, Special Collections
Department, Manuscripts Division, University of
Virginia Library)

and others asserted that they could not possibly work well with Russian Communists or a Labour government in Britain. The confirmation hearings were
strenuous and occasionally amusing, but in the end the whole team won the
approval of the Senate. They were all dedicated and able men.[6]

Even before the new team was assembled, Stettinius had enlisted
MacLeish to organize a broad campaign of public education and promotion
to ensure strong support for the United Nations. This was a marked departure
from traditional State Department activities, but MacLeish carried it off with
energy and skill, drawing on the wide resources available to him in academic
circles, magazine and newspaper journalism, book publishing, radio broad-
casting, and Hollywood. Nearly two million copies of a pamphlet entitled
"Questions and Answers on the Dumbarton Oaks Proposals" were distributed
to civic groups throughout the country. MacLeish organized teams of State
Department experts who gave more than five hundred speeches in six months
to church, labor, business, and professional leaders in all the major cities. He
arranged an informal exchange of views between Stettinius and leading writers and editors, and reinforced this with thorough briefings for the nation's

best-known lecturers on international affairs. He arranged a series of informative radio lectures over the NBC network and persuaded the movie industry to produce a documentary film on the virtues of the United Nations.[7]

The single aim of this extensive effort was to build sustained public support for the admittedly less-than-perfect Dumbarton Oaks proposals. Its main themes were (1) the impracticality of isolationism in a shrinking world, as evidenced by the attack on Pearl Harbor and by new weapons like the German V-2 rocket which was even then causing panic and destruction in London, and (2) the need to use force to prevent new aggressions. At the same time, care was taken to avoid any implication that American sovereignty would be compromised. Stettinius called the idea of a superstate "wholly repugnant," and MacLeish said, "The practical choice at this time is clearly between an organization of the type proposed at Dumbarton Oaks and international anarchy." At the same time, State Department spokesmen sought to couple realism with a sense of pioneering into a new and more hopeful era: if immediate prospects for the United Nations were limited and imperfect, they projected the expectation that experience with the proposed new forms of international cooperation would bring lasting peace to future generations.[8]

There were serious doubters and dissenters, even among convinced internationalists. In February 1945, the Catholic Association for International Peace called the proposals a "death sentence" for small nations, and soon thereafter the Catholic bishops warned that the chasm separating the values of democracy and Communism made it impossible for the two systems to cooperate within any world organization. Religious pacifists inveighed against the emphasis on force to maintain the peace and argued for total disarmament as the only road to salvation. To counter these negatives, Senator Ball, acknowledging the many flaws in the Dumbarton Oaks proposals, warned against the dangers of perfectionism. And a Democratic National Committee handbook put the matter succinctly: "Remember that the choice is not between the proposed world organization and some other one. The choice is between the proposed one and none. If Dumbarton Oaks is discarded, we must begin to prepare for World War III."[9]

Widening Cracks in the Alliance

Immediately following adjournment of the Dumbarton Oaks Conference, the State Department set out to find some new formulation of the veto issue that could break the ominous Washington-Moscow deadlock. In November, Stettinius met with the Senate Committee of Eight to explain the impasse and put forward a new U.S. position: the veto would apply to any proposed action for sanctions or force, but could not be used to prohibit the discussion of any matter, if seven members of the eleven-member Security Council voted to place the matter on the agenda. Senator Vandenberg thought that this compromise was an "unconscionable" surrender to the Russians, but nevertheless agreed to support it along with his fellow Senators. Further bipartisan consultations led to support for the position by Republican and Democratic leaders in the House, and also by Dewey and John Foster Dulles.[10]

With this encouragement, FDR cabled Stalin on December 5, urging his acceptance of the new U.S. proposal, arguing that it was necessary for great nations to exhibit "those enduring qualities of moral leadership which can raise the whole level of international relations the world over." In presenting the message, Ambassador Harriman asked for a prompt reply, but Stalin waited three weeks before delivering a categorically negative answer. "The principle of unity of action must be preserved from the inception of any dispute. . . . There must be no exceptions . . . otherwise, the entire organization would be emasculated."[11]

This issue did not, of course, exist in isolation. Since the bitter exchanges between Roosevelt and Stalin over the Warsaw uprising in August, the situation in Eastern Europe had grown more volatile, producing increased tension in relations between Russia and the British and Americans, and growing distrust of Russia throughout American and British society. On October 1, Finland and Bulgaria had quit the Axis, and Russian forces had occupied both countries. Concurrently the Red Army was invading the Balkans, overrunning Estonia, Latvia, and Lithuania, and advancing through Hungary and Yugoslavia to the borders of Greece and Turkey. Churchill was suddenly so concerned about control in southeastern Europe that he insisted on an immediate Big Three conference, but for FDR, in the midst of a presidential campaign, this was a practical impossibility. Churchill thereupon went to see Stalin alone, with Ambassador Harriman sitting in as the U.S. observer. Churchill's primary aim was to preserve the British position in Greece and to avoid a British-Russian collision in the Balkans. Meeting the Moscow dictator, he pushed across the table a single half-sheet of paper with a stark handwritten list giving Russia 90 percent predominance in Romania and 75 percent in

Bulgaria, Britain 90 percent in Greece, and dividing Yugoslavia and Hungary 50–50 between Russia and the West. Stalin paused only a moment before making a large tick on the paper with a blue pencil and passing it back to Churchill. After a long silence, Churchill said, "Might it not be thought rather cynical if it seemed we had disposed of these issues, so fateful to millions of people, in such an offhand manner?" He proposed to burn the paper. "No, you keep it," said Stalin.[12]

When informed of this agreement by Churchill, FDR did not object, but it did not alleviate his primary concern, which was that the pursuit of traditional spheres-of-influence diplomacy by both his major allies would deepen Americans' sense of confusion and disillusionment. This, in turn, could revive isolationist feelings and thus erode support for the United Nations. Roosevelt understood that the balance between isolationist and internationalist sentiment remained basically unstable and was unusually sensitive to events, especially to events which affronted American idealism and distaste for power politics. The President's fears were confirmed when Stalin refused his plea to postpone recognition of the Lublin Poles in December, and when Churchill sent British troops to Greece to establish a conservative government against the armed opposition of Communist-dominated rebels. Churchill's orders to the troop commander—to fire on any armed opposition to British authority—disturbed some Americans. Religious editors decried "the reversion to power politics," and the New Republic feared the shape of the postwar world was "being set along the lines of old fashioned imperialism." Heavy fighting ensued in Greece, but Stalin lived up to his October bargain and refused to aid the Communist guerrillas.[13]

Reflecting this uneasiness in public opinion, Senator Ball and his B2-H2 cosponsors proposed to ask Congress to vote for the immediate creation of a United Nations Council, but the President was able to persuade them to desist, out of a concern that congressional hearings on the subject would inevitably include attacks on Russian and British policy, and thus expose severe cracks in the Alliance on the eve of the next round of critical Big Three talks. A leading isolationist, Senator Burton Wheeler (D-Montana), had already declared Dumbarton Oaks "a grim hoax" that left Russia and Britain free "to connive or fight for the spoils."[14]

In his State of the Union address on January 6, 1945, the President sought to restore a sense of proportion to the debate. Refusing to minimize the glaring divisions in the Alliance caused by the emergence of dramatically divergent interests and value systems, he pleaded for patience and understanding. "We must not let these differences . . . blind us to our more important common and continuing interests in winning the war and building the peace." He denounced imperialism and power politics, but issued a grim reminder of what "perfectionism" had cost the nation in 1920. "In our disillusionment after the last war, we gave up the hope of achieving a better peace because we had not the courage to fulfill our responsibilities in an admittedly imperfect world. We must not let that happen again, or we shall follow the same tragic road again—the road to a third world war."[15]

The speech had a generally salutary effect on public opinion, and won the praise of leading editors and commentators for its historical perspective, firm reasoning, and moderation. Polls indicated that 60 percent of the country now endorsed participation in the United Nations, even if the new organization fell short of satisfying American aims. These responses encouraged the President, but he realized that sustained American support for the United Nations depended on the outcome of the next Big Three talks. Also, preliminary planning for the next major conference had brought home to him how unbending Stalin could be. He had hoped for a meeting in the Mediterranean, but Stalin, pleading ill health, refused to leave the Soviet Union, and urged a conference on the Black Sea coast. The dictator's insistence coldly ignored all considerations of the American President's health and physical limitations and his constitutional obligation to remain in contact with the Congress, but FDR finally agreed to meet at Yalta on the Crimean coast (February 4–11) following his fourth inauguration. When he told Churchill he would stop at Malta en route, the Prime Minister cabled, "No more let us falter! From Malta to Yalta! Let nobody alter!"[16]

Yalta

The President recognized the need to resolve four major issues at Yalta: (1) agreement on the treatment of a defeated Germany; (2) Russian participation in the Pacific war; (3) establishment of the United Nations organization; and (4) control of Poland. It was apparent that Stalin possessed superior leverage on the three latter issues.[17]

Allied military strategy was generally set, and victories across the globe were generating a powerful momentum. In Europe, Paris had been liberated the previous August, and the Germans had been driven completely out of France by the end of September. The Anglo-American assault on the German fortifications known as the Siegfried Line began in October and made steady progress until mid-December, when Hitler launched a desperate, last-ditch counteroffensive in the Ardennes forest which became known as the Battle of the Bulge. The Allied forces were caught off guard and suffered their heaviest losses of the war, but had regained all the lost ground by the time the Yalta talks began. Victory in Europe now appeared imminent, but the Alliance was divided by basically different approaches to treatment of the German enemy.[18]

In the Pacific, American air, sea, and land forces were pushing to the threshold of Japan's inner citadel. General Douglas MacArthur's large armies had landed in the Philippines in October 1944. American B-29 bombers had begun heavy raids on Japan in November from the captured island bases of Saipan and Tinian. The bloody invasions of Iwo Jima (February 1945) and Okinawa (April) were in train. Despite these advances, however, U.S. military planners believed that the war against Japan could last for eighteen months after Germany surrendered, even with large-scale Russian participation. Without the weight of Russian armies to engage 2 million Japanese troops in Manchuria, they estimated that the war might last indefinitely, with unbearable losses. Because American development of the atomic bomb was not yet sufficiently advanced to carry weight in U.S. military calculations, large-scale Russian help was considered imperative.[19]

To bring the United Nations into being, it was necessary to resolve both the veto issue and the quixotic matter of Stalin's demand for extra seats in the General Assembly. As to Poland, FDR understood there was no practical way to deny Russian military and political dominance there or throughout Eastern Europe—Stalin held the whip hand. The President was accordingly prepared to settle for essentially paper agreements that spoke of "self-determination" and "free elections"—agreements, that is, aimed at mollifying American opinion and thus preserving American support for the United Nations. FDR had no illusions that such words could change the harsh facts or deflect Moscow from its determination to exercise total control, but he needed them to obtain Senate ratification of a United Nations treaty. U.S. participation and leadership in an operative United Nations was, in his mind, the supreme key to peace.[20]

Sir Alexander Cadogan, W. Averell
Harriman, and Anthony Eden on board
the U.S.S. *Quincy*, en route to Yalta in late
January 1945. (Courtesy Franklin Roosevelt
Library)

Regarding Yalta, Churchill told Harry Hopkins in late January that ten
years of research could not have unearthed a worse place to meet. He himself
planned to counter the typhus and lice that thrived there by bringing an adequate supply of whiskey. The retreating German Army had generally stripped
the city and inflicted heavy structural damage. The American delegation was
lodged in the Lavadia Palace, a fifty-room summer house built for Czar
Nicholas in 1910 on a bluff overlooking the Black Sea. It offered beautiful vis-
tas and extensive gardens, but its furnishings had come hastily from the Hotel
Metropole in Moscow and it possessed only one bathroom, which was a part
of the President's commodious first-floor suite. There was no shortage of bed-
bugs, which bit ministers, generals, butlers, and privates alike with a total disregard for rank.[21]

On February 6, the third day of the conference, Stettinius presented the
new American proposal for resolving the veto deadlock, after surmounting
several earlier obstacles. On the sea voyage from Norfolk, Virginia, to Malta,
he had to deflect an effort by James Byrnes to revert to the earlier formula
under which no party to a dispute could exercise a veto. On arriving in Yalta
he discovered that Churchill agreed with Stalin that the veto power should be

absolute. To turn the Prime Minister around required the support of Anthony Eden, who told Churchill bluntly that if the Big Three insisted on an absolute veto, the smaller nations would refuse to participate and there would be no United Nations.[22]

The first Russian reaction to the American proposal was flatly negative, but Molotov announced acceptance the next day, as Stettinius grinned happily. Molotov further sweetened the spoon by announcing that Russia had also reduced its demand for extra seats in the General Assembly—from sixteen to three, "or at least two," of the Soviet Republics: the Ukraine, White Russia, and Lithuania. FDR, who had told both Stettinius and the Senate Committee of Eight that he was "unalterably opposed" to any extra seats, suggested that the question be left for decision by the U.N. organizing conference, but Stalin refused. The matter was then referred to the three foreign ministers, who met for an hour and proposed that the United States and Britain ask the U.N. organizing conference to grant General Assembly membership to the Ukraine and White Russia.[23]

All three heads of state agreed to the proposal, but even this did not end the bizarre episode. Byrnes was so upset by this concession and so fearful of its negative impact on domestic politics that he persuaded FDR, on the last day of the conference, to ask his Russian and British counterparts to support a future American request for three votes in the General Assembly. In an exercise that had now descended to ward-level political logrolling, they agreed to do so.[24]

The conference failed to resolve basic differences of approach to the treatment of Germany, but FDR agreed to equip eight additional French divisions and to provide a French zone of occupation in Germany, in order to avoid a potential power vacuum if, as he believed, it turned out that American public opinion would not support "an appreciable American force in Europe" for more than two years. Stalin confirmed that Russia would enter the war against Japan within three months after Germany's surrender, but only in return for major concessions, including control of Outer Mongolia, transfer of the Kurile Islands from Japan, return of the southern half of Sakhalin Island, and extensive rights to railroads and harbors in Manchuria. On Poland, instead of accommodating the Anglo-American desire for a coalition of London and Lublin Poles, which would have greatly helped Roosevelt's domestic political problem, Stalin agreed only to a "reorganization" of the Lublin group into a provisional government, coupled with a vague promise of later "free" elections. When Admiral Leahy saw this formulation, he said, "Mr. President, this is so elastic that the Russians can stretch it all the way from Yalta to Washington without technically breaking it." FDR replied, "I know, Bill—I know it. But it's the best I can do for Poland at this time."[25]

With decisions taken on all the major issues, there was no difficulty in agreeing that the United States should host an organizing conference to launch the United Nations, in late April. Various sites were under consideration, but on February 9 Stettinius awoke with a vision of San Francisco. "I saw golden sunshine, and as I lay there on the shores of the Black Sea in the Crimea, I could almost feel the fresh and invigorating air from the Pacific."[26] On February 10, just before the final dinner, the President announced that the organizing conference would be held in San Francisco in the spring. Stettinius, Eden, and Molotov raised their glasses of vodka in a toast to success, while the three heads of state beamed their approval.[27]

As the conference ended, the mood of the U.S. delegation was one of exhilaration and confidence. "We really believed in our hearts that this was the dawn of the new day we had been praying for," Hopkins said later. The Russians had proved that they could be "reasonable and farseeing," and everyone in the delegation from FDR on down was confident of getting along with them peacefully "for as far into the future as anyone could imagine."[28]

The final communiqué, naturally designed to put the best face on the conference decisions, said that the Big Three would occupy Germany after the war and stamp out every trace of Nazism; "free" elections would ensure "democratic" governments in Eastern Europe; all nations who had signed the United Nations Declaration would be invited to a conference at San Francisco on April 25; an agreement had been reached on a voting formula for the Security Council, but would not be disclosed until approved by the other permanent member, China, and also by France—a potential permanent member. There was no mention of Stalin's agreement to enter the war against Japan, nor of the large concessions (many at the expense of China) granted to Russia for this commitment. Nor was there any hint of the deal on extra seats in the General Assembly. On this last matter, FDR was almost obsessively concerned about secrecy, insisting on personally explaining the concession to Congressional leaders before it became public knowledge.[29]

The initial press comments, based on the Yalta communiqué, were

FDR at Yalta, February 1945.
(Courtesy Franklin Roosevelt Library)

euphoric. *Time* ran a picture of Roosevelt and Stalin with the caption "Eight Great Days on the Russian Riviera."[30] *Newsweek* asserted that no citizen of Russia, Britain, or America "could complain that his country had been sold down the river."[31] Clark Eichelberger, head of the United Nations Association, said that the results of the conference "have surpassed the hopes of the idealists and to a great extent confounded the cynics."[32] Numerous Republicans, including Herbert Hoover, made favorable comments. Senator Vandenberg, less impressed, complained about the ambiguities of the Polish agreement.[33]

The President enjoyed a leisurely and restful voyage home aboard the cruiser U.S.S. *Quincy*, but the trip was marred by the death en route of his appointments secretary, "Pa" Watson, who succumbed to a heart attack.[34] On the advice of Byrnes and Vice President Truman, he decided to make his report to the American people by addressing a joint session of Congress on

March 1. For the first time ever, he addressed the legislators sitting down, in a plush chair in the well of the House, for which he asked the indulgence of his listeners by saying it "makes it a lot easier for me" not to have to stand (in ten-pound leg braces)—also, that he had "just completed a fourteen-thousand-mile trip." A packed chamber gave him a standing ovation, but was shocked by how thin and aged he appeared, despite a good tan from the weeks at sea. He spoke for nearly an hour in an informal, chatty manner, but his speech was halting, and he slurred some words. His right hand trembled, making it necessary for him to turn the pages of his speech awkwardly with his left hand.[35]

Calling the Yalta Conference a turning point—"I hope in our history and therefore in the history of the world"—FDR said that whether it could bring forth lasting results "lies to a great extent in your hands." The Senate and the American people would soon face "a great decision that will determine the fate of the United States—and of the world—for generations to come." Everyone should understand there was no middle ground. "We shall have to take the responsibility for world collaboration, or we shall have to bear the responsibility for another world conflict." The Yalta agreements "ought" to spell the end of unilateral actions, exclusive alliances, spheres of influence, and balances of power that "have been tried for centuries—and have always failed." It was time to substitute "a universal organization," and the President was confident that the Congress and the American people would accept the Yalta agreements as laying the foundations of "a permanent structure of peace."[36]

In private, Roosevelt was less confident. When Adolf Berle, who distrusted Russian intentions, questioned him on the achievements of the conference, he threw up his arms and said, "Adolf, I didn't say the result was good. I said it was the best I could do." The agreement on Poland was entirely dependent on Stalin's word, for there was no practical way to confront Russian power in Eastern Europe. In part, this stance was dictated by the basic need for Russian military cooperation to finish the war against Germany and then join the war against Japan; in larger part it reflected FDR's judgment that establishing the United Nations organization was the overarching strategic goal, the absolute first priority. He faced, as he viewed it, a delicate problem of balance. To prevent a U.S. reversion to isolationism after the war, U.S. participation in a new world organization was the sine qua non, but the United Nations could not be brought into being without genuine Russian cooperation, and that depended on Western accommodation to unpalatable manifestations of the Soviet Communist system in Eastern Europe.[37]

Roosevelt's Final Crisis

Following the Yalta Conference, polls showed that Americans who favored U.S. participation in the United Nations had risen from 60 to 80 percent, and that those "satisfied" with Allied cooperation had increased from 46 to 64 percent. At the same time, only 30 percent had heard of the Dumbarton Oaks proposals, and 38 percent thought another war was likely within twenty-five years. FDR was thus keenly aware that mass enthusiasm for a new world order rested on a shaky base, but he was determined to minimize official expressions of doubt as events moved toward the consequential organizing conference in San Francisco.[38]

While still at Yalta, the President and Stettinius had agreed on the makeup of the American delegation to San Francisco. It would consist of seven persons, with an emphasis on congressional and bipartisan representation: Senators Tom Connally and Arthur Vandenberg; Representatives Sol Bloom (D-New York) and Charles Eaton (R-New Jersey); Virginia Gildersleeve, dean of Barnard College; and Lieutenant Commander Harold Stassen. The Secretary of State would chair the delegation. FDR, who disliked Vandenberg, preferred Senator Warren Austin (R-Vermont), but Stettinius convinced him that Vandenberg was the pivotal Republican figure. As chairman of the House Foreign Affairs Committee, Bloom was hard to ignore, but he was brash and superficial; Eaton was too old and infirm to be very helpful. Gildersleeve, intelligent and resourceful, had been involved in both official and private postwar planning since 1942. Stassen, the thirty-seven-year-old former governor of Minnesota, was a liberal Republican and firm internationalist who reflected the views of millions of young Americans in the armed forces. After Vandenberg's request to name John Foster Dulles as his chief aide was finessed, Dulles was invited to serve as nonpartisan adviser to the entire delegation.[39]

Stettinius revealed the agreed voting formula for the Security Council, as approved at Yalta, in a speech delivered in Mexico City on March 5, and it was broadly accepted. Dulles called it a "statesmanlike solution to a knotty problem."[40] To the *New Republic* it merely reflected the reality that any attempt to

Lieutenant Commander Harold Stassen, former governor of
Minnesota, was appointed by FDR as a U.S. delegate to the
San Francisco conference.

impose sanctions on major powers "undoubtedly means war." Isolationists
who continued to posture against the "undemocratic" nature of any veto were
reminded by a conservative columnist that they were also adamant to defend
American sovereignty, which was the precise purpose of the veto. In logic,
they couldn't have it both ways.[41]

Members of the American delegation had no objections to the voting formula, but they were appalled when the President, in his second meeting with
them on March 23, revealed the deal to support the Russian request for two
extra votes in the General Assembly and Stalin's willingness to back a similar
American bid. They listened in stunned silence as FDR explained, uncon-
vincingly, that they were not legally bound by the commitment, that the final
decision was up to them. This effort to "stack" the Assembly "will raise hell,"
Vandenberg recorded in his diary, and "could easily dynamite San Francisco—
or subsequent Senate approval of the entire treaty."[42]

Some disenchanted delegate then leaked the story, which appeared on
March 29 on the front page of the *New York Herald-Tribune*. The revelation
provoked a firestorm of harsh criticism and anguished disbelief, causing chaos
among the press secretaries at the White House and the State Department,
few of whom knew the facts and none of whom was authorized to make a
statement. The President, passing through Washington from Hyde Park en

route to Warm Springs, Georgia, for the last time, finally authorized confirmation of the story. But he stressed that the "ultimate decision" rested with the San Francisco conference and that the United States had an equal claim to extra seats. On April 2, Stettinius persuaded the President to announce that the United States would not seek extra seats at San Francisco, a renunciation that Vandenberg and others strongly urged—but the damage had been done. A hitherto supportive press now reverted to cynicism. The Big Three had "practiced to deceive their Allies and the world," said Time, and Arthur Krock asked the question that would haunt the Democrats for years afterward: "What will be the date-line on the leak of the next Yalta secret?"[43] In the wake of this embarrassing episode, a rash of press stories suggested that the Administration was planning to postpone the San Francisco conference, but Stettinius confirmed that the meeting would open as scheduled on April 25.

Although the President sought to shrug off this episode as a matter of no importance—the General Assembly "is an investigatory body only"—his insensitivity deepened the doubts and weakened the fragile hopes of millions who yearned, however unrealistically, for a new organization based on the principle of equality for all nations, large and small. In tactical terms, it would have been better to have disclosed the deal immediately after Yalta where its negative aspects might have been readily absorbed by the larger positive points of the communiqué. Why did he delay? A reasonable inference is that he was made hesitant by the discouraging indication in mid-March that Gromyko rather than Molotov would head the Russian delegation to San Francisco, a clear sign that Stalin attached diminishing importance to the organizing conference. Taken together with other evidence of growing Russian intransigence and hostility—in barring all non-Lublin Poles from participating in a new Polish regime, in purging and deporting non-Communists in Rumania, in accusing the British and Americans of negotiating the surrender of Italian troops "behind the back of the Soviet Union"—FDR apparently decided not to reveal an awkward concession to Russian sensibilities that he had felt it necessary to make in the context of give-and-take at Yalta. Whatever the rationale, Robert Sherwood thought that it was the kind of political mistake that Roosevelt usually left to his opponents.[44]

Denied any chance to reduce his workload by the crushing pressures of post-Yalta events, an exhausted FDR went to Warm Springs on March 29 to

FDR working with Grace Tully on the terrace of his cottage
at Warm Springs, Georgia, a few days before his death on
April 12, 1945. (Courtesy Franklin Roosevelt Library)

rest and try to regain some measure of his strength. He had lost more weight,
his color was poor, and his attention span grew shorter daily. On March 30,
William Hassett, who had succeeded "Pa" Watson as appointments secretary,
anxiously informed FDR's doctor that "He is slipping away from us and no
earthly power can keep him here." The doctor's prognosis was less dire, but he
admitted that the patient was "in a precarious condition." On April 6, the
President asked Archibald MacLeish to prepare a speech which he intended to
make to the opening session of the San Francisco conference. But on April 12,
about one-fifteen P.M., as he sat perusing documents and posing for a portrait,
FDR pressed his left hand to his temple, complained of "a terrific headache,"
and slumped in his chair. He had suffered a massive cerebral hemorrhage, and
efforts to revive him were unavailing.[45]

The nation and much of the world went into mourning. Churchill felt as
if he had been struck a physical blow. Stalin, who received the news with
apparently genuine distress, held Harriman's hand for more than thirty sec-
onds before inviting the Ambassador to sit down. Chiang Kai-shek left his
breakfast untouched to pray. Goebbels told Hitler, "My Fuhrer, I congratulate
you. Roosevelt is dead. It is written in the stars that the second half of April

will be the turning point for us." To internationalists, the fallen leader promptly became a martyr and symbol of their cause. Intoned the *New Republic*, "Franklin Roosevelt at rest in Hyde Park is a more powerful force for America's participation in a world organization than was President Roosevelt in the White House."[46]

16

Contention and Compromise
at San Francisco

The new American President, Harry S Truman, promptly
ended press speculation that the San Francisco conference
would be postponed owing to FDR's death. It would be
held "as President Roosevelt had directed," and Secretary of
State Stettinius added that the United States would press
toward "the establishment of a world organization endowed
with the strength to keep the peace for generations." Truman was a convinced internationalist who believed that the
United States could not evade the responsibilities of its
abundant power. He had been a key supporter of the B2-
H2 resolution in the Senate, and as Vice President had said
in a radio address of February 23, 1945, that "America can
no longer sit smugly behind a mental Maginot Line."[1]

As the 282 delegates from forty-six nations began gathering at San Francisco for the April 25 conference, it was
clear that Big Three relations had never been more tense or
strained, and that many small nations were strongly opposed to the concentration of power granted to the permanent members of the Security Council by the proposals
before them. It was evident that major issues would have to
be resolved or compromised both among the permanent
five and between them collectively and the smaller nations,
if the conference were to succeed. These questions included
control of Poland, the extent of the veto power, the author-

ity of the General Assembly, and the extra General Assembly seats for White Russia and the Ukraine. Taking no chances, the United States used electronic intelligence to intercept the diplomatic messages of all the foreign delegations (except Britain and Russia) at San Francisco. Washington thus had advance knowledge of the negotiating positions of the participating nations. It used this information to set the agenda, guide the debate, and press for a U.N. Charter that was consistent with the U.S. blueprint.[2]

The mood at the conference opening was subdued, even grim; there were no bands or gala ceremonies, and the onlookers who crowded the streets outside the San Francisco Opera House were solemn and quiet. President Truman decided not to attend the opening session, but addressed the delegates by radio, welcoming them to America and encouraging them in their momentous task: "We must build a new world," he told them, "a far better world—one in which the eternal dignity of man is respected."[3]

Organizing the Conference

Before any substantive issues could be addressed, however, the conference was forced to deal with another Russian surprise—the assertion that equality among the four sponsoring powers required that there be four presidents of the conference. To underline his demand, Soviet Foreign Minister V. M. Molotov threatened to go home unless his view prevailed. This ploy alarmed the American delegates, who saw it as an effort to set a precedent for permanent multiple management of the United Nations organization. Stettinius told President Truman that, if Molotov's view prevailed, it might be impossible to establish a single U.N. Secretary General. Fortunately, British Foreign Secretary Anthony Eden broke the deadlock by proposing that there be four presidents, but that Stettinius should double as "chairman of the presidents." Molotov's prompt acceptance of this artful diplomatic device suggested that Moscow's concern for equality was mainly symbolic, for it left management of the conference largely in American hands.[4]

A Steering Committee composed of the chairman of each national delegation was then formed, together with a smaller Executive Committee of fourteen delegation heads including the five permanent members of the Security Council. In practice, most of the critical decisions were taken by the Big Five

Soviet Foreign Minister V. M. Molotov and Ambassador
Andrei Gromyko at the San Francisco conference. (Edward
R. Stettinius, Jr., Papers, Special Collections Department,
Manuscripts Division, University of Virginia Library)

in the Secretary of State's penthouse atop the Fairmont Hotel, after consultation with selected chairmen of other delegations.

This concentration of power caused widespread discontent among the
many smaller delegations, for whom the Australian Foreign Minister, Herbert
Evatt, soon made himself the most visible and disputatious spokesman. In
collaboration with New Zealand, Evatt introduced a resolution requiring
General Assembly concurrence before the Security Council could take enforcement action, except in cases of "extreme emergency." He also champi-
oned a veto-free process for amending the U.N. Charter.[5] But Stettinius,
whose marching orders from Truman were to establish the United Nations as
swiftly as possible as a principal vehicle of U.S. foreign policy, proved to be a
tough and resourceful conference manager who never hesitated to exert what-

ever pressures were necessary to hold the delegations in line and keep the proceedings moving toward the realization of American objectives. At one point, he persuaded Truman to ask the Australian prime minister to rein in the outspoken Evatt.[6]

Poland

On Poland, the Yalta agreement provided for the establishment of a new and mutually acceptable provisional government, in which the London Poles would be represented, even though the Lublin Poles would predominate. The Western powers had hoped that such a government could be formed by March 5, in time to be invited to San Francisco, but when the deadline passed without any progress, no invitation was issued to Poland. Russian displeasure at this rebuff had been signaled by the announcement that Gromyko, not Molotov, would head the Moscow delegation, which threw sudden cold water on the prospect for Russian cooperation at San Francisco.[7]

Churchill had sent a sour cable to FDR, saying that Molotov's withdrawal "leaves a bad impression on me." Did it mean that the Russians were "going to run out," or were they "trying to blackmail us"? The cable reaffirmed that the Dumbarton Oaks proposals rested on the concept of Great Power unity, but there was no unity on Poland, "which is, after all, a major problem of the postwar settlement." Were the Great Powers then in the position of "building the whole structure of future world peace on foundations of sand"? Sharing the Prime Minister's frustration, but recognizing his limited leverage, FDR had tried a soft approach to Stalin, expressing the hope that Molotov might at least attend "the vital opening sessions" at San Francisco, as his total absence would be construed as a lack of Russian interest in "the great objectives of this conference." This plea did not move Stalin, nor did a joint Anglo-American appeal which stressed that failure to agree on Poland could gravely imperil "any real chance of getting the world organization established on lines that will commend themselves to our respective public opinions."[8]

It took Roosevelt's death on April 12 to bring about a change in Moscow's position on the level of Russian representation at San Francisco. When a somber Stalin had asked Harriman what might be done to ease U.S.-Russian relations, the Ambassador replied that it would be a good thing to send Molotov to San Francisco. Stettinius followed with an invitation for Molotov to attend a pre-conference meeting in Washington of the Big Three foreign ministers. Stalin accepted both of these suggestions.

Russian amiability did not last long, however, or extend beyond matters of procedure. Only a few days after FDR's death, Moscow blatantly asked the United States to invite the Lublin Poles to San Francisco as the officially recognized Polish Government. As there had been no attempt to form a provisional coalition with the non-Communist London faction, as agreed at Yalta, the U.S. response was a categorical rejection. The State Department declared publicly: "Poland is a member of the United Nations, and of right should be at San Francisco. However, the view of the United States Government remains that an invitation to the Conference at San Francisco should be extended only to a Provisional Government of National Unity formed in accordance with the Crimea agreement."[9]

Undeterred, the Russians officially recognized the Lublin faction and signed a treaty of mutual assistance on April 22, the very day that Molotov arrived in Washington. Bolstered by strong warnings from Harriman of Russia's predatory drive in Eastern Europe—"We must clearly recognize that the Soviet program is the establishment of totalitarianism, ending personal liberty and democracy as we know and respect it"—the fledgling American President and his advisers met with the Russian foreign minister in the Oval Office. Truman told Molotov that, while he desired progress on Poland, he would recognize no government that failed to provide free elections. When Molotov began to argue that Allied unity required that the Big Three governments treat each other as equals, and that the London Poles had worked against the Red Army, Truman cut him short. He was not interested in propaganda, he said. The United States was prepared to carry out all agreements reached at Yalta, and he expected Russia to do the same. According to Charles E. Bohlen, Molotov turned "ashy" and tried to divert the talk to another subject, but Truman ended the meeting with a brusque request that the U.S. views be promptly conveyed to Stalin. Secretary of War Stimson and General Marshall, who were concerned about assuring Russian entrance into the Japanese war, reacted uneasily to the vigor of the new President's confrontational stance. Even Harriman was slightly taken aback. The Polish question remained in deadlock.[10]

The X Matter and Argentina

The United States had pledged in the Yalta agreements to support General Assembly membership for White Russia and the Ukraine, and was now eager to honor this commitment as a means of pressuring Russia to meet its own Yalta commitments—especially with regard to Poland. But there lurked in the background the prospect that the Latin American delegations would refuse to vote with the U.S. on this issue, unless there was also strong American support for the admission of Argentina. The Buenos Aires government, which had maintained a pro-Hitler neutrality throughout the war, posed a serious political problem for Washington, for Americans generally regarded it as an enemy state. Truman wanted to postpone the issue and was opposed to allowing Argentina to sign the Declaration by United Nations, even after it declared war on the Axis belatedly on March 27, 1945.[11]

Molotov, however, insisted on placing the White Russia/Ukraine issue on the agenda of the first Steering Committee meeting on April 26, and moved for the election of both republics, in accordance with the Yalta decisions. The American, British, and Chinese delegates supported the motion, a few others spoke favorably, and it was unanimously approved. Molotov then asked that these two "sovereign" entities be invited to the conference. At that point, the Colombian delegate objected to immediate action and won sufficient support to have the question referred to the smaller Executive Committee for further consideration.[12]

Molotov had temporarily overreached, but only on the secondary question of whether the two Soviet republics should be invited to the conference—they had already been accepted for General Assembly membership. He then further roiled the situation by pressing the provocative issue of Poland. Czech Foreign Minister Jan Masaryk, obviously speaking at Russia's behest, urged that the Lublin Poles also be invited to the conference. This was a clear violation of the Yalta agreements, and a proposal put forward with the knowledge that the United States and Britain were categorically opposed. An agitated Senator Arthur Vandenberg quickly passed Stettinius a proposed rejoinder, and the Secretary of State accepted it without hesitation and used it to respond to Molotov "with great emphasis." Stettinius said, "I remind the Conference that we have just honored our own Yalta engagements on behalf of Russia," but the creation of "a new and representative Polish Provisional Government" is an equal obligation of the Yalta participants. "Until that happens, it would be a sordid exhibit of bad faith" to recognize the Lublin Poles. Eden staunchly supported Stettinius. Molotov had overreached again, but had also succeeded in partially linking Poland with the question of Argentina and the two Soviet republics.[13]

Two days later, on April 28, a committee of foreign ministers from Mexico, Chile, Brazil, and Venezuela urged that Argentina be invited to San Francisco with Russian support, in the same spirit of cooperation as the Latin American delegates had shown in supporting General Assembly membership for White Russia and the Ukraine. But Molotov declared that the admission of "fascist" Argentina was hardly comparable—the Soviet republics, he declared, had fought "heroically" against the common enemy, whereas Argentina had helped the Axis; it would be an "incomprehensible" action unless Poland were also invited. The foreign ministers reminded him that the Polish question was in the hands of the Big Three—beyond the jurisdiction of the conference—and strongly hinted that they would vote against an invitation to the Soviet republics if Argentina were not also invited. Molotov refused to budge, which moved the deadlocked question to the smaller Executive Committee.[14]

The Latin American resistance to inviting the Soviet republics forced the United States to make a categorical commitment to Argentina, as it could not deliver on its Yalta commitment to support the two Soviet republics without the help of Latin American votes. After further negotiation, invitations to all three nations were approved at a plenary session of the conference, but not before Molotov delivered another lengthy anti-Argentina speech, this time in a public forum. The approval was the work of Stettinius and Nelson Rockefeller, the State Department Coordinator of Latin American Affairs. As Walter Lippmann noted, these two men forged a "solid block" of twenty Latin American votes that enabled them to "steamroller" the opposition, but there was widespread public sympathy for Molotov's arguments, and this provided the Russian delegation with a temporary public relations victory.[15]

Liberal elements of the American press expressed concern about the threat to U.S.-Soviet relations created by the "reprehensible" American effort to "force" the admission of a "fascist" state on the United Nations.[16] Senators Carl Hatch and Joseph H. Ball, both strong U.N. supporters, termed the action "a cynical repudiation" of the cause for which the Allies were fighting. From retirement, Hull denounced the decision and privately blamed Stettinius.[17]

On balance, however, the showdown on Argentina helped to clear the diplomatic air. Russia was impressed by the U.S. determination to muster support for its objectives. Molotov thereafter avoided public confrontation and showed himself more ready to debate issues without rancor. Stettinius was proving to be a surprisingly able diplomat, working smoothly to preserve the fragile unity of the sponsoring powers, but ever ready to be blunt and stubborn with Russia, Britain, and the smaller nations in defense of U.S. objectives. The principal American goal was to bring the United Nations into being without delay and with the full participation of the Big Three. President Truman was scheduled to meet with Churchill and Stalin at Potsdam in August, and he wanted the San Francisco conference brought to a successful close before he tackled serious and growing tensions in the wartime alliance.[18]

No one had any illusions about the growing tensions. On May 3, the British learned that the Russians had arrested sixteen Polish leaders of the London regime who had gone to Moscow to negotiate, and intended to put them on trial for aiding the Nazis. Eden and Stettinius bluntly denounced the Russian government for betraying its obligation to treat the negotiators decently. The issue of Poland remained in bitter contention between East and West.[19]

Four-Power Amendments

On May 2, Eden, Molotov, Stettinius, and Chinese Foreign Minister T. V. Soong began two days of continuous meetings to consider and agree upon amendments to the Dumbarton Oaks proposals that the Big Four would submit to the conference. U.S. amendments included proposals urged on the delegation by James Shotwell and Clark Eichelberger for a declaration on human rights in the charter and a broadening of the Economic and Social Council to include a commission on human rights. These were approved by the four foreign ministers, along with twenty-five other amendments. None of them changed the fundamental nature of the proposed United Nations organization, but all tended to make it more open and democratic.[20]

On May 5, Stettinius met with the full group of private American experts organized by Shotwell and Eichelberger to thank them for their contributions, calm their anxiety about the evident discord in Big Three relations, and urge upon them a sense of proportion. It was a notable performance. "Regardless of any situation," he told them, "we must succeed at San Francisco in agreeing on the foundation and framework, and building on that. Let us get over this hurdle, and get unanimity on the basic thinking of a world organization; then let us take up these world political problems, one by one, as we come to them."[21]

The Recurrent Regional Impulse

To understand the next major difficulty that confronted the San Francisco conference, it is necessary to summarize developments and decisions that took place three months earlier at a Pan-American conference held in Mexico City (February 21 to March 5). Stettinius had gone directly from Yalta to Mexico to urge hemispheric support for the Dumbarton Oaks proposals, and to make sure that six of the Latin American nations (who were considered "associate" U.N. members, even though they had declared their "nonbelligerency" in the war) would be eligible to participate at San Francisco. The latter aim was met when all six declared war on the Axis before March 1. (Argentina, which had declared "neutrality" and was considered pro-Nazi, did not declare war until March 27.)[22]

A complementary U.S. aim was to achieve a moderate strengthening of the Pan-American system by providing machinery for handling the "peaceful settlement of disputes" and for assuming "initial responsibility" for enforcing peace in the hemisphere, consistent with the authority of the U.N. Security Council. According to the Dumbarton Oaks proposals, regional organizations could take enforcement action only after being authorized to do so by the Security Council.

The United States understood that the Latin Americans were anxious to strengthen the autonomy of regional organizations, but Stettinius and his colleagues were "astonished" to find that they now wanted to establish a full-fledged regional security system to deal with threats from both within and outside the hemisphere; moreover, they wanted this to be essentially independent of the U.N., and to be put in place speedily, in order to present the San Francisco conference with a fait accompli. In short, the Latin nations, which had historically viewed the Monroe Doctrine as "a sort of club over their heads" held by their large northern neighbor, were now not only willing but eager to participate fully in hemisphere defense. The principal cause of this dramatic shift was their growing fear of Communism. They were concerned that, if exclusive jurisdiction for keeping the peace were vested in the Security Council, it would open a Pandora's box of outside interference in Latin America, especially of Communist infiltration.[23]

In one sense, the United States was pleased by the new Latin American stance, but it presented two serious problems: first, it raised again the inherently difficult question of whether the U.S. President could deploy American armed forces on behalf of a regional security system without approval in each case by the Congress; second, it presented the disturbing likelihood that a relatively autonomous security system in the Western Hemisphere would encourage the creation of similar systems in other regions, resulting in a serious erosion of the central authority of the United Nations. This eleventh-hour Latin American challenge revived the debates of 1942 and 1943 when Sumner Welles and Winston Churchill advanced approaches to collective security based on the primacy of regional organizations that were rejected by Roosevelt, Hull, and senior officials in both the State Department and the Foreign Office.[24]

The situation revealed at Mexico City thus presented a dilemma of some consequence and demanded a prompt solution that would reconcile the global and regional approaches. After long negotiations outside the formal proceedings of the conference, and with FDR's final approval, an agreement known as the Act of Chapultepec (named for the castle where the negotiations were conducted) was reached. The key provision, inherited from conferences at Buenos Aires in 1936 and Lima in 1938, stated that an attack on one state in the hemisphere would be considered an attack on all and would demand immediate collective consultation, but it fell short of requiring an automatic military response. Moreover, the agreement would apply only until the end of the war; thereafter, new arrangements would be negotiated.[25]

The State Department believed that the Chapultepec negotiations had laid to rest the issue of Latin American security, but a new "regional" crisis now descended on the San Francisco conference. One of the charter amendments put forward by the four sponsoring powers exempted Russia from Security Council jurisdiction, if Moscow decided that it was necessary to invoke its bilateral treaties with several Eastern European countries against renewed German aggression. Molotov had argued that, until the U.N. could demonstrate its ability to prevent a German resurgence, Russia must be free to take direct enforcement action without prior U.N. authorization. Debate among the sponsoring powers had narrowed the exemption to "measures against enemy states in the war" or measures "in regional arrangements directed against renewal of aggressive policy on the part of such states"—and only until the United Nations was charged by its members with "the responsibility for preventing further aggression."[26]

Although this amendment applied only to current enemy states and only for a transitional period, the Latin American delegates reacted with anger and resentment. That Russia should be granted an exemption for enforcement action in Eastern Europe, while no similar special arrangement would be accorded the Pan-American system, seemed an outrageous case of unequal treatment. Colombian Foreign Minister Alberto Lleras Camargo charged that, as things now stood, all regional arrangements were at the mercy of the permanent members of the Security Council; in future disputes within Latin America, the contending parties would be forced to seek the support of a permanent member who could veto adverse U.N. action, and this would lead inevitably to outside interference in hemisphere affairs "to an extent which has never happened before." He complained to Leo Pasvolsky, special assistant to the Secretary of State, that the United States was trying to scuttle the Act of Chapultepec. This was hardly the case, but the Latin Americans were moved by their resentment of Molotov's rude behavior and their mounting fear of Communism.[27]

When Pasvolsky advised Stettinius that his efforts to mediate Latin American concerns had failed, because they wanted a regional bloc "completely free of world arrangements," the Secretary's inclination was to override their objections with a demonstration of firm Big Three solidarity. But this tactic was tripped up by the volatility of domestic politics. Nelson Rockefeller, who perceived an explosive state of mind in the Latin American delegations, talked to Vandenberg, and the Senator wrote a letter to Stettinius. In it he warned that, unless new ways were found to safeguard the Pan-American system, the Monroe Doctrine would be undermined and that would pose "a threat to Senate confirmation of the entire San Francisco Charter." Stettinius was irritated by Rockefeller's initiative and angered by the Senator's letter, but Vandenberg's political clout could not be ignored.[28]

The ensuing debate in the full delegation on May 7 found the U.S. officials still troubled and divided. Vandenberg proposed an addition to the
"Russian exemption" amendment which would give a similar specific exemp-
tion to the Act of Chapultepec, and this was supported by several. But John
Foster Dulles thought that too much insistence on an explicit exemption for
the Pan-American system could create trouble in Europe. Russia, he predicted,
would agree to a U.S. demand for exempting a regional security system in the
Americas, but would use this to justify excluding the U.N.—and the United
States—from influence in Europe. Pasvolsky agreed with Dulles that a strong
United Nations with global jurisdiction was the best available vehicle for dealing effectively with Russia's intertwined national and ideological ambitions;
moreover, that any more exemptions for regional arrangements would feed the
demand for them, which in turn would destroy the credibility of the global
organization.[29]

With the U.S. delegation thus deeply divided, Stettinius met on May 8
with a group of Latin American leaders who were entirely united—"resolute,"
in the words of their joint statement, "that they must not sacrifice the American system."[30] A damp fog swirling outside the picture windows of the penthouse seemed an apt reinforcement of the confusion and misunderstanding
within, for at the heart of the impasse lay a profound irony: the United States
stood accused of abandoning the Monroe Doctrine, the unilateral declaration
of 1823 long viewed by Latin Americans as a cloak for U.S. oppression. The
accusation was without foundation—the United States would, in its own
interest, defend the Western Hemisphere by every means—but the new Latin
American fear of Communism and of untried U.N. procedures had produced
an anxiety which insisted that the global superpower give first priority to Latin
American concerns.[31]

Stettinius now decided that it was necessary to turn to the White House
for help, and he asked Dulles to prepare a memorandum for President Truman. To reject the Latin American contentions, Dulles wrote, "would seriously impair our Latin American relations," but to accept them would gravely
weaken the authority of the Security Council and "invite Russian domination
of all Europe." The U.S. faced a Hobson's choice.[32]

The memorandum arrived in Washington on May 8, the momentous day
of Germany's unconditional surrender and in the midst of an intense review
of U.S.-Russian relations by the President and his key advisers. Distrust of

Moscow's intentions was now the dominant view. The American officials agreed to send a strong signal of U.S. disapproval by cutting back Lend-Lease aid, and they began a highly confidential research effort to ascertain whether it might be possible to repudiate the extensive Far East concessions made to Stalin at Yalta.[33] In that context, the heavyweight Washington advisers gave strong support to a policy of protecting the Pan-American system from Security Council interference. Secretary of War Stimson and Secretary of the Navy Forrestal had recently succeeded in securing absolute U.S. control over the Pacific bases wrested from the Japanese, and they and the Joint Chiefs of Staff now argued for the right "in the first instance" to take necessary military action in the hemisphere "free of any veto in the Security Council," even though they considered the Latin fears of infiltration and aggression to be exaggerated. No clear decision was taken in Washington; in effect, the dilemma was passed back to Stettinius in San Francisco, where he loyally shouldered the burden.[34]

The Concept of Self-Defense

The time had come, the Secretary of State told his delegation, for the United States to stop being "pushed around" by "a lot of small American republics who are dependent on us in many ways. . . . We must provide leadership."[35] The needed conceptual solution appears to have been provided by Lieutenant Commander Harold Stassen, the former governor of Minnesota who had recently returned from duty on the staff of Admiral William F. ("Bull") Halsey in the Pacific theater. Stassen developed the argument that every nation possessed an inherent right of self-defense, which could be invoked if a veto in the Security Council threatened to stultify an effective response to aggression—against Latin America or any other area. Although Vandenberg feared that if such a right were expressed in the U.N. Charter it would encourage nations to ignore the U.N. security system and rely on their own power, a new formula, based on the concept of self-defense, was drafted by Dulles, Pasvolsky, James Dunn, and Isaiah Bowman. It said that, in the event of an attack against any U.N. member state, such member "shall possess the right to take measures of self-defense," and this right "shall apply to understandings and arrangements like those embodied in the Act of Chapultepec." However, the taking of such measures "shall not affect the authority and responsibility of the Security Council" to take any action it deemed necessary at any time.[36]

When this American proposal was presented to the Steering Committee on May 12, Eden brusquely attacked it as a paper "clearly of Latin American origin," which would lead to "regionalism of the worst kind," producing "regional movements all over the world." He predicted that it would wreck the conference, and he deplored the fact that such an obstacle had "come so late in the day." He then passed a note to Stettinius, asking for a private talk, and shortly thereafter the Secretary declared a short recess. With the Russians out of earshot, Eden made plain that his real objection to the American proposal was that, by its direct reference to Chapultepec, it appeared to limit self-defense measures to formal regional organizations. He wanted a broader formula, flexible enough to permit Britain, alone or with selected allies, to respond, for example, to a Russian attack on Turkey.[37]

After several more arduous drafting efforts, the Big Five agreed to language which met Eden's requirement: "Nothing in this Charter shall invalidate the right of self-defense against armed attack, either individual or collective, in the event of the Security Council failing to take the necessary steps to maintain or restore international peace and security."[38] The new formula implicitly authorized the right of hemisphere self-defense, and Vandenberg advised that he would nail this down by inserting "an interpretive reservation" in the ratification process indicating that the U.S. Senate construed the language "to specifically include Chapultepec."[39]

This addition was entirely acceptable to Eden, but the stubborn, fearful Latin Americans still insisted on specific reference to Chapultepec in the charter amendment. An exasperated Stettinius called on their spokesman, Lleras Camargo of Colombia, to free himself and his colleagues from "a small hemispheric view" and understand that, although the United States would firmly safeguard the Western Hemisphere, that could not be the only concern of a great power with global responsibilities. The matter was not resolved until May 15, however, when President Truman promised to hold a new Pan-American conference within a year to consider a firm postwar treaty of implementation growing out of the agreements reached at Chapultepec.[40]

Final reconciliation of the global and regional approaches to international security was reflected in Article 51 of the U.N. Charter, which read: "Nothing in the present Charter shall impair the inherent right of individual or collective self-defence if an armed attack occurs against a Member of the United Nations, until the Security Council has taken the measures necessary to maintain international peace and security." This became the legal basis for the several regional blocs established during the Cold War—especially NATO, SEATO, CENTO, and even the Warsaw Pact.[41]

One historian later remarked that, while tedious and time-consuming, this whole episode provided perhaps the most successful application at San Francisco of "the old-fashioned art of diplomatic negotiation."[42] Much of the credit belonged to Stettinius for a strong and tenacious performance. Vandenberg, who had doubted the Secretary's ability, ended up admiring his judgment and drive. *Time* magazine, which had often criticized Stettinius, noted that his work at San Francisco had won the respect of seasoned diplomats from many countries.[43]

The Recurrent Veto Crisis

The most serious, as well as the most dramatic, controversy at San Francisco occurred over the veto question in the Security Council. Here, unlike the debate over global versus regional emphasis (where there was a willingness to negotiate the modification of texts), the controversy centered on the proper interpretation of the Yalta agreements. Failure to reach a meeting of minds on this issue threatened the conference with total breakdown and therefore a stillborn United Nations.

There is little doubt that there was genuine concurrence among the three heads of government at Yalta, but when the agreed-upon voting formula was finally put into writing, it was ambiguous. And the smaller powers, who deeply resented the enormous authority conferred on the Great Powers by the veto, were determined to exploit any differences between them in an effort to win liberalizing changes in the formula. The Yalta text said that permanent members of the Security Council could veto enforcement decisions but not procedural matters, although "procedural matters" was not defined. Fearing that this ambiguity would permit a permanent member to veto even the discussion of a dispute, forty-five smaller nations, led by the redoubtable Australian Foreign Minister Herbert Evatt, addressed a list of twenty-three questions to the sponsoring powers—for example, would the Security Council discuss matters "freely and without limitation"? Would it decide on terms for the "peaceful settlement" of disputes free of the veto? Would the veto apply to the nomination of a candidate for Secretary-General?[44]

It was soon apparent that the sponsoring powers would have to address these questions seriously or risk wholesale dissension among the smaller nations. Stettinius, pressed by Truman to wind up the conference and perceiving danger in any attempt to reopen the Yalta agreements, hoped to "nip this thing in the bud" by presenting the dissenters with a Great Power united front. Part of his strategy was to wean the French away from their strong support for the smaller nations on the veto question. He accomplished this by flattering Parisian pretensions to Great Power status, telling the members of the French delegation that their true interests coincided with those of the permanent members of the Security Council. His diplomacy here was aided by U.S. electronic intelligence, which had revealed ambivalence at the Quai d'Orsay.[45]

But a number of obstacles to full agreement remained. First, within the American delegation, strong support developed for abolishing the veto on all "peaceful settlement" decisions (which would clearly alter the Yalta agreement). Next, Andrei Gromyko told Stettinius that Russia interpreted the Yalta formula as giving it a veto on whether the council could take up a particular question or dispute.[46]

Stettinius flew to Washington on May 23 to report these disturbing developments directly to the President. Truman thought that it would be unwise for the United States to change its position on "peaceful settlement," but that it should insist absolutely that discussion of all matters should be free of the veto. Met with this firm U.S. position, Gromyko referred the issue to Moscow, and the conference marked time for five days while the delegates waited for Stalin's reply from halfway around the world. On June 2, the answer came back: Russia's "final position" was insistence on an absolute veto. On hearing this, Vandenberg confided to his diary that Russia demanded a veto "even on free speech in the Council, [which] collides with the grim conviction of almost every other Power at Frisco. It is 'Yalta' carried to the final, absurd extreme. . . . We all knew that we had reached the zero hour of this great adventure."[47]

That same day, Stettinius read to Gromyko the State Department's March 24 "interpretative statement" of the Yalta agreements which held that a permanent power could not employ its veto to prevent discussion of an issue.

The Secretary noted that this was also the position of Britain and China, and that Russia had registered no disagreement at the time. An irritated Gromyko insisted that the U.S. statement was "a retreat from Yalta." Stettinius heatedly told him that, if the Russian view prevailed, there would be no U.N. Charter. "I did not mince matters at all," for it was vital that "the importance of our stand could not be misunderstood."[48]

The Fateful Hopkins Mission

With the conference now in peril of total breakdown, with all of the unmeasurable consequences, Stettinius telephoned the President to suggest that Harry Hopkins, who was already in Moscow on a mission to find a solution to the Polish problem, be asked to take up the veto issue directly with Stalin. Truman approved, and Stettinius then drafted a cable for Hopkins via U.S. Ambassador W. Averell Harriman. Saying "we have reached a very serious crisis in the Conference at San Francisco," he sketched out the dilemma, characterized the Russian position as a "farce," and urged Hopkins to tell Stalin "in no uncertain words" that the United States "could not possibly join an organization based on so unreasonable an interpretation" of the Security Council veto.[49]

While they waited for the fateful further word from Moscow, the strain of the deadlock began to tell on the American delegation. Only a few had been informed of the new initiative, and their anxiety was reinforced by several concurrent developments. A front-page story by James Reston in the *New York Times* of June 3 minutely described the blowup over the veto, which seemed to deepen a growing public disillusionment, as reflected in opinion polls: while 85 percent of Americans now believed that the United States should join the U.N., only 40 percent thought that the San Francisco conference would succeed, and those who thought the United Nations could prevent war for at least a generation had dropped from 49 to 32 percent since the opening of the conference. Trust in the Russians stood at 45 percent, down 10 percent since Yalta and still falling.

If this were not enough bad news, the egregious General de Gaulle, now head of the provisional government of France, profoundly embarrassed the British and Americans by sending troops to restore French interests in Syria and Lebanon, a move that resulted in open warfare and the killing of many civilians. A senior American diplomat decried the fact that, while those at San Francisco were devising measures to prevent aggression, "France is openly pursuing tactics similar to those used by the Japanese in Manchukuo and by the Italians in Ethiopia." Fortunately, Churchill moved beyond hand-wringing. On May 31, he sent de Gaulle a curt ultimatum, warning that British troops would act to restore order and urging France to cease fire "in order to avoid collision between British and French forces." This bold act restored peace in the Levant and cut short the embarrassment to the proceedings at San Francisco.[50]

Stettinius and Truman remained steady during this stressful period, but suggestions originating in the State Department and the American delegation were made that the conference should be brought to swift conclusion without attempting to settle the veto issue—that is, both the Russian and Anglo-American interpretations should merely be entered into the record book. Senators Connally and Vandenberg recognized this notion as unworkable and politically unacceptable—"a climax in humiliation" for the United States.[51] At the same time, Vandenberg warned Stettinius that, unless action were promptly taken to restore confidence in the San Francisco proceedings, the GOP might feel obliged to end its bipartisan cooperation and condemn the Administration's failure. To keep the Senator from any damaging statement or action, Stettinius revealed to him the Hopkins initiative in Moscow.[52]

On June 6, after four nerve-wracking days, Hopkins brought up the veto issue during his last meeting with Stalin in the Kremlin. When he had explained the American position and indicated that it was supported by Britain and China, the dictator seemed puzzled. An exchange between Stalin and Molotov made it clear to both Hopkins and Harriman that Stalin had not been informed of his own government's current position on the issue, nor did he understand that it was a matter of serious controversy with the United States. After being briefed, however, he commented casually that it was an insignificant matter, and told Molotov to accept the American position. The incident suggests that Molotov and other hardliners in the Russian Foreign Ministry were indeed trying to alter the Yalta agreement to prevent any U.N. challenge or embarrassment to Russian policies. It also makes clear both the decisive importance of the Hopkins mission—to make the full implications of the deadlock crystal clear to the one man who could overrule the Russian bureaucracy—and the grave consequences for the United Nations if the mission had failed.[53]

Stettinius, who learned of Stalin's assent before word reached Gromyko, had the unique pleasure of informing the Soviet ambassador of a decision taken by his own government. The Russian received the news with good grace and gave his full cooperation in the drafting of a joint press release announcing the end of the veto crisis. The American delegation was relieved and overjoyed, and messages of congratulation and satisfaction passed between Truman, Stettinius, Cordell Hull, and Under Secretary of State Joseph Grew.[54]

Resolution of the veto crisis ended any chance that the smaller nations could win further liberalizing changes in the voting formula. Foreign Minister Evatt of Australia made one more effort to free the "settlement of peaceful disputes" from the veto, but he was dramatically rebuffed by Senator Connally, who told him that any further change would "tear up the Charter." To illustrate, Connally then ripped the pages he was holding in his hands and flung the shredded scraps on the floor.[55] Despite the acute differences between and among the Big Five, they recognized the unacceptable disorder that would flow from efforts of the smaller nations to relax the requirement for Great Power unanimity in decisions of the Security Council. Aroused by the intensity and bitterness of the attack of the smaller states on the measures they had so laboriously negotiated at Dumbarton Oaks, Yalta, and elsewhere, and aware that the burden of ensuring future peace rested primarily on their shoulders, the Big Five instinctively closed ranks against all further attempts to alter the structure or rules relating to the Security Council.[56]

As a concession to the smaller nations, the United States and Britain did support their last-minute rearguard proposal to permit the General Assembly to "discuss any matter within the sphere of international relations," but here the Russians balked again, delaying the end of the conference by three days before accepting language that confined Assembly discussion to matters "within the scope of the present Charter." Truman had announced his plan to attend the closing ceremony on June 23, following a state visit to the Pacific Northwest, but the final wrangle put off his speech until June 26.[57] To the assembled delegates he said, "Let us not fail to grasp this supreme chance to establish a world-wide rule of reason — to create an enduring peace under the guidance of God."[58]

Less than a week later, President Truman personally delivered the charter to the Senate. In the ensuing hearings before the Foreign Relations Committee, there was solid support for it from a broad spectrum of American society.

President Truman addressing the San Francisco conference on June 26, 1945.
(Courtesy Harry S Truman Library)

On July 28, the Senate voted to ratify the United Nations treaty by a vote of eighty-nine to two. The dissenting votes came from William Langer (R-North Dakota) and Henrik Shipstead (R-Minnesota) who denounced the United Nations as an unlawful superstate.[59] Decisively influenced by Nelson Rockefeller's offer of a choice site on the East River, the permanent headquarters of the United Nations was established in New York City.

A Summing Up

The U.N. Charter as finally approved at San Francisco retained the basic structure and character of the Dumbarton Oaks agreements. The Security Council, dominated by the Big Five, had exclusive jurisdiction for keeping the peace, whereas the General Assembly was confined essentially to the discussion of problems. Members agreed to supply armed forces to the Security Council through separate bilateral agreements, and these troops would be used—subject to the voting procedures in the Security Council—to counter aggression. The Economic and Social Council was given a wider role, and the charter included a draft statute for a new International Court of Justice. A Trusteeship Council was created, but with narrowly defined powers. Although it looked forward to the eventual freedom and self-government of all colonial peoples, it did not require the dissolution of the British, French, Dutch, Belgian, or Portuguese overseas empires, and it permitted the United States to control the Pacific islands wrested from the Japanese. A long, eloquent preamble, written by Field Marshall Jan Smuts, the prime minister of South Africa, provided a context of moral purpose that was missing from the Dumbarton Oaks agreements, but this did not alter the core fact that the charter amounted to the formalization of the Great Power wartime alliance.

The aging Cordell Hull—who would receive the 1945 Nobel Peace Prize for his contributions to the United Nations—declared the charter "one of the great milestones in man's upward climb toward a truly civilized existence." But *Time* magazine's balanced assessment seemed closer to reality: it called the San Francisco document "a charter written for a world of power, tempered by a little reason," a world system "divided into power spheres" established in the hope of setting limits to the rivalry between Russia and the West, and of thus sparing the world another catastrophic war.[60] Only those who naively believed in "genuine collective security" would be disappointed.[61]

Most Americans, tempered by the harsh experience of the war, seemed to agree. Liberal journalists expressed "restrained optimism." The *Nation* cautioned idealists not to "turn their backs on San Francisco and wander off into cynicism," for with the creation of the United Nations "the battle for effective world organization has not been lost; it is only beginning."[62]

Epilogue

With victory in Europe proclaimed on May 8, 1945, with the United Nations Charter unanimously approved by the San Francisco conference on June 25 and ratified by the U.S. Senate on July 28, and with the Pacific war moving toward climax, the American people were forming some fairly definite ideas about the kind of postwar world that they wanted and that seemed within reach.

Most agreed that U.S. repudiation of the League of Nations had been a serious mistake, for the League's consequent failure was a major cause of World War II. And Pearl Harbor had shown that the Atlantic and Pacific oceans were no longer effective barriers against direct attack. From these lessons Americans drew the conclusion that the United States must now maintain its leadership role in forming a new world organization whose primary purpose must be to prevent another terrible war. Accordingly, they favored U.S. participation in some kind of collective security system, based on real power, including the continuing military power of the United States. They were prepared for political and military cooperation with the three other most powerful nations—Britain, the Soviet Union, and China—for they assumed that, whatever their differences might be, these nations shared the American desire to avoid further world wars.

As historian Robert Divine has noted, "this stress on security revealed the continuing strength of nationalism" and, indeed, of a continuing form of isolationism. Americans in 1945 were not interested in another Wilsonian crusade to uplift humankind and achieve democracy and equality for all nations. They did not respond to Henry Wallace's call to sponsor a global New Deal funded by America. After a first flush of enthusiasm, they found little appeal in a world federation or other proposals for world government, for they were instinctively wary of surrendering American sovereignty, especially to an untried world body. According to a 1945 Gallup Poll, Americans wanted international arrangements that would "make sure there are no more world wars," but, according to Divine, they also "yearned for a magic formula which would permit them to live in peace without constant involvement abroad." Basically, the American people wanted to make the world safer for the United States.[1]

The extraordinary American exertions to meet the Soviet Communist challenge after 1947—especially the Marshall Plan, the creation of NATO, and the organization of U.N. resistance in Korea—were a reinforcement, a logical application of this basic attitude that had emerged from the crucible of the war. These actions reflected a broad, enlightened self-interest, and they were taken—with a determination born of painful experience—to avoid a recurrence of the dangerously unfavorable global balance of power that had confronted the United States in 1940. Americans agreed that it was important to encourage democracy and greater equality everywhere, but the impetus was not Wilsonian idealism. Basically, it was the felt need to create a world in which American values—and thus America—could survive and prosper.[2]

From the perspective of fifty years after the United Nations came into existence, the popular hope that the organization would become the central arena for the management of world affairs and the effective guarantor of world peace has clearly not been realized. In fact, such an expectation was always a utopian vision, and it is ironic that much of the euphoria was generated on the American side by leaders who were keenly aware of the inherent limitations.

As World War II ended, world leaders understood that the emerging United Nations organization would be, unavoidably, a mirror image of the prevailing system of nation-states, each acknowledged by international law as sovereign in its territories and institutions. In addition to the Big Power victors, the middle-sized and smaller nations were firmly unwilling to subordinate their identities, their interests, or their sovereign decisions to anything resembling world federation or world government. This was a basic fact of international life in 1945, and has hardly changed. Compelling economic, technological, and social developments have steadily eroded "real" national sovereignty—meaning the ability of individual states to control or influence outcomes—yet nationalism remains the most tenacious force in world affairs.

Also in 1945, there was a wide range of views among the forty-six original members as to what the United Nations was intended to be. Stalin's government was willing to join, in the belief that the principle of Big Power unity (undergirded by the veto provisions) would obligate the Americans and the British to accept Russian hegemony (including Russian methods) in Eastern Europe. Stalin thus viewed the U.N. as a potentially useful vehicle for enhancing Russian prestige without hampering Russian interests or ambitions. The British and French embraced the U.N. as an improvement over the League of Nations, primarily because the full participation of the United States promised a stronger and more effective collective security system. They viewed the U.N. as a useful addition to the range of instruments available to traditional diplomacy, but not as a replacement for them. The Chinese, aware of their almost total dependence on American goodwill, were ready to accept all U.S. proposals for U.N. organization and procedures. The smaller nations viewed the U.N. as a means of strengthening their collective influence and security vis-à-vis the Big Powers and worked hard to reinforce the illusory notion of the "sovereign equality" of all nations.

President Franklin Roosevelt's approach was decisively influenced by recent American history—the Senate's rejection of the League treaty in 1920 and the deep-seated American isolationism of the twenties and thirties. He came to believe that only by presenting the United Nations as a definitive replacement for traditional diplomacy could he persuade the American people to support a leading and sustained U.S. role in world affairs after victory over Germany and Japan. As he said in his address to a joint session of Congress after the Yalta Conference, it was time to substitute "a universal organization" for the exclusive alliances, spheres of influence, and power balances that "have been tried for centuries—and have always failed."[3]

If he really believed that the U.N. could and would become the central arena for managing international affairs—and the specific evidence is thin—it was because he viewed the Security Council as a direct extension of the Big Three wartime alliance. The main lesson he drew from the League failure was that responsibility for world peace depended exclusively on the few nations that possessed real power and that they must "run the world" for an indefinite transitional period after victory; he considered the lesser nations irrelevant to the international policing function. In his view, Big Power cooperation was imperative for settling or suppressing conflicts between and among the lesser nations, especially conflicts that might lead to wider war. It is thus a fair inference that he viewed the Security Council as the most convenient forum for ensuring this.

At the same time, he understood that there was no mechanistic remedy for unresolved conflict between Big Powers. He saw the prevention of Big Power conflict as the supreme political challenge of the postwar period; if cooperation between them broke down, then the world would split into rival power blocs and probably blunder into another global war.

During the war, he consistently warned the American people that power was the only decisive counter to aggression. At the same time, the pervasive disillusionment among Americans at what they regarded as the cynicism and corruption of traditional diplomacy pushed him to present the United Nations as an arrangement that would render that age-old practice essentially obsolete. Here he borrowed Woodrow Wilson's thesis: fractious international problems had proven beyond resolution within an unregulated nation-state system, but they could be resolved within the framework of a universal body operating on the principles of justice and legitimate police power. The key to success, he argued, was full U.S. participation and determined U.S. leadership.

The First Five Years

The triumphal wave of victory in the war against the Axis raised the tidal hopes of humankind everywhere for a new era of enduring peace, and the embryonic United Nations achieved a series of notable successes in the first five years of its existence without having to resort to the direct use of force. In 1946, debate in the Security Council, amplified by the world media, persuaded Moscow to withdraw Russian troops from northern Iran and pushed Paris to remove French forces from Syria and Lebanon. In 1947, the Security Council played a major role in the decolonization of Indonesia. In 1947–48, the General Assembly endorsed the Zionists' claim to statehood for Israel (after Britain had terminated its untenable League Mandate), and this led to a prompt broad-based recognition of Israeli sovereignty that could hardly have happened in the absence of a United Nations organization. The former Italian colonies of Eritrea, Somalia, and Libya were granted independence by the General Assembly in 1949.[4]

These real achievements, however, hardly affected the serious interests of any of the Big Powers, and as the East-West distrust hardened, it became clear that no permanent member of the Security Council, including the United States, was willing to submit issues involving its own vital interests to U.N. jurisdiction. With the onset of the Cold War—marked by ruthless Russian unilateralism in Eastern Europe, East-West deadlock on policy toward Germany, Russian pressures on Turkey, and Russian-backed Communist efforts to overturn the existing order in France and Italy—the contending forces swiftly resolved themselves into two hostile blocs, as FDR had predicted. This development marginalized the U.N. as an instrument of collective security for the next forty years, but it remained a unique forum for bringing to bear the pressure of world opinion on major issues of the Cold War. In addition, the U.N. became the focal point (through the creation of subsidiary or specialized organs, like the World Health Organization, UNICEF, the Commission for Refugees, and the International Civil Aviation Organization) for the coordination of global problems less affected by political and ideological controversy.

A Bipolar World

Led by the United States, the Western bloc turned inevitably to economic aid agreements, military alliances, and other devices of traditional diplomacy as the only available means to build bulwarks for security and survival. These efforts produced the fundamental strategy of containment and the closely linked doctrine of nuclear deterrence together with the panoply of implementing policies and programs, including the Truman Doctrine for Greece and Turkey, the Point Four Program of technical assistance, the Marshall Plan, the European Union, the North Atlantic Alliance, the Berlin airlift, and later a string of lesser regional alliances (SEATO, CENTO, ANZUS).

The first crucial postwar test of the world community's will to repel direct aggression came in June 1950 with North Korea's armed invasion of South Korea. It is important to recall that President Truman ordered U.S. air and naval forces into action, then appealed to the United Nations to provide all assistance "necessary to repel the armed attack and restore international peace . . . in the area." Because the Soviets had been boycotting the Security Council for several months to protest the fact that the defeated Chiang Kai-shek government still occupied the China seat, the Soviet delegate was not present to cast a veto when the crucial vote was taken to authorize a U.N. "police action" in Korea, late in the evening of June 27. Owing to that fortuitous circumstance, what began as a purely American response was transformed into a broad international military coalition fighting under the righteous banner of the United Nations. American ground forces were committed to the fighting a week later. The American military effort was paramount and decisive throughout the conflict, but modest to moderate military force contributions came from fifteen other nations. That fact lent substance to the world's perception that a concerted resistance to naked aggression—the first major collective security effort undertaken by the League or the United Nations—was being mounted in the name of humankind.[5]

What would have happened if the Soviet delegate had been present to veto the proposed "police action"? At three A.M. on June 25, when President Truman was informed of the attack, he told Secretary of State Dean Acheson, "Dean, we've got to stop those sons of bitches no matter what." When Truman returned to Washington from Missouri the next day, he told his assembled advisers, "By God, I'm going to let them have it." Asked years later whether he would have acted to beat back the aggression even without a U.N. endorsement, he replied, "No doubt about it."[6] It is thus virtually certain that the United States would have persevered, alone if necessary, while making every effort to generate political support and military force contributions from a broad base of non-Communist nations—just as it did within the framework of the U.N. mandate. It is also probable that such efforts would have succeeded in raising a representative fighting coalition, which would surely have found a way to associate its armed resistance with the cause of peace. The essential point here is that an effective response—whether or not authorized by the U.N.—depended decisively on the United States. With or without a Soviet veto, a passive U.S. reaction to the attack on South Korea would have resulted in another stillbirth for collective security.

In the 1956 Suez Canal crisis, U.S. political and economic pressure was the decisive factor in forcing Israel, Britain, and France to break off their joint military attack on Egypt, thereby resolving the situation. The U.N. played a useful, though subordinate, role by forming the first "blue helmet" peace-keeping unit that provided a respectable fig leaf to cover the humiliating forced withdrawal of the British, French, and Israeli troops.[7]

Beginning in 1960, under the aggressive leadership of Secretary-General Dag Hammarskjöld, the U.N. played the dominant role in a confused, pro-tracted, highly controversial U.N. military effort in the Congo, first, to retrieve order from chaos in that newly independent nation, then, to defeat the seces-sion of Katanga province. Hammarskjöld was killed in an airplane crash near the town of Ndola in September 1961, en route to a meeting with the Katan-gan leader. The secession was finally suppressed in January 1963, but the united Congo (now Zaire) soon fell into, and remains in, the hands of one of the most tyrannical, corrupt, and avaricious regimes in Africa.[8]

During the Cuban missile crisis of October 1962, the U.N. provided a dramatic forum for the United States to present revealing aerial photographs of Russian missile sites in Cuba, the existence of which the Soviets continued to deny. But it was U.S. power—President John F. Kennedy's readiness to risk nuclear war to force removal of the missiles and his direct exchanges with Russian Premier Nikita Khrushchev—which resolved the single most danger-ous superpower confrontation of the Cold War.[9]

After the Cold War

With the dramatic breakup of the Soviet Union, following seismic shifts in Russian foreign policy under Gorbachev—including major concessions to the Western position on nuclear arms control, removal of Moscow's support for Communist governments in Eastern Europe, and acceptance of a unified Ger-many—the world entered a new phase of history. In theory at least, this seemed to provide fresh opportunity for the United Nations to become the central arena of international policy and action which its supporters had pre-dicted for it in 1945. But the world, as the Cold War ended, was a far differ-ent place from the one the U.N. founders had known and confronted. Mem-bership in the United Nations had increased from 46 to 185, and most of the newcomers were among the world's least politically stable and economically viable societies. There was an ongoing global revolution in communications, as well as a population explosion occurring primarily in the poorest and most backward countries. Both factors widened the gap between rich and poor nations and made environmental degradation an issue of increasing scientific and political concern.

There were also dramatic changes in the distribution of world power and influence. In 1945, the Big Three—the United States, Britain, and the Soviet Union—dominated the scene; indeed, they had imposed the structure and procedures of the United Nations organization on the rest of the world. By 1996, however, of the five permanent members of the Security Council, only the United States remained a military-economic superpower. The former Soviet Union was a broken jigsaw puzzle, politically fragmented and economically chaotic, notwithstanding Russian and Ukrainian retention of a large nuclear weapons capability. Britain and France, effectively shorn of their overseas empires, were declining middle-sized powers of limited military and economic strength. The People's Republic of China, which had overthrown the Chiang Kai-shek regime, was a clumsy giant of large, perhaps hostile potential which appeared to have little sense of obligation to the world community or to the U.N. Charter. This growing disparity between authority and real power in the Security Council was underlined by the fact that Germany and Japan, while required to pay higher U.N. dues than several of the permanent members, remained outside the inner circle, as did other rising regional powers like India and Brazil.

The new era also ushered in a markedly more cautious approach to intervention in local and regional conflicts, a posture which seemed to reflect general agreement that the threat of major war had greatly receded. During the Cold War both superpowers meddled in such disturbances almost reflexively, for they perceived them as chess pieces in a zero-sum power game whose manipulation was necessary to avoid a potential loss in power or territory or to advance its own ideological agenda. But absent the Cold War dynamic, this felt necessity has weakened, despite an upsurge of local and regional turmoil. Great Power interests are now being construed in stricter, more traditional terms, accompanied by a new sensitivity to military casualties.

From under the melting political geography of the Cold War, local and regional conflicts have re-emerged in virulent new and old forms—from civil wars and savage ethnic bloodbaths to fratricides that are producing anarchy and mass starvation and threatening genocide. The reality of dozens of national and subnational motivations, interacting simultaneously yet no longer restrained by intrusive Cold War policies orchestrated from Washington and Moscow, has come as a shock to the international nervous system. As President Bill Clinton acknowledged in his speech to the United Nations on September 27, 1993, the end of the Cold War "simply removed the lid from many cauldrons of ethnic, religious, and territorial animosity."[10]

Overloading the United Nations

Recognizing this potentially ominous law-and-order deficit, yet reluctant to intervene directly, the leading nations have sought to cope with these eruptions by thrusting the United Nations forward as principal peacekeeper and peace enforcer. In 1988, less than 10,000 U.N. "blue helmets" were deployed in a few places (principally the Middle East) to patrol ceasefire lines. By 1994, the emotional pressures for international action (magnified by the pervasive medium of global television) were severely testing and sometimes overwhelming proportion and judgment. In that year, the U.N. security system was trying to manage a mix of seventeen peacekeeping and peace enforcement operations involving 80,000 "blue helmets." Only in Bosnia did these operations involve troops from any of the five permanent members of the Security Council.

In its haste to be responsive to starvation, anarchy, and chaos in weak and "failed" states, the Security Council (meaning especially the five permanent members) stretched both the U.N. authority to intervene and the definition of "threat to peace." At the same time, it has been cavalier about balancing commitments against available resources. Political pressures have operated to plant the U.N. flag, then to look around for the necessary troops, equipment, logistical support, and money. Predictably, the unprecedented demands have exposed the truth that not every member nation has an equal interest in providing troops and money to oppose a specific aggression, or to rescue a specific situation from anarchy. The result of rising demands for U.N. intervention has been a growing political and financial resistance among the member states. By late 1995, the general willingness to "let the U.N. do it" had led to several conspicuous U.N. failures and had produced a donor fatigue which thrust the organization into the worst financial crisis of its fifty-year history. Of the 185 members, some 70 owed $3.3 billion in back dues and peacekeeping assessments, of which $1.4 billion was owed by the United States and another $1 billion by Russia. The U.S. and Russian defaults were the most visible and consequential, but 68 other nations, representing more than one-third of the U.N. membership, were also in arrears.[11]

Necessary But Problematical Reform

In late 1996, the United Nations remains in serious financial trouble, even though the number of security operations has been curtailed. Part of the problem is a growing consensus, especially in the developed world, that the organization as a whole—embracing both peacekeeping and the multiplicity of non-security functions—has become a grossly ineffective bureaucracy. The U.N. structure still lacks adequate management controls, even after the appointment of a strong Under Secretary-General for Administration and Finance in 1993. And undeniably it is staffed primarily on the principle of international political patronage, which means that, while some U.N. officials are conspicuously able professionals, many are incompetent, and most are virtually irremovable.

Since 1945, the central staff secretariat has grown from 1,500 to 14,000 (excluding a number of large special agencies like the World Bank, the World Health Organization, the International Atomic Energy Agency, and several thousand consultants).[12] The organization has also spawned nearly one hundred agencies, subagencies, regional offices, special funds, and commissions. Most of these are not integral parts of the central U.N. organization established by the charter, but are quasi-independent entities with their own budgets and advisory groups, subject only to minimal oversight by the Security Council. Some, like the World Health Organization (which helped to eradicate smallpox) and the Commission for Refugees (which is trying to help 18 million refugees) are recognized as extremely valuable. Moreover, the U.N. role in combatting threats to the global environment and helping to control international drug traffic is increasingly appreciated. But many functions and agencies are of marginal usefulness; their missions overlap, and their operations are marked by a lack of coordination. In 1995, the U.N. as a whole spent about $10.5 billion—about $3.5 billion for headquarters and peacekeeping and peace enforcement operations, and about $7 billion for the multiplicity of special agencies.[13]

Professor Paul Kennedy of Yale, who headed a team of scholars retained by the U.N. Secretariat to study the future of the organization, wrote in October 1995 that the world community faces an urgent decision: either to reduce its demands on the U.N., thereby giving it a "decent chance" to carry on a lower level of activity within existing resources; or to expand available resources so the organization can meet what Kennedy and his team see as inexorably growing demands from member states who cannot cope with the technological pace, population growth, and environmental pressures of the twenty-first century. Kennedy believes that, "in light of global circumstances," opting for expanded resources and a larger U.N. would be the "wiser" choice.[14]

Expansion of U.N. resources and activities in any reasonable time frame looks like a remote possibility. At U.S. insistence, the General Assembly adopted a "no-growth" 1996–97 budget of $2.6 billion for the central organization, which has required the U.N. to reduce its staff by more than one thousand people. The sums expended by both the central organization and the special agencies are not a great deal of money in relation to the wide array of political, economic, environmental, and humanitarian problems with which the organization is charged (it is dwarfed, for example, by the U.S. defense budget of $262 billion). But among member states who pay the largest dues and assessments, there is a lack of confidence in the utility or efficiency of many U.N. operations. This translates to resistance to bearing further burdens until the U.N. has undergone serious reform.

Unfortunately, the U.S.-led effort to force reform by tightening the purse-strings will engender more ill will between the developed "North" and the less developed "South." The North wants reform leading to a more coherent, more efficient U.N. operation, but the South sees reform as a self-serving rationale for reducing the continuing transfer of assets from rich to poor nations—a transfer it has come to regard as a basic entitlement. The nations of the South, who are often the founders and beneficiaries of special U.N. subagencies, look upon efforts toward improving efficiency and accountability as deliberate discrimination. Given this fundamental divergence of view, the outlook for achieving sensible U.N. reforms by general agreement is bleak. Previous efforts, like the 1969 Capacity Study led by Sir Robert Jackson and the 1987 Group of Eighteen Study endorsed by the General Assembly, have been fatally watered down or talked to death. Even such basic reform measures as a single consolidated budget and a one-term limit for U.N. executive agency heads have proven beyond agreement.

Proposals in 1995 by two reputable U.S. legislators, Senator Nancy Kassebaum (R-Kansas) and Congressman Lee Hamilton (D-Indiana), support the U.N. as an "indispensable institution" and probably represent the strongest pro-U.N. sentiment in the Congress; at the same time, these legislators believe that the U.N. must be pruned and reformed in order to obtain future U.S. funding—and their proposals for reform are drastic. They would boil the U.N. down to a few "core" agencies like the World Bank, the International Atomic Energy Agency, the World Health Organization, and the High Commission for Refugees.[15]

Behind these pro-U.N. moderates stand harsh American critics and detractors, especially Republican members of Congress whose overriding goal is budget reduction and who view the U.N. as a threat to U.S. sovereignty. Senator Jesse Helms has declared that the U.S. should deliver an ultimatum to the organization: "reform or die".[16] Conversely, polls consistently show that a substantial majority of the American people believes that the U.N. contributes directly to important U.S. international interests, especially the sharing of peacekeeping and related security tasks. Such polls support the view that the U.S. should pay in full the back dues and assessments for which it is legally obligated, then press for a set of basic reforms. Unfortunately, the majority view is passive and unorganized, while the anti-U.N. minority view is focused and strident. In the American political system, only the President is capable of transforming latent majority support into an effective political force. Thus far, President Clinton has declined to confront the U.N. opponents.

Prospects for serious reform or solid financial solvency are thus highly problematical.

Peacekeeping Versus Peace Enforcement

The current political and financial crisis was brought to a head by Security Council decisions regarding Somalia and Bosnia. Faced in both cases with highly charged emotional pressures for action, the Security Council plunged into humiliation and tragedy by using rhetoric its major members were unwilling to match with the political and military strength required to defeat genocidal aggression. This was a scandalous moral failure of Western Europe and the United States. In particular, they failed by attempting to finesse the distinction between peacekeeping and peace enforcement. In the new era, the difference between the two is of central importance. *Peacekeeping* means essentially monitoring truce arrangements that the adversaries have agreed to observe, and that therefore require only small, lightly armed U.N. troop units and involve little risk of casualties. *Peace enforcement* involves combat operations to suppress violence and defeat aggression; it means taking sides, waging war, and accepting casualties as well as unexpected financial costs. Peace enforcement can be conducted only by nations that have the common interest, the will, and the means to carry it through.

Where U.N. operations have been confined to small-scale peacekeeping activities, like monitoring agreed ceasefire lines (as in the Sinai or Namibia), or supervising elections (as in Cambodia and Haiti), they have generally stabilized the immediate situation and improved prospects for the future. However, where the U.N. has undertaken actions involving coercive military force on any significant scale, it has been effective only when it delegated direct operating responsibility to an outside military coalition with the will and the means to prevail.

The response to the attack on South Korea (1950) and to Iraq's invasion of Kuwait (1991) were conducted under the strategic direction of the United States, by U.S. military forces moderately augmented by the forces of a number of like-minded nations. These ad hoc coalitions operated under a very broad delegation of authority from the Security Council, and were not subject to day-to-day U.N. supervision. In effect, they borrowed the U.N. flag and fought on their own terms, with their own command and force structures. The only clear-cut enforcement operation managed directly by the U.N. involved the defeat of the Katanga secession (1961–63); while this achieved its goal, it was engulfed in such confusion and controversy that the Security Council shied away from enforcement operations for the next three decades.[17]

The U.N. failures in Somalia and Bosnia are directly related to the Security Council's readiness, witting or unwitting, to blur peacekeeping with peace enforcement, and to the fact that the United States was not fully committed to enforcement action when the use of significant military force became the recognized requirement to carry out the U.N. mandate.

Neither the United States nor the U.N. made an effort to redeem the U.N. failure in Somalia, but the moral and military debacle in Bosnia produced a belated American realization that the situation there posed a serious threat to the continued cohesion of NATO, to U.S. leadership therein, and to stability and democracy in Europe. To restore and protect Europe, the United States had fought two world wars in this century and then sustained the

NATO alliance for forty years. Somalia was strategically peripheral; Europe was central to U.S. national interests.

By the late summer of 1995, the Bosnian enterprise was drifting and rudderless, with all concerned accepting a corrosive loss of both U.N. and NATO credibility as preferable to the risks of a stronger policy. At that point, the Clinton Administration finally moved to take a leading role, determined for its own reasons to create conditions that would force a settlement. The reasons included several realizations: that the Western Europeans were inherently incapable of resolving the situation by themselves; that meeting the U.S. pledge to help extricate a beleaguered U.N. force in Bosnia carried greater military and political risks than sending U.S. troops to enforce a peace settlement; that Clinton's reelection could be jeopardized if a Bosnian settlement was not reached before the summer of 1996.

There followed serious U.S.-led NATO air strikes which forced the Serbs to the bargaining table, and intensive U.S.-led negotiations in Dayton, Ohio, which produced a fragile diplomatic agreement in November 1995. These successes set the stage for the NATO decision to send 60,000 troops (including 20,000 Americans) to police the agreed settlement and monitor new elections. These achievements—whether or not they produce an enduring Balkan peace—constituted an impressive demonstration of American power. They reaffirmed the truth that the U.S. remains the necessary guarantor of European peace, as well as the one decisive balance wheel in the international system. At the same time, they revealed Europe's continuing disunity and its dependence on American leadership. In the process, the U.N. was relegated to a distinctly subordinate role.

These developments are connected to three enduring realities: (a) unless the weight of U.S. political and military power is available to support a U.N. or NATO effort, no enforcement action on any significant scale can be carried through to a settlement; (b) like other sovereign nations, the United States will judge its own interests in a given situation, sometimes with timely wisdom, sometimes with myopic judgment; (c) broadly speaking, the U.S. Government and the American people lack confidence in the U.N.'s ability to manage military operations and prefer to avoid becoming enmeshed in the vagaries of the U.N. decision-making process in situations involving the use of force.

Limiting the U.N. Police Role to Peacekeeping

These realities raise the question of whether the United Nations can or should be responsible for maintaining international peace. On October 10, 1995, Secretary-General Boutros Boutros-Ghali, who had led the charge for U.N. interventions in Somalia and Bosnia, said in an interview, "Enforcement is beyond the power of the U.N. because members contribute troops on the understanding that their role will be limited to peacekeeping, and the troops will be protected." He added, "If it goes beyond passive measures, and the troops are endangered, their governments will pull them out. In the future, if peace enforcement is needed, it should be conducted by countries with the will to do it."[18]

Other observers have reached the same conclusion. Senator Kassebaum and Congressman Hamilton believe that the term *peace enforcement* should be struck from the U.N. vocabulary, and future U.N. peacekeeping "should be limited to classic operations in which Blue Helmets stand between suspicious parties only after diplomacy has secured a peace to be kept." Who then would fight to defeat aggression? The Kassebaum-Hamilton response echoes Boutros-Ghali: "Situations that require more robust military action are better handled directly by the member states."[19]

At first glance, these statements are stunning—they amount to a basic repudiation of the first principle on which both the League of Nations and the United Nations were founded. The cardinal premise of Woodrow Wilson and the League Covenant was that every member nation would equally and energetically support every League decision to oppose aggression—and that world peace depended on such a unified response. The U.N. Charter is even more explicit. It obligates all member nations to "make available to the Security Council . . . armed forces" and other facilities and assistance (Article 43), in order that the U.N. can take "effective collective measures for the prevention and removal of threats to the peace, and for the suppression of acts of aggression" (Article 1) including "such action by air, sea, or land forces as may be necessary to restore international peace and security" (Article 42). Both the League and the United Nations were perceived by their founders as the very embodiment of international collective security. The U.N. Charter designates the Security Council as the world police commissioner, the central organizer and manager of peace-loving coalitions organized to fight for humankind against aggressors.[20]

On reflection, however, the statements are less startling. There has always been a chasm between the formal prescriptions for collective security and the realities. Woodrow Wilson's high-flown assumption was conclusively disproved by the League failure to halt the march of the dictators during the 1930s. And the tepid, uneven response of U.N. members to obligations under Article 43 has revealed the inherent unreality of expecting member states of widely different size and orientation to provide troops, more or less automatically, to meet any situation in which the Security Council might decide to intervene. Only a handful of nations—notably Canada, Australia, the Netherlands, and the Scandinavian countries—have met this obligation fully, by earmarking and training specific units for U.N. duty. Most members have reserved their sovereign right to decide, in each case, whether a particular U.N. intervention affects their interests enough to warrant sending troops. The United States has formally declined to make a blanket Article 43 commitment.

Also, as previously noted, the only large-scale U.N. peace enforcement operations—the Korean War and the Gulf War—were conducted by ad hoc coalitions entirely dependent on the leadership and military power of the United States. Moreover, they were fought under a broad delegation of U.N. authority which essentially freed the coalitions from the complexities of U.N. oversight. The U.N. provided an important framework of moral and legal consensus for these actions to protect and restore the existing order, but the United States was required to do the heavy lifting.

Throughout the Cold War, the United States played a broad containing, buttressing, protecting role by acting alone, through the U.N., or through various regional alliances. Every collective action was decisively undergirded by U.S. power; multilateralism was mostly nominal, for none of the alliances (including NATO) was credible without the U.S. commitment. During this long period, the United States showed a readiness to act to stabilize the existing order, even on issues where its own vital interests were not directly involved, but it was not inexorably bound to any particular vehicle for action. The U.N., the regional alliances, and unilateral intervention were different strategic or tactical options available to meet different circumstances.

The world balance of power situation is essentially the same today. Like it or not, no other nation or combination of nations possesses anything approaching the power and mobility—the global reach—of U.S. air, sea, and ground forces, supported by sealift, airlift, fixed wing and helicopter air cover, satellite reconnaissance, and other forms of intelligence gathering. Without U.S. leadership and participation, there can be no effective response to serious aggression or other serious threats to general peace.

A formal decision to confine future U.N. security missions to essentially passive peacekeeping would be a practical adjustment to reality, but it would not be a responsible one unless the U.S. Government and the American people understood and accepted the corollary truth: that the United States is the ultimate guarantor of the peace. At present, the American political system is still trying to claim what it believes is a deserved respite from the heavy international burdens it carried during the Cold War. It is still trying to work out some new reconciliation between the demands of its domestic problems and the enduring implications of dominant U.S. power for peace or war for the present and the future.

Given the power realities and the responsibility they impose, the United States would be wise to make an effective United Nations a major goal and tenet of U.S. foreign policy. In particular, it should support a more efficient U.N. peacekeeping system, recognizing that duties like patrolling ceasefire lines and monitoring elections often prevent or delay the deterioration of situations into open conflicts that require a warfighting response. However, even a more coherent peacekeeping system will have to operate within resource limits—troops and money—which will require a selective response, for the U.N. cannot mount or sustain simultaneous peacekeeping operations everywhere. But the acute North-South differences in priorities are likely to complicate nearly every decision. For example, Boutros Boutros-Ghali has asserted that the Security Council's readiness to engage in Bosnia, but not in Liberia, Sudan, Rwanda, or Tajikistan, are examples of Western discrimination.

The challenge to the American political system is to recognize both the fundamental importance of the United Nations organization and its inherent limitations. The corollary is to acknowledge the enduring necessity for the dominant world power to play a steady balancing role, both inside and outside the U.N. The United States should take a leading role in an effort to strengthen and sustain a U.N. peacekeeping system that is deliberately designed to reduce the need for U.S.-led military efforts; at the same time, the United States cannot avoid responsibility as the ultimate guarantor of world peace and the existing order. Civilization requires a police force. The best available combination—namely, the United Nations strongly supported by the United States—is the very formula for world stability and peace that Franklin D. Roosevelt fought with all his strength to achieve more than half a century ago.

Appendix

Charter of the United Nations

WE THE PEOPLES OF THE UNITED NATIONS DETERMINED

to save succeeding generations from the scourge of war, which twice in our lifetime has brought untold sorrow to mankind, and

to reaffirm faith in fundamental human rights, in the dignity and worth of the human person, and in the equal rights of men and women and of nations large and small, and

to establish conditions under which justice and respect for the obligations arising from treaties and other sources or international law can be maintained, and

to promote social progress and better standards of life in larger freedom,

AND FOR THESE ENDS

to practice and live together in peace with one another as good neighbors, and

to unite our strength to maintain international peace and security, and

to ensure, by the acceptance of principles and the institution of methods, that armed force shall not be used, save in the common interest, and

to employ international machinery for the promotion of the economic and social advancement of all peoples,

HAVE RESOLVED TO COMBINE OUR EFFORTS TO ACCOMPLISH THESE AIMS.

Accordingly, our representative Governments, through representatives assembled in the city of San Francisco, who have exhibited their full powers found to be in good and due form, have agreed to the present Charter of the United Nations and do hereby establish an international organization known as the United Nations.

Chapter I. Purposes and Principles
Article 1

The Purposes of the United Nations are:

1. To maintain international peace and security, and to that end: to take effective collective measures for the prevention and removal of threats to the peace, and for the suppression of acts of aggression or other breaches of the peace, and to bring about by peaceful means, and in conformity with the principles of justice and international law, adjustment or settlement of international disputes or situations which might lead to a breach of the peace;

2. To develop friendly relations among nations based on respect for the principle of equal rights and self-determination of peoples, and to take other appropriate measures to strengthen universal peace;

3. To achieve international co-operation in solving international problems of an economic, social, cultural, or humanitarian character, and in promoting and encouraging respect for human rights and for fundamental freedoms for all without distinction as to race, sex, language, or religion; and

4. To be a centre for harmonizing the actions of nations in the attainment of these common ends.

Article 2

The Organization and its Members, in pursuit of the Purposes stated in Article 1, shall act in accordance with the following principles.

1. The Organization is based on the principle of the sovereign equality of all its Members.

2. All Members, in order to ensure to all of them the rights and benefits resulting from membership, shall fulfill in good faith the obligations assumed by them in accordance with the present Charter.

3. All Members shall settle their international disputes by peaceful means in such a manner that international peace and security, and justice, are not endangered.

4. All Members shall refrain in their international relations from the threat of use of force against the territorial integrity or political independence of any state, or in any other manner inconsistent with the Purposes of the United Nations.

5. All Members shall give the United Nations every assistance in any action it takes in accordance with the present Charter, and shall refrain from giving assistance to any state against which the United Nations is taking preventive or enforcement action.

6. The Organization shall ensure that states which are not members of the United Nations act in accordance with these Principles so far as may be necessary for the maintenance of international peace and security.

7. Nothing contained in the present Charter shall authorize the United Nations

to intervene in matters which are essentially within the domestic jurisdiction of any state or shall require the Members to submit such matters to settlement under the present Charter; but this principle shall not prejudice the application of enforcement measures under Chapter VII.

Chapter II. Membership
Article 3

The original Members of the United Nations shall be the states which, having participated in the United Nations Conference on International Organization at San Francisco, or having previously signed the Declaration by United Nations of 1 January 1942, sign the present Charter and ratify it in accordance with Article 110.

Article 4

1. Membership in the United Nations is open to all other peace-loving states which accept the obligations contained in the present Charter and, in the judgement of the Organization, are able and willing to carry out these obligations.

2. The admission of any such state to membership in the United Nations will be effected by a decision of the General Assembly upon the recommendation of the Security Council.

Article 5

A Member of the United Nations against which preventative or enforcement action has been taken by the Security Council may be suspended from the exercise of the rights and privileges of membership by the General Assembly upon the recommendation of the Security Council. The exercise of these rights and privileges may be restored by the Security Council.

Article 6

A Member of the United Nations which has persistently violated the Principles contained in the present Charter may be expelled from the Organization by the General Assembly upon the recommendation of the Security Council.

Chapter III. Organs
Article 7

1. There are established as the principal organs of the United Nations: a General Assembly, a Security Council, an Economic and Social Council, a Trusteeship Council, an International Court of Justice, and a Secretariat.

2. Such subsidiary organs as may be found necessary may be established in accordance with the present Charter.

Article 8

The United Nations shall place no restrictions on the eligibility of men and women to participate in any capacity and under conditions of equality in its principal and subsidiary organs.

Chapter IV. The General Assembly
Composition
Article 9

1. The General Assembly shall consist of all the Members of the United Nations.

2. Each Member shall have not more than five representatives in the General Assembly.

Functions and Powers
Article 10

The General Assembly may discuss any questions or any matters within the scope of the present Charter, and, except as provided in Article 12, may make recommendations to the Members of the United Nations or to the Security Council or to both on any such questions or matters.

Article 11

1. The General Assembly may consider the general principles of co-operation in the maintenance of international peace and security, including the principles governing disarmament and the regulation of armaments, and may make recommendations with regard to such principles to the Members or to the Security Council or both.

2. The General Assembly may discuss any questions relating to the maintenance of international peace and security brought before it by any Member of the United Nations in accordance with Article 35, paragraph 2, and, except as provided in Article 12, may make recommendations with regard to any such questions to the state or states concerned or to the Security Council or to both. Any such question on which action is necessary shall be referred to the Security Council by the General Assembly either before or after discussion.

3. The General Assembly may call the attention of the Security Council to situations which are likely to endanger international peace and security.

4. The powers of the General Assembly set forth in this Article shall not limit the general scope of Article 10.

Article 12

1. While the Security Council is exercising in respect of any dispute or situation the functions assigned to it in the present Charter, the General Assembly shall not make any recommendation with regard to that dispute or situation unless the Security Council so requests.

2. The Secretary-General, with the consent of the Security Council, shall notify the General Assembly at each session of any matters relative to the maintenance of international peace and security which are being dealt with by the Security Council and shall similarly notify the General Assembly, or the Members of the United Nations if the General Assembly is not in session, immediately the Security Council ceases to deal with such matters.

Article 13

1. The General Assembly shall initiate studies and make recommendations for the purpose of:

a. promoting international co-operation in the political field and encouraging the progressive development of international law and its codification;

b. promoting international co-operation in the economic, social, cultural, educational, and health fields, and assisting in the realization of human rights and fundamental freedoms for all without distinction as to race, sex, language, or religion.

2. The further responsibilities, functions, and powers of the General Assembly with respect to matters mentioned in paragraph 1(b) above are set forth in Chapters IX and X.

Article 14

Subject to the provisions of Article 12, the General Assembly may recommend measures for the peaceful adjustment of any situation, regardless of origin, which it deems likely to impair the general welfare or friendly relations among nations, including situations resulting from a violation of the provisions of the present Charter setting forth the Purposes and Principles of the United Nations.

Article 15

1. The General Assembly shall receive and consider annual and special reports from the Security Council; these reports shall include an account of the measures that the Security Council has decided upon or taken to maintain the international peace and security.

2. The General Assembly shall receive and consider reports from other organs of the United Nations.

Article 16

The General Assembly shall perform such functions with respect to the international trusteeship system as are assigned to it under Chapters XII and XIII, including the approval of the trusteeship agreements for areas not designated as strategic.

Article 17

1. The General Assembly shall consider and approve the budget of the Organization.

2. The expenses of the Organization shall be borne by the Members as apportioned by the General Assembly.

3. The General Assembly shall consider and approve any financial and budgetary arrangements with specialized agencies referred to in Article 57 and shall examine the administrative budgets of such specialized agencies with a view to making recommendations to the agencies concerned.

Voting
Article 18

1. Each member of the General Assembly shall have one vote.

2. Decisions of the General Assembly on important questions shall be made by a two-thirds majority of the members present and voting. These questions shall include: recommendations with respect to the maintenance of international peace and security, the election of the non-permanent members of the Security Council, the election of the members of the Economic and Social Council, the election of members of the Trusteeship Council in accordance with paragraph 1(c) of Article 86, the admission of new Members to the United Nations, the suspension of the rights and privileges of membership, the expulsion of Members, questions relating to the operation of the trusteeship system, and budgetary questions.

3. Decisions on other questions, including the determination of additional categories of questions to be decided by a two-thirds majority, shall be made by a majority of the members present and voting.

Article 19

A Member of the United Nations which is in arrears in the payment of its financial contributions to the Organization shall have no vote in the General Assembly if the amount of its arrears equals or exceeds the amount of the contributions due from it for the preceding two full years. The General Assembly may, nevertheless, permit such a Member to vote if it is satisfied that the failure to pay is due to conditions beyond the control of the Member.

Procedure
Article 20

The General Assembly shall meet in regular annual sessions and in such special sessions as occasion may require. Special sessions shall be convoked by the Secretary-General at the request of the Security Council or of a majority of the Members of the United Nations.

Article 21

The General Assembly shall adopt its own rules of procedure. It shall elect its President for each session.

Article 22

The General Assembly may establish such subsidiary organs as it deems necessary for the performance of its functions.

Chapter V. The Security Council
Composition
Article 23

1. The Security Council shall consist of fifteen members of the United Nations. The [People's] Republic of China, France, the Union of Soviet Socialist Republics, the United Kingdom of Great Britain and Northern Ireland, and the United States of America shall be permanent members of the Security Council. The General Assembly shall elect ten other Members of the United Nations to be non-permanent members of the Security Council, due regard being specially paid, in the first instance to the contribution of Members of the national peace and security and to the other purposes of the Organization, and also to equitable geographical distribution.

2. The non-permanent members of the Security Council shall be elected for a term of two years. In the first election of the non-permanent members after the increase of the membership of the Security Council from eleven to fifteen, two of the four additional members shall be chosen for a term of one year. A retiring member shall not be eligible for immediate re-election.

3. Each member of the Security Council shall have one representative.

Functions and Powers
Article 24

1. In order to ensure prompt and effective action by the United Nations, its members confer on the Security Council primary responsibility for the maintenance

of international peace and security, and agree that in carrying out its duties under this responsibility the Security Council acts on their behalf.

2. In discharging these duties the Security Council shall act in accordance with the Purposes and Principles of the United Nations. The specific powers granted to the Security Council for the discharge of these duties are laid down in Chapters VI, VII, VIII, and XII.

3. The Security Council shall submit annual, and when necessary, special reports to the General Assembly for its consideration.

Article 25

The members of the United Nations agree to accept and carry out the decisions of the Security Council in accordance with the present Charter.

Article 26

In order to promote the establishment and maintenance of international peace and security with the least diversion for armaments of the world's human and economic resources, the Security Council shall be responsible for formulating, with the assistance of the Military Staff Committee referred to in Article 47, plans to be submitted to the Members of the United Nations for the establishment of a system for the regulation of armaments.

Voting
Article 27

1. Each member of the Security Council shall have one vote.

2. Decisions of the Security Council on procedural matters shall be made by an affirmative vote of nine members.

3. Decisions of the Security Council on all other matters shall be made by an affirmative vote of the nine members including the concurring votes of the permanent members; provided that, in decisions under Chapter VI, and under paragraph 3 of Article 52, a party to a dispute shall abstain from voting.

Procedure
Article 28

1. The Security Council shall be so organized as to be able to function continuously. Each member of the Security Council shall for this purpose be represented at all times at the seat of the Organization.

2. The Security Council shall hold periodic meetings at which each of its mem-

bers may, if it so desires, be represented by a member of the government or by some other specially designated representative.

3. The Security Council may hold meetings at such places other than the seat of the Organization as in its judgement will best facilitate its work.

Article 29

The Security Council may establish such subsidiary organs as it deems necessary for the performance of its functions.

Article 30

The Security Council shall adopt its own rules of procedure, including the method of selecting its President.

Article 31

Any Member of the United Nations which is not a member of the Security Council may participate, without vote, in the discussion of any question brought before the Security Council whenever the latter considers that the interests of that Member are specially affected.

Article 32

Any Member of the United Nations which is not a member of the Security Council or any state which is not a Member of the United Nations, if it is a party to a dispute under consideration by the Security Council, shall be invited to participate, without vote, in the discussion relating to the dispute. The Security Council shall lay down such conditions as it deems just for the participation of a state which is not a Member of the United Nations.

Chapter VI. Pacific Settlement of Disputes
Article 33

1. The parties to any dispute, the continuance of which is likely to endanger the maintenance of international peace and security, shall, first of all, seek a solution by negotiation, enquiry, mediation, conciliation, arbitration, judicial settlement, resort to regional agencies or arrangements, or other peaceful means of their own choice.

2. The Security Council shall, when it deems necessary, call upon the parties to settle their dispute by such means.

Article 34

The Security Council may investigate any dispute, or any situation which might lead to international friction or give rise to a dispute, in order to determine whether the continuance of the dispute or situation is likely to endanger the maintenance of international peace and security.

Article 35

1. Any Member of the United Nations may bring any dispute, or any situation of the nature referred to in Article 34, to the attention of the Security Council or of the General Assembly.

2. A state which is not a Member of the United Nations may bring to the attention of the Security Council or of the General Assembly any dispute to which it is a party if it accepts in advance, for the purposes of the dispute, the obligations of pacific settlement provided in the present Charter.

3. The proceedings of the General Assembly in respect of matters brought to its attention under this Article will be subject to the provisions of Articles 11 and 12.

Article 36

1. The Security Council may, at any stage of a dispute of the nature referred to in Article 33 or a situation of like nature, recommend appropriate procedures or methods of adjustment.

2. The Security Council should take into consideration any procedures for the settlement of the dispute which have already been adopted by the parties.

3. In making recommendations under this Article the Security Council should also take into consideration that legal disputes should as a general rule be referred by the parties to the International Court of Justice in accordance with the provisions of the Statute of the Court.

Article 37

1. Should the parties to a dispute of the nature referred to in Article 33 fail to settle it by the means indicated in that Article, they shall refer it to the Security Council.

2. If the Security Council deems that the continuance of the dispute is in fact likely to endanger the maintenance of international peace and security, it shall decide whether to take action under Article 36 or to recommend such terms of settlement as it may consider appropriate.

Article 38

Without prejudice to the provisions of Articles 33 to 37, the Security Council may, if all the parties to any dispute so request, make recommendations to the parties with a view to a pacific settlement of the dispute.

Chapter VII. Action with Respect to Threats to the Peace, Breaches of the Peace, and Acts of Aggression
Article 39

The Security Council shall determine the existence of any threat to the peace, breach of the peace, or act of aggression and shall make recommendations, or decide what measures shall be taken in accordance with Articles 41 and 42, to maintain or restore international peace and security.

Article 40

In order to prevent an aggravation of the situation, the Security Council may, before making the recommendations or deciding upon the measures provided for in Article 39, call upon the parties concerned to comply with such provisional measures as it deems necessary or desirable. Such provisional measures shall be without prejudice to the rights, claims, or position of the parties concerned. The Security Council shall duly take account of failure to comply with such provisional measures.

Article 41

The Security Council may decide what measures not involving the use of armed force are to be employed to give effect to its decisions, and it may call upon the Members of the United Nations to apply such measures. These may include complete or partial interruption of economic relations and of rail, sea, air, postal, telegraphic, radio, and other means of communication, and the severance of diplomatic relations.

Article 42

Should the Security Council consider that measures provided for in Article 41 would be inadequate or have proved to be inadequate, it may take such action by air, sea, or land forces as may be necessary to maintain or restore international peace and security. Such action may include demonstrations, blockade, and other operations by air, sea, or land forces of Members of the United Nations.

Article 43

1. All Members of the United Nations, in order to contribute to the maintenance of international peace and security, undertake to make available to the Security Council, on its call and in accordance with a special agreement or agreements, armed forces, assistance, and facilities, including right of passage, necessary for the purpose of maintaining international peace and security.

2. Such agreement or agreements shall govern the numbers and types of forces, their degree of readiness and general location, and the nature of the facilities and assistance to be provided.

3. The agreement or agreements shall be negotiated as soon as possible on the initiative of the Security Council. They shall be concluded between the Security Council and Members or between the Security Council and groups of Members and shall be subject to ratification by the signatory states in accordance with their respective constitutional processes.

Article 44

When the Security Council has decided to use force it shall, before calling upon a Member not represented on it to provide armed forces in fulfillment of the obligations assumed under Article 43, invite that Member, if the Member so desires, to participate in the decisions of the Security Council concerning the employment of contingents of that Member's armed forces.

Article 45

In order to enable the United Nations to take urgent military measures, Members shall hold immediately available national air-force contingents for combined international enforcement action. The strength and degree of readiness in these contingents and plans for their combined action shall be determined, within the limits laid down in the special agreement or agreements referred to in Article 43, by the Security Council with the assistance of the Military Staff Committee.

Article 46

Plans for the application of armed force shall be made by the Security Council with the assistance of the Military Staff Committee.

Article 47

1. There shall be established a Military Staff Committee to advise and assist the Security Council on all questions relating to the Security Council's military require-

ments for the maintenance of international peace and security, the employment and command of forces placed at its disposal, the regulation of armaments, and possible disarmament.

2. The Military Staff Committee shall consist of the Chiefs of Staff of the permanent members of the Security Council or their representatives. Any Member of the United Nations not permanently represented on the Committee shall be invited by the Committee to be associated with it when the efficient discharge of the Committee's responsibilities requires the participation of that Member in its work.

3. The Military Staff Committee shall be responsible under the Security Council for the strategic direction of any armed forces placed at the disposal of the Security Council. Questions relating to the command of such forces shall be worked out subsequently.

4. The Military Staff Committee, with the authorization of the Security Council and after consultation with appropriate regional agencies, may establish regional subcommittees.

Article 48

1. The action required to carry out the decisions of the Security Council for the maintenance of international peace and security shall be taken by all the Members of the United Nations or by some of them, as the Security Council may determine.

2. Such decisions shall be carried out by the Members of the United Nations directly and through their action in the appropriate international agencies of which they are members.

Article 49

The members of the United Nations shall join in affording mutual assistance in carrying out the measures decided upon by the Security Council.

Article 50

If preventive or enforcement measures against any state are taken by the Security Council, any other state, whether a Member of the United Nations or not, which finds itself confronted with special economic problems arising from carrying out those measures shall have the right to consult the Security Council with regard to a solution of those problems.

Article 51

Nothing in the present Charter shall impair the inherent right of individual or collective self-defence if an armed attack occurs against a Member of the United

Nations, until the Security Council has taken measures necessary to maintain international peace and security. Measures taken by Members in the exercise of this right of self-defence shall be immediately reported to the Security Council and shall not in any way affect the authority and responsibility of the Security Council under the present Charter to take at any time such action as it deems necessary in order to maintain or restore international peace and security.

Chapter VIII. Regional Arrangements
Article 52

1. Nothing in the present Charter precludes the existence of regional arrangements for dealing with such matters relating to the maintenance of international peace and security as are appropriate for regional action, provided that such arrangements or agencies and their activities are consistent with the Purposes and Principles of the United Nations.

2. The Members of the United Nations entering into such arrangements or constituting such agencies shall make every effort to achieve public settlement of local disputes through such regional arrangements or by such regional agencies before referring them to the Security Council.

3. The Security Council shall encourage the development of pacific settlement of local disputes through such regional arrangements or by such regional agencies either on the initiative of the states concerned or by reference from the Security Council.

4. This Article in no way impairs the application of Articles 34 and 35.

Article 53

1. The Security Council shall, where appropriate, utilize such regional arrangements or agencies for enforcement action under its authority. But no enforcement action shall be taken under regional arrangements or by regional agencies without the authorization of the Security Council, with the exception of measures against any enemy state, as defined in paragraph 2 of this Article, provided for pursuant to Article 107 or in regional arrangements directed against renewal of aggressive policy on the part of any such state, until such time as the Organization may, on request of the Governments concerned, be charged with the responsibility for preventing further aggression by such a state.

2. The term *enemy state* as used in paragraph 1 of this Article applies to any state which during the Second World War has been an enemy of any signatory of the present Charter.

Article 54

The Security Council shall at all times be kept fully informed of activities under-taken or in contemplation under regional arrangements or by regional agencies for the maintenance of international peace and security.

Chapter IX. International Economic and Social Co-operation
Article 55

With a view to the creation of conditions of stability and well-being which are necessary for peaceful and friendly relations among nations based on respect for the principle of equal rights and self-determination of peoples, the United Nations shall promote:

a. higher standards of living, full employment, and conditions of economic and social progress and development;

b. solutions of international economic, social, health, and related problems; and international cultural and educational co-operation; and

c. universal respect for, and observe of, human rights and fundamental freedoms for all without distinction as to race, sex, language, or religion.

Article 56

All members pledge themselves to take joint and separate action in co-operation with the Organization for the achievement of the purposes set forth in Article 55.

Article 57

1. The various specialized agencies, established by intergovernmental agreement and having wide international responsibilities, as defined in their basic instruments, in economic, social, cultural, educational, health, and related fields, shall be brought into relationship with the United Nations in accordance with the provisions of Article 63.

2. Such agencies thus brought into relationship with the United Nations are here-inafter referred to as specialized agencies.

Article 58

The Organization shall make recommendations for the co-ordination of the poli-cies and activities of the specialized agencies.

Article 59

The Organization shall, where appropriate, initiate negotiations among the states concerned for the creation of any new specialized agencies required for the accomplishment of the purposes set forth in Article 55.

Article 60

Responsibility for the discharge of the functions of the Organization set forth in this Chapter shall be vested in the General Assembly and, under the authority of the General Assembly, in the Economic and Social Council, which shall have for this purpose the powers set forth in Chapter X.

Chapter X. The Economic and Social Council
Composition
Article 61

1. The Economic and Social Council shall consist of fifty-four Members of the United Nations elected by the General Assembly.

2. Subject to the provisions of paragraph 3, eighteen members of the Economic and Social Council shall be elected each year for a term of three years. A retiring member shall not be eligible for immediate re-election.

3. At the first election after the increase in the membership of the Economic and Social Council from twenty-seven to fifty-four members, in addition to the members elected in place of the nine members whose term of office expires at the end of that year, twenty-seven additional members shall be elected. Of these twenty-seven additional members, the term of office of nine members so elected shall expire at the end of two years, in accordance with arrangements made by the General Assembly.

4. Each member of the Economic and Social Council shall have one representative.

Functions and Powers
Article 62

1. The Economic and Social Council may make or initiate studies and reports with respect to international economic, social, cultural, educational, health, and related matters and may make recommendations with respect to any such matters to the General Assembly, to the Members of the United Nations, and to the specialized agencies concerned.

2. It may make recommendations for the purpose of promoting respect for, and observance of, human rights and fundamental freedoms for all.

3. It may prepare draft conventions for submission to the General Assembly, with respect to matters falling within its competence.

4. It may call, in accordance with the rules prescribed by the United Nations, international conferences on matters falling within its competence.

Article 63

1. The Economic and Social Council may enter into agreements with any of the agencies referred to in Article 57, defining the terms on which the agency concerned shall be brought into relationship with the United Nations. Such agreements shall be subject to approval by the General Assembly.

2. It may co-ordinate the activities of the specialized agencies through consultation with and recommendations to such agencies and through recommendations to the General Assembly and to the Members of the United Nations.

Article 64

1. The Economic and Social Council may take appropriate steps to obtain regular reports from the specialized agencies. It may make arrangements with the Members of the United Nations and with the specialized agencies to obtain reports on the steps taken to give effect to its own recommendations and to recommendations on matters falling within its competence made by the General Assembly.

2. It may communicate its observations on these reports to the General Assembly.

Article 65

The Economic and Social Council may furnish information to the Security Council and shall assist the Security Council upon its request.

Article 66

1. The Economic and Social Council shall perform such functions as fall within its competence in connexion with the carrying out of the recommendations of the General Assembly.

2. It may, with the approval of the General Assembly, perform services at the request of Members of the United Nations and at the request of specialized agencies.

3. It shall perform such other functions as are specified elsewhere in the present Charter or as may be assigned to it by the General Assembly.

Voting
Article 67

1. Each member of the Economic and Social Council shall have one vote.

2. Decisions of the Economic and Social Council shall be made by a majority of the members present and voting.

Procedure
Article 68

The Economic and Social Council shall set up commissions in economic and social fields and for the promotion of human rights, and such other commissions as may be required for the performance of its functions.

Article 69

The Economic and Social Council shall invite any Member of the United Nations to participate, without vote, in its deliberations on any matter of particular concern to that Member.

Article 70

The Economic and Social Council may make arrangements for representatives of the specialized agencies to participate, without vote, in its deliberations and in those of the commissions established by it, and for its representatives to participate in the deliberations of the specialized agencies.

Article 71

The Economic and Social Council may make suitable arrangements for consultation with non-governmental organizations which are concerned with matters within its competence. Such arrangements may be made with international organizations and, where appropriate, with national organizations after consultation with the Member of the United Nations concerned.

Article 72

1. The Economic and Social Council shall adopt its own rules of procedure, including the method of selecting its President.

2. The Economic and Social Council shall meet as required in accordance with its rules, which shall include provision for the convening of meetings on the request of a majority of its members.

Chapter XI. Declaration Regarding Non-Self-Governing Territories
Article 73

Members of the United Nations which have or assume responsibilities for the administration of territories whose peoples have not yet attained a full measure of self-government recognize the principle that the interests of the inhabitants of these territories are paramount, and accept as a sacred trust the obligation to promote the utmost, within the system of international peace and security established by the present Charter, the well-being of the inhabitants of these territories, and, to this end:

a. to ensure, with due respect for the culture of the peoples concerned, their political, economic, social, and educational advancement, their just treatment, and their protection against abuses;

b. to develop self-government, to take due account of the political aspirations of the peoples, and to assist them in the progressive development of their free political institutions, according to the particular circumstances of each territory and its peoples and their varying stages of advancement;

c. to further international peace and security;

d. to promote constructive measures of development, to encourage research, and to co-operate with one another and, when and where appropriate, with specialized international bodies with a view to the practical achievement of the social, economic, and scientific purposes set forth in this Article; and

e. to transmit regularly to the Secretary-General for information purposes, subject to such limitation as security and constitutional considerations may require, statistical and other information of a technical nature relating to economic, social, and educational conditions in the territories for which they are respectively responsible other than those territories to which Chapters XII and XIII apply.

Article 74

Members of the United Nations also agree that their policy in respect of the territories to which this Chapter applies, no less than in respect of their Metropolitan areas, must be based on the general principle of good-neighborliness, due account being taken of the interests and well-being of the rest of the world, in social, economic, and commercial matters.

Chapter XII. International Trusteeship System
Article 75

The United Nations shall establish under its authority an international trusteeship system for the administration and supervision of such territories as may be placed thereunder by subsequent individual agreements. These territories are hereinafter referred to as trust territories.

Article 76

The basic objectives of the trusteeship system, in accordance with the Purposes of the United Nations laid down in Article 1 of the present Charter, shall be:

a. to further international peace and security;

b. to promote the political, economic, social, and educational advancement of the inhabitants of the trust territories, and their progressive development towards self-government or independence as may be appropriate to the particular circumstances of each territory and its peoples concerned, and as may be provided by the terms of each trusteeship agreement;

c. to encourage respect for human rights and for fundamental freedoms for all without distinction as to race, sex, language, or religion, and to encourage recognition of the interdependence of the people of the world; and

d. to ensure equal treatment in social, economic, and commercial matters for all Members of the United Nations and their nationals, and also equal treatment for the latter in the administration of justice, without prejudice to the attainment of the foregoing objectives and subject to the provisions of Article 80.

Article 77

1. The trusteeship system shall apply to such territories in the following categories as may be placed thereunder by means of trusteeship agreements:

a. territories now held under mandate;

b. territories which may be detached from enemy states as a result of the Second World War; and

c. territories voluntarily placed under the system by states responsible for their administration.

2. It will be a matter for subsequent agreement as to which territories in the foregoing categories will be brought under the trusteeship system and upon what terms.

Article 78

The trusteeship system shall not apply to territories which have become Members of the United Nations, relationship among which shall be based on respect for the principle of sovereign equality.

Article 79

The terms of trusteeship for each territory to be placed under the trusteeship system, including any alteration or amendment, shall be agreed upon by the states directly concerned, including the mandatory power in the case of territories held under mandate by a Member of the United Nations, and shall be approved for in Articles 83 and 85.

Article 80

1. Except as may be agreed upon in individual trusteeship agreements, made under Articles 77, 79, and 81, placing each territory under the trusteeship system, and until such agreements have been concluded, nothing in this Chapter shall be construed in or of itself to alter in any manner the rights whatsoever of any states or any peoples or the terms of existing international instruments to which Members of the United Nations may respectively be parties.

2. Paragraph 1 of this Article shall not be interpreted as giving grounds for delay or postponement of the negotiation and conclusion of agreements for placing mandated and other territories under the trusteeship system as provided for in Article 77.

Article 81

The trusteeship agreement shall in each case include the terms under which the trust territory will be administered and designate the authority which will exercise the administration of the trust territory. Such authority, hereinafter called the administering authority, may be one or more states or the Organization itself.

Article 82

There may be designated, in any trusteeship agreement, a strategic area or areas which may include part or all of the trust territory to which the agreement applies, without prejudice to any special agreement or agreements made under Article 43.

Article 83

1. All functions of the United Nations relating to strategic areas, including the approval of the terms of the trusteeship agreements and of their alteration or amendment, shall be exercised by the Security Council.

2. The basic objectives set forth in Article 76 shall be applicable to the people of each strategic area.

3. The Security Council shall, subject to the provisions of the trusteeship agreements and without prejudice to security considerations, avail itself of the assistance of the Trusteeship Council to perform those functions of the United Nations under the trusteeship system relating to political, economic, social, and educational matters in the strategic areas.

Article 84

It shall be the duty of the administering authority to ensure that the trust territory shall play its part in the maintenance of international peace and security. To this end the administering authority may make use of volunteer forces, facilities, and assistance from the trust territory in carrying out the obligations towards the Security Council undertaken in this regard by the administering authority, as well as for local defence and the maintenance of law and order within the trust territory.

Article 85

1. The functions of the United Nations with regard to trusteeship agreements for all areas not designated as strategic, including the approval of the terms of the trusteeship agreements and of their alteration or amendment, shall be exercised by the General Assembly.

2. The Trusteeship Council, operating under the authority of the General Assembly, shall assist the General Assembly in carrying out these functions.

Chapter XIII. The Trusteeship Council
Composition
Article 86

1. The Trusteeship Council shall consist of the following Members of the United Nations:

a. those Members administering trust territories;

b. such of those Members mentioned by name in Article 23 as are not administering trust territories; and

c. as many other Members elected for three-year terms by the General Assembly as may be necessary to ensure that the total number of members of the Trusteeship Council is equally divided between those Members of the United Nations which administer trust territories and those which do not.

2. Each member of the Trusteeship Council shall designate one specially qualified person to represent it therein.

Functions and Powers
Article 87

The General Assembly and, under its authority, the Trusteeship Council, in carrying out their functions, may:

a. consider reports submitted by the administering authority;

b. accept petitions and examine them in consultation with the administering authority;

c. provide for periodic visits to the respective trust territories at times agreed upon with the administering authority; and

d. take these and other actions in conformity with the terms of the trusteeship agreements.

Article 88

The Trusteeship Council shall formulate a questionnaire on the political, economic, social, and educational advancement of the inhabitants of each trust territory, and the administering authority for each trust territory within the competence of the General Assembly shall make an annual report to the General Assembly upon the basis of such questionnaire.

Voting
Article 89

1. Each member of the Trusteeship Council shall have one vote.

2. Decisions of the Trusteeship Council shall be made by a majority of the members present and voting.

Procedure
Article 90

1. The Trusteeship Council shall adopt its own rules of procedure, including the method of selecting its President.

2. The Trusteeship Council shall meet as required in accordance with its rules, which shall include provision for the convening of meetings on the request of a majority of its members.

Article 91

The Trusteeship Council shall, when appropriate, avail itself of the assistance of the Economic and Social Council and of the specialized agencies in regard to matters with which they are respectively concerned.

Chapter XIV. The International Court of Justice
Article 92

The International Court of Justice shall be the principal judicial organ of the United Nations. It shall function in accordance with the annexed Statute, which is based upon the Statute of the Permanent Court of International Justice and forms an integral part of the present Charter.

Article 93

1. All Members of the United Nations are ipso facto parties to the Statute of the International Court of Justice.

2. A state which is not a Member of the United Nations may become a party to the Statute of the International Court of Justice on conditions to be determined in each case by the General Assembly upon the recommendation of the Security Council.

Article 94

1. Each member of the United Nations undertakes to comply with the decision of the International Court of Justice in any case to which it is a party.

2. If any party to a case fails to perform the obligations incumbent upon it under a judgment rendered by the Court, the other party may have recourse to the Security Council, which may, if it deems necessary, make recommendations or decide upon measures to be taken to give effect to the judgment.

Article 95

Nothing in the present Charter shall prevent Members of the United Nations from entrusting the solution of their differences to other tribunals by virtue of agreements already in existence or which may be concluded in the future.

Article 96

1. The General Assembly or the Security Council may request the International Court of Justice to give an advisory opinion on any legal question.

2. Other organs of the United Nations and specialized agencies, which may at any time be so authorized by the General Assembly, may also request advisory opinions of the Court on legal questions arising within the scope of their activities.

Chapter XV. The Secretariat
Article 97

The Secretariat shall comprise a Secretary-General and such staff as the Organization may require. The Secretary-General shall be appointed by the General Assembly upon the recommendation of the Security Council. He shall be the chief administrative officer of the Organization.

Article 98

The Secretary-General shall act in that capacity in all meetings of the General Assembly, of the Security Council, of the Economic and Social Council, and of the Trusteeship Council, and shall perform such other functions as are entrusted to him by these organs. The Secretary-General shall make an annual report to the General Assembly on the work of the Organization.

Article 99

The Secretary-General may bring to the attention of the Security Council any matter which in his opinion may threaten the maintenance of international peace and security.

Article 100

1. In the performance of their duties the Secretary-General and the staff shall not seek or receive instructions from any government or from any other authority external to the Organization. They shall refrain from any action which might reflect on their position as international officials responsible only to the Organization.

2. Each Member of the United Nations undertakes to respect the exclusively international character of the responsibilities of the Secretary-General and the staff and not to seek to influence them in the discharge of their responsibilities.

Article 101

1. The staff shall be appointed by the Secretary-General under regulations established by the General Assembly.

2. Appropriate staffs shall be permanently assigned to the Economic and Social Council, the Trusteeship Council, and, as required, to the other organs of the United Nations. These staffs shall form a part of the Secretariat.

3. The paramount consideration in the employment of the staff and in the determination of the conditions of service shall be the necessity of securing the highest standards of efficiency, competence, and integrity. Due regard shall be paid to the importance of recruiting the staff on as wide a geographical basis as possible.

Chapter XVI. Miscellaneous Provisions
Article 102

1. Every treaty and every international agreement entered into by any Member of the United Nations after the present Charter comes into force shall as soon as possible be registered with the Secretariat and published by it.

2. No party to any such treaty or international agreement which has not been registered in accordance with the provisions of paragraph 1 of this Article may invoke that treaty or agreement before any organ of the United Nations.

Article 103

In the event of a conflict between the obligations of the Members of the United Nations under the present Charter and their obligations under any other international agreement, their obligations under the present Charter shall prevail.

Article 104

The Organization shall enjoy in the territory of each of its Members such legal capacity as may be necessary for the exercise of its functions and the fulfillment of its purposes.

Article 105

1. The Organization shall enjoy in the territory of each of its Members such privileges and immunities as are necessary for the fulfillment of its purposes.

2. Representatives of the Members of the United Nations and officials of the Organization shall enjoy such privileges and immunities as are necessary for the independent exercise of their function in connexion with the Organization.

3. The General Assembly may make recommendations with a view to determining the details of the application of paragraphs 1 and 2 of this Article or may propose conventions to the Members of the United Nations for this purpose.

Chapter XVII. Transitional Security Arrangements
Article 106

Pending the coming into force of such special agreements referred to in Article 43 as in the opinion of the Security Council enable it to begin the exercise of its responsibilities under Article 42, the parties to the Four-Nation Declaration, signed at Moscow, 30 October 1943, and France, shall, in accordance with the provisions of paragraph 5 of that Declaration, consult with one another and as occasion requires with other Members of the United Nations with a view to such joint action on behalf of the Organization as may be necessary for the purpose of maintaining international peace and security.

Article 107

Nothing in the present Charter shall invalidate or preclude action, in relation to any state which during the Second World War has been an enemy of any signatory to the present Charter, taken or authorized as a result of that war by the Governments having responsibility for such action.

Chapter XVIII. Amendments
Article 108

Amendments to the present Charter shall come into force for all Members of the United Nations when they have been adopted by a vote of two-thirds of the members of the General Assembly and ratified in accordance with their respective constitutional processes by two-thirds of the Members of the United Nations, including all the permanent members of the Security Council.

Article 109

1. A General Conference of the Members of the United Nations for the purpose of reviewing the present Charter may be held at a date and place to be fixed by a two-thirds vote of the members of the General Assembly and by a vote of any nine members of the Security Council. Each Member of the United Nations shall have one vote in the conference.

2. Any alteration of the present Charter recommended by a two-thirds vote of the conference shall take effect when ratified in accordance with their respective constitutional processes by two-thirds of the Members of the United Nations including all permanent members of the Security Council.

3. If such a conference has not been held before the tenth annual session of the General Assembly following the coming into force of the present Charter, the proposal to call such a conference shall be held if so decided by a majority vote of the members of the General Assembly and by a vote of any seven members of the Security Council.

Chapter XIX. Ratification and Signature
Article 110

1. The present Charter shall be ratified by the signatory states in accordance with their respective constitutional processes.

2. The ratifications shall be deposited with the Government of the United States of America, which shall notify all the signatory states of each deposit as well as the Secretary-General of the Organization when he has been appointed.

3. The present Charter shall come into force upon the deposit of ratifications by the [People's] Republic of China, France, Union of Soviet Socialist Republics, the United Kingdom of Great Britain and Northern Ireland, and the United States of America, and by a majority of the other signatory states. A protocol of the ratifications deposited shall thereupon be drawn up by the Government of the United States of America which shall communicate copies thereof to all the signatory states.

4. The states signatory to the present Charter which ratify it after it has come into force will become original Members of the United Nations on the date of the deposit of their respective ratifications.

Article 111

The present Charter, of which the Chinese, French, Russian, English, and Spanish texts are equally authentic, shall remain deposited in the archives of the Government of the United States of America. Duly certified copies thereof shall be transmitted by that Government to the Governments of the other signatory states.

IN FAITH WHEREOF the representatives of the Governments of the United Nations have signed at the present Charter.

DONE at the city of San Francisco the twenty-sixth day of June, one thousand nine hundred and forty-five.

Notes

Chapter One
The Ghost of Woodrow Wilson

1. For Wilson's continued influence in American foreign policy long after his death, see Thomas Knock, *To End All Wars: Woodrow Wilson and the Quest for a New World Order* (New York: Oxford University Press, 1992). For the lessons policymakers learned from the League of Nations fight when creating the United Nations, see Evan Luard, *A History of the United Nations*, vol. 1: *The Years of Western Domination, 1945–1955* (New York: St. Martin's Press, 1982), pp. 3–16; and David Steigerwald, *Wilsonian Idealism* (Ithaca: Cornell University Press, 1994), pp. 139–50.

2. Knock, *To End All Wars*, p. 272.

3. Sumner Welles, *The Time for Decision* (New York: Harper & Brothers, 1944), p. 3.

4. Walter Lippmann, *U.S. War Aims* (Boston: Little, Brown, 1944), pp. 181–82.

5. The best works about Wilson and the treaty fight are Lloyd E. Ambrosius, *Woodrow Wilson and the American Diplomatic Tradition: The Treaty Debate in Perspective* (Cambridge: Cambridge University Press, 1987); Kurt Wimer, "Woodrow Wilson Tries Conciliation: An Effort that Failed," *Historian* 25 (1963), pp. 419–38; and William C. Widenor, *Henry Cabot Lodge and the Search for an American Foreign Policy* (Berkeley: University of California Press, 1979), pp. 104–28.

6. Gene Smith, *When the Cheering Stopped: The Last Years of Woodrow Wilson* (New York: Time, 1964), p. 43.

7. Ibid., p. 53.

8. Ibid., p. 54.

9. Thomas A. Baily, *Woodrow Wilson and the Great Betrayal* (New York: Macmillan, 1944), pp. 185–86; Widenor, *Henry Cabot Lodge*, pp. 266–353; and Robert A. Divine, *Second Chance: The Triumph of Internationalism in American Policy during World War II* (New York: Atheneum, 1967), pp. 8–9.

10. Jerrold M. Post and Robert S. Robins, *When Illness Strikes the Leader: The Dilemma of the Captive King* (New Haven: Yale University Press, 1993), pp. 85–90. For Wilson's physician's account, see Cary Grayson, *Woodrow Wilson: An Intimate Memoir* (New York: Holt, Rinehart, and Winston, 1960).

11. Smith, *When the Cheering Stopped,* pp. 58–59.

12. J. Tumulty, *Woodrow Wilson As I Knew Him* (New York: Doubleday, Page, 1921), pp. 434–45. Also see Lloyd E. Ambrosius, "Woodrow Wilson's Health and the Treaty Fight," *International History Review* 9 (February 1987), pp. 73–84.

13. Smith, *When the Cheering Stopped,* pp. 119–20.

14. Kenrick A. Clements, *Woodrow Wilson: World Statesman* (Boston: G. K. Hall, 1987), pp. 219–20.

15. For information on Woodrow Wilson's second wife, Edith Bolling Galt, see her own often inaccurate *My Memoir* (Indianapolis: Bobbs-Merrill, 1938), and Ishbel Ross, *Power and Grace: The Life of Mrs. Woodrow Wilson* (New York: Putnam, 1975).

16. Smith, *When the Cheering Stopped,* pp. 142–44.

17. Ibid, p. 148.

18. Arthur Link, *Woodrow Wilson: Revolution, War, and Peace* (Arlington Heights, Ill.: Harlan-Davidson Press, 1979), pp. 126–27.

19. Smith, *When the Cheering Stopped,* p. 58. For the election of 1920 see Wesley M. Bagby, *The Road to Normalcy: The Presidential Campaign and Election of 1920* (Baltimore: Johns Hopkins University Press, 1962).

20. For FDR's varying views of the League see Willard Range, *Franklin D. Roosevelt's World Order* (Athens: University of Georgia Press, 1959), pp. 162–70; Eleanor Roosevelt, *The Autobiography of Eleanor Roosevelt* (New York: Harper, 1958), p. 101; Robert Dallek, *Franklin D. Roosevelt and American Foreign Policy, 1932–1945* (New York: Oxford University Press, 1979), pp. 13–14; and Georg Schild, *Bretton Woods and Dumbarton Oaks: American Economic and Political Postwar Planning in the Summer of 1944* (New York: St. Martin's Press, 1995), pp. 19–21.

21. Georg Schild, "The Roosevelt Administration and the United Nations," *World Affairs* (Summer 1995), pp. 26–34.

22. Sumner Welles, *Seven Decisions That Shaped History* (New York: Harper & Brothers, 1951), p. 176.

23. Frank Freidel, *Franklin Roosevelt: The Triumph* (Boston: Little, Brown, 1956), pp. 248–54, 308–11.

24. Ruth B. Russell, *A History of the United Nations Charter: The Role of the United States, 1940–1945* (Washington, D.C.: Brookings Institution, 1958), pp. 978–89.

25. Franklin Roosevelt, "Plan to Preserve World Peace," reprinted as appendix to Eleanor Roosevelt, *This I Remember* (New York: Harper & Brothers, 1949), pp. 353–66. FDR never entered the contest because his wife was one of the jurors. James Shotwell won first place for his article, which called for making war illegal.

26. Schild, "The Roosevelt Administration and the United Nations."

Chapter Two
A Grim Road to War

1. For histories of what led to the Atlantic Charter Conference, see Douglas Brinkley and David Facey-Crowther (eds.), *The Atlantic Charter* (New York: St. Martin's Press, 1994), and Theodore A. Wilson, *The First Summit: Roosevelt and Churchill at Placentia Bay, 1941,* revised edition (Lawrence: University Press of Kansas, 1991).

2. Harley A. Notter, *Postwar Foreign Policy Preparation, 1939–1945* (Washington, D.C.: U.S. Department of State, publication 3580, 1950), pp. 13–19.

3. David Reynolds, *The Creation of the Anglo-American Alliance, 1937–1941: A Study in Competitive Cooperation* (Chapel Hill: University of North Carolina Press, 1982), pp. 7–36.

4. William L. Langer and S. Everett Gleason, *The Challenge to Isolation, 1937–40* (New York: Harper & Brothers, 1952), p. 32; Notter, *Postwar Foreign Policy Preparation*, pp. 13–19; and Winston Churchill, *The Second World War*, 6 vols. (Boston: Houghton Mifflin, 1948–53), vol. 1, *The Gathering Storm*, pp. 280–81.

5. Churchill, *Gathering Storm*, pp. 212–15.

6. Hugh Thomas, *The Spanish Civil War* (New York: Viking Press, 1961).

7. Churchill, *Gathering Storm*, p. 29.

8. Divine, *Second Chance*, p. 29.

9. Notter, *Postwar Foreign Policy Preparation*, pp. 27–31.

10. Dallek, *Franklin Roosevelt and American Foreign Policy*, pp. 210–17; Julian G. Hurtsfield, *America and the French Nation* (Chapel Hill: University of North Carolina Press, 1986), pp. 3–15; and Richard Lewis, *Churchill as War Leader* (New York: Carroll and Graf, 1991), pp. 15–21.

11. Notter, *Postwar Foreign Policy Preparation*, pp. 27–31; Dallek, *Franklin Roosevelt and American Foreign Policy*, pp. 218–20; and Townsend Hoopes and Douglas Brinkley, *Driven Patriot: The Life and Times of James Forrestal* (New York: Knopf, 1992), pp. 115–16.

12. Dallek, *Franklin D. Roosevelt and American Foreign Policy*, pp. 241–46.

13. Akira Iriye, *Across the Pacific: An Inner History of American-East Asian Relations* (New York: Harcourt, Brace, and World, 1967).

14. Franklin Roosevelt, "The Quarantine-Aggressor Speech," October 5, 1937. President's Personal File 1820 (speech file), speech 1093, FDR Library, Hyde Park, N.Y.

15. Welles, *Seven Decisions That Shaped History*, pp. 68–76.

16. Divine, *Second Chance*, pp. 30–33. Also see Cordell Hull, *The Memoirs of Cordell Hull*, 2 vols. (New York: Macmillan, 1948), vol. II, pp. 1626–28.

17. Dulles is quoted in Divine, *Second Chance*, p. 37. Also see Ronald W. Pruessen, *John Foster Dulles: The Road to Power* (New York: Free Press, 1982), pp. 187–217.

18. Henry Luce, "The American Century," *Life*, February 17, 1941, pp. 61–65.

19. Clarence Streit, *Union Now* (New York: Harper & Brothers, 1939).

20. Divine, *Second Chance*, pp. 38–39.

21. James MacGregor Burns, *Roosevelt: The Soldier of Freedom* (New York: Harcourt Brace Jovanovich, 1970), pp. 3–29.

22. Ibid., pp. 20–21. Also see Welles, *Seven Decisions That Shaped History*, pp. 70–82.

23. Franklin D. Roosevelt, speech on May 27, 1940. Also Dallek, *Franklin D. Roosevelt and American Foreign Policy*, pp. 220–32.

24. Steve Neal, *Dark Horse: A Biography of Wendell Willkie* (Garden City, N.Y.: Doubleday, 1984), pp. 142–80.

25. Hoopes and Brinkley, *Driven Patriot*, pp. 28–29; and Mark Lincoln Chadwin, *The Warhawks: American Interventionists Before Pearl Harbor* (New York: Norton, 1968), pp. 148–49.

26. Waldo Heinrichs, *Threshold of War: Franklin D. Roosevelt and American Entry into World War II* (New York: Oxford University Press, 1988), pp. 13–117.

27. Robert E. Sherwood, *Roosevelt and Hopkins: An Intimate History* (New York: Harper & Brothers, 1948), p. 343.

28. Heinrichs, *Threshold of War*, pp. 118–45.

29. Jonathan G. Utley, *Going to War with Japan, 1937–1941* (Knoxville: University of Tennessee Press, 1985), pp. 138–82; and Heinrichs, *Threshold of War*, pp. 147–79.

Chapter Three

Argentia and the Atlantic Charter

1. Argentia Bay was also known as Placentia Bay. The meeting was held offshore near the town of Argentia. Assistant Navy Secretary Roosevelt and First Lord of the Admiralty Churchill had met briefly in 1919.

2. The Four Freedoms address of January 1941 can be found in Samuel I. Rosenman (ed.), *The Public Papers and Addresses of Franklin D. Roosevelt*, 13 vols. (New York: Macmillan, 1938–1950), vol. 9, p. 672. For FDR's New Year's Day drafting of the speech see Stuart Murray and James McCabe (eds.), *Norman Rockwell's Four Freedoms: Images that Inspire a Nation* (Stockbridge, Mass.: Berkshire House, 1993), pp. 3–7.

3. William Allen White quoted in William vanden Heuvel, "The Four Freedoms," in *Norman Rockwell's Four Freedoms*, p. 108. For the connection between the Four Freedoms speech and the Lend-Lease bill see Langer and Gleason, *The Undeclared War: 1939–1940* (New York: Harper & Row, 1952), p. 253.

4. Sumner Welles, *Where Are We Heading?* (New York: Harper & Brothers, 1946), p. 6.

5. Theodore A. Wilson, *The First Summit: Roosevelt and Churchill at Placentia Bay, 1941*, revised ed. (Lawrence: University Press of Kansas, 1991), pp. 1–20.

6. Sherwood, *Roosevelt and Hopkins*, p. 354.

7. Ibid., pp. 354–55.

8. Lloyd Gardner, "The Atlantic Charter: Idea and Reality, 1942–45," in Douglas Brinkley and David R. Facey-Crowther (eds.), *The Atlantic Charter* (New York: St. Martin's Press, 1994), pp. 44–81; Welles, *Where Are We Heading?* pp. 10–16; and Wilson, *First Summit*, pp. 81–90.

9. Wilson, *First Summit*, p. 22; and Benjamin Welles, "Sumner Welles," unpublished manuscript.

10. Quotes are from Sherwood, *Roosevelt and Hopkins*, p. 9. For a brilliant analysis of how polio changed FDR, see Geoffrey C. Ward, *A First-Class Temperament: The Emergence of Franklin Roosevelt* (New York: Harper & Row, 1989).

11. Ibid., pp. 141–43.

12. Ibid. For destroyers-for-bases deal see Robert Shogan, *Hard Bargain* (New York: Scribner, 1995); and Reynolds, *Creation of the Anglo-American Alliance, 1937–41*, pp. 121–32.

13. FDR to King George VI, November 22, 1940, Presidential letters, vol. 4, p. 1084.

14. Warren F. Kimball, *The Most Unsordid Act: Lend-Lease, 1939–1941* (Baltimore: Johns Hopkins University Press, 1969).

15. Winston Churchill, *The Second World War*, 6 vols. (Boston: Houghton Mifflin, 1948–53), vol. 3, *The Grand Alliance*, p. 431.

16. Sherwood, *Roosevelt and Hopkins*, p. 363. Also see Joseph Lash, *Roosevelt and Churchill, 1939–1941: The Partnership That Saved the West* (New York: Norton, 1976), pp.

397–404; Theodore A. Wilson, "The First Summit: FDR and the Riddle of Personal Democracy," in Brinkley and Facey-Crowther (eds.), *The Atlantic Charter,* pp. 1–31.

17. For an understanding of the intimate relationship these two leaders forged during World War II see Warren F. Kimball (ed.), *Churchill and Roosevelt: The Complete Correspondence, 1939–1945,* 3 vols. (Princeton: Princeton University Press, 1984).

18. George McJimsey, *Harry Hopkins: Ally of the Poor and Defender of Democracy* (Cambridge, Mass.: Harvard University Press, 1987); and Sherwood, *Roosevelt and Hopkins.*

19. Sherwood, *Roosevelt and Hopkins,* p. 350.

20. Irvin F. Gellman, *Secret Affairs: Franklin Roosevelt, Cordell Hull, and Sumner Welles* (Baltimore: Johns Hopkins University Press, 1995), pp. 20–30.

21. *New York Times,* August 3, 1941.

22. Gellman, *Secret Affairs,* p. 146.

23. Sherwood, *Roosevelt and Hopkins,* p. 135.

24. Benjamin Welles, "Sumner Welles."

25. *Time,* August 11, 1941.

26. Gellman, *Secret Affairs,* pp. 262–80.

27. Sumner Welles, *Where Are We Heading?* pp. 8–9.

28. Churchill, *Grand Alliance,* pp. 262–80.

29. Welles, *Where Are We Heading?* pp. 13–14; and Benjamin Welles, "Sumner Welles."

30. Dallek, *Franklin Roosevelt and American Foreign Policy,* pp. 283–300; and Sherwood, *Roosevelt and Hopkins,* pp. 359–64.

31. Sherwood, *Roosevelt and Hopkins,* p. 361.

32. The text of the Atlantic Charter can be found in Brinkley and Facey-Crowther (eds.), *The Atlantic Charter,* pp. xvii–xviii.

33. Welles, *Where Are We Heading?* p. 15.

34. Welles, *Where Are We Heading?* p. 4, and *Seven Decisions That Shaped History,* p. 178.

35. Welles, *Where Are We Heading?* p. 15.

36. Sherwood, *Roosevelt and Hopkins,* p. 360.

37. Welles, *Where Are We Heading?* pp. 15–18.

38. Anthony Eden, *The Reckoning: The Memoirs of Sir Anthony Eden, Earl of Avon* (Boston: Houghton Mifflin, 1965), p. 296; and Elisabeth Barker, *Churchill and Eden at War* (New York: St. Martin's Press, 1978), pp. 235–41.

39. Sherwood, *Roosevelt and Hopkins,* pp. 362–63.

40. David Reynolds, "The Atlantic 'Flop': British Foreign Policy and the Churchill-Roosevelt Meeting of August 1941," in Brinkley and Facey-Crowther (eds.), *The Atlantic Charter,* p. 146.

41. Welles, *Seven Decisions That Shaped History,* pp. 179–81.

Chapter Four
Postwar Planning Begins

1. Notter, *Postwar Foreign Policy Preparation,* pp. 14–20.

2. Robert D. Schulzinger, *The Wise Men of Foreign Affairs: The History of the Council on Foreign Relations* (New York: Columbia University Press, 1984).

3. Divine, *Second Chance,* pp. 32–33.

4. Divine, *Second Chance,* p. 32; and Notter, *Postwar Foreign Policy Preparation,* pp. 20–21.

5. Benjamin Welles, "Sumner Welles," unpublished manuscript.

6. Hull, *Memoirs,* vol. II, pp. 1083–94.

7. Dean Acheson, *Present at the Creation: My Years in the State Department* (New York: Norton, 1969), pp. 37–38.

8. Divine, *Second Chance,* pp. 47–48.

9. Robert C. Hilderbrand, *Dumbarton Oaks: The Origins of the United Nations in the Search for Postwar Security* (Chapel Hill: University of North Carolina Press, 1990), pp. 15–16.

10. Gellman, *Secret Affairs,* pp. 262–80; and Welles, *Seven Decisions That Shaped History,* pp. 115–16.

11. Hull, *Memoirs,* vol. II, pp. 1632–33. Also see Douglas Brinkley, "Dean Acheson and the Atlantic Community," in Francis Heller and John Gillingham (eds.), *NATO and the Atlantic Alliance* (New York: St. Martin's Press, 1993), pp. 28–54.

12. Welles, *Seven Decisions That Shaped History,* pp. 123–26.

13. Eden, *The Reckoning,* pp. 370–71.

14. Welles, *Seven Decisions That Shaped History,* p. 139.

15. Ibid.

16. Schild, *Bretton Woods and Dumbarton Oaks,* pp. 13–15; and Welles, *Seven Decisions That Shaped History,* pp. 123–35.

17. Schild, *Bretton Woods and Dumbarton Oaks,* pp. 49–59; and Notter, *Postwar Foreign Policy Preparation,* pp. 78–81. For profiles of Pasvolsky see the Edward Stettinius Dumbarton Oaks Notebooks, Stettinius Papers, University of Virginia, Charlottesville, Va.

18. Russell, *History of the United Nations Charter,* pp. 99–100.

19. Benjamin Welles, "Sumner Welles."

20. Welles, *Seven Decisions That Shaped History,* pp. 126–27; and Lydia V. Pozdeeva, "The Soviet Union: Territorial Diplomacy," in David Reynolds, Warren F. Kimball, and A. O. Chubarian (eds.), *Allies at War: The Soviet, American, and British Experience, 1939–1945* (New York: St. Martin's Press, 1994), pp. 356–85.

21. American Embassy London (Sir Stafford Cripps) to State Department Cable 1095 (March 9, 1942), Sumner Welles Papers, FDR Presidential Library, Hyde Park, N.Y.

22. FDR to Sumner Welles, handwritten, n.d., Benjamin Welles papers, Washington, D.C.

23. Eden, *The Reckoning,* p. 376; Benjamin Welles, "Sumner Welles."

24. FDR quoted in Benjamin Welles, "Sumner Welles."

25. *Foreign Relations of the United States* (hereafter *FRUS*), FDR-Stalin, April 11, 1942, 538, 542–43, and 560.

26. FDR-Molotov conversation, *FRUS,* May 1942, vol. III, pp. 575–83; and Forrest C. Pogue, *George C. Marshall: Ordeal and Hope, 1939–1942* (New York: Viking Press, 1966), pp. 325–28.

27. Benjamin Welles, "Sumner Welles;" and Sherwood, *Roosevelt and Hopkins.*

Chapter Five
The Widening Public Debate

1. Franklin D. Roosevelt, Address to the Congress on the State of the Union, January 6, 1942, FDR speeches, FDR Presidential Library (hereafter FDRL); and George Orwell, *The War Commentaries,* W. J. West (ed.), (New York: Viking Penguin, 1985), p. 201.

2. Charles DeBendetti, "Peace Was His Profession: James T. Shotwell and American

Internationalism," in Frank T. Merli and Theodore Wilson (eds.), *Makers of American Diplomacy* (New York: Charles Scribner's Sons, 1974), pp. 87–100. For Shotwell's views on postwar peace see James T. Shotwell, *The Autobiography of James T. Shotwell* (Indianapolis: Bobbs-Merrill, 1961).

3. Divine, *Second Chance,* pp. 53–54.

4. Ronald Pruessen, *John Foster Dulles,* pp. 190–217; Townsend Hoopes, *The Devil and John Foster Dulles* (Boston: Little, Brown, 1973), pp. 55–56.

5. Divine, *Second Chance,* pp. 58–59. "Union Now" was a phrase Streit used in mantra-like fashion; he published two different books whose titles include the phrase.

6. Nicholas J. Spykman, *America's Strategy in World Politics* (New York: Harcourt Brace, 1942).

7. Herbert Hoover and Hugh Gibson, *The Problems of Lasting Peace* (Garden City, N.Y.: Doubleday, 1942).

8. Walter Lippmann, *U.S. Foreign Policy: Shield of the Republic* (Boston: Little, Brown, 1943). For the importance of the book see Ronald Steel, *Walter Lippmann and the American Century* (Boston: Little, Brown, 1980), pp. 405–11.

9. Divine, *Second Chance,* pp. 126–27.

10. Henry A. Wallace, "The Price of Free World Victory," *Free World,* 3 (June 1942), pp. 9–13; and *New York Times,* May 9, 1942. The speech is most easily found in Henry A. Wallace, *Democracy Reborn* (Cornwall, N.Y.: Reynold & Hitchcock, 1944), pp. 190–200.

11. Divine, *Second Chance,* pp. 66–79. Also see Richard J. Walton, *Henry Wallace, Harry Truman and the Cold War* (New York: Viking Press, 1976), pp. 1–32, and John Morton Blum (ed.), *The Price of Vision: The Diary of Henry A. Wallace, 1942–1946* (Boston: Houghton Mifflin, 1973).

12. Divine, *Second Chance,* p. 79.

13. *Newsweek,* January 25, 1943, p. 34.

14. *New York Times,* June 1, 1943; and Benjamin Welles, "Sumner Welles." That June Columbia University Press published a collection of Welles's pro-U.N. speeches under the title *The World of the Four Freedoms.*

15. *New York Times,* May 31, 1942; and Sumner Welles, *The World of the Four Freedoms* (New York: Columbia University Press, 1943), pp. 70–78.

16. Hull, *Memoirs,* vol. II, p. 1229.

17. Fred L. Israel (ed.), *The War Diary of Breckinridge Long: Selections from the Years 1939–1945* (Lincoln: University of Nebraska Press, 1966), pp. 271–77.

18. Beatrice Bishop Berle and Francis Jacobs (eds.), *Navigating the Rapids, 1918–1971: From the Papers of Adolf A. Berle* (New York: Harcourt, Brace & Jovanovich, 1973), p. 415, diary entry from June 24, 1942.

19. Cordell Hull, radio address, July 23, 1942, *Vital Speeches* 8 (August 1, 1942), pp. 611–13; *New York Times,* July 26, 1942.

20. Divine, *Second Chance,* pp. 67–68.

21. Neal, *Dark Horse,* pp. 231–92; and Divine, *Second Chance,* pp. 69–89.

22. Wendell Willkie, radio address, October 26, 1942, *Vital Speeches* 9 (November 1, 1942), pp. 34–39; and Donald Bruce Johnson, *The Republican Party and Wendell Willkie* (Urbana: University of Illinois Press, 1960), pp. 214–28.

23. Divine, *Second Chance,* pp. 71–74.

Chapter Six
Progress in 1943

1. Franklin Roosevelt, "The New Year's Day Statement on War and Peace" (also press conference 871) in Samuel I. Rosenman (ed.), *Public Papers and Addresses of Franklin D. Roosevelt* (New York: Harper & Brothers, 1950), pp. 3–6. Also see Russell, *History of the United Nations Charter,* p. 100.

2. Quoted in Herbert Feis, *Churchill, Roosevelt, Stalin: The War They Waged and the Peace They Sought* (Princeton: Princeton University Press, 1957), pp. 108–11.

3. Ernest K. Lindley, "The Roosevelt Doctrine," *Newsweek,* January 18, 1943, p. 34.

4. Divine, *Second Chance,* pp. 89–90.

5. Roscoe Drummond, "Senator Ball of Minnesota," *American Mercury,* 60, May 1945, pp. 530–33; and Divine, *Second Chance,* p. 92. For the full Ball Resolution text, see "Organization of the United Nations," Senate Resolution 114, *Congressional Record,* vol. 89, pt. 2, 78th Cong., 1st sess., March 16, 1943, pp. 2030, 2031.

6. Divine, *Second Chance,* p. 95.

7. Ibid., pp. 95–97.

8. *New Yorker,* May 15, 1943, p. 11. Also Divine, *Second Chance,* p. 84.

9. Hull, *Memoirs,* vol. II, p. 1639.

10. Welles, *Where Are We Heading?* p. 23.

11. Welles, *Seven Decisions That Shaped History,* p. 184.

12. Welles, *Where Are We Heading?* p. 23.

13. Ibid.

14. Benjamin Welles, "Sumner Welles;" and Welles, *Seven Decisions That Shaped History,* pp. 185–86.

15. Churchill quoted in Stanley Meisler, *United Nations: The First Fifty Years* (New York: Atlantic Monthly Press, 1995), p. 3.

16. Russell, *History of the United Nations Charter,* p. 103; and Winston Churchill, *The Second World War,* 6 vols. (Boston: Houghton Mifflin, 1948–53), vol. 4, *Hinge of Fate,* p. 562.

17. British Information Services, *British Speeches of the Day,* vol. I, April 1943, pp. 1–10.

18. Dallek, *Franklin D. Roosevelt and American Foreign Policy,* pp. 406–41.

19. Hilderbrand, *Dumbarton Oaks,* pp. 24–25.

20. Ibid. Also Russell, *History of the United Nations Charter,* pp. 92–122.

21. *FRUS,* 1943, vol. III, p. 39.

22. Russell, *History of the United Nations Charter,* pp. 92–122.

23. William H. McNeill, *America, Britain, and Russia: Their Cooperation and Conflict, 1941–1946* (New York: Oxford University Press, 1953), p. 321.

24. Churchill, *Hinge of Fate,* p. 802.

25. Russell, *History of the United Nations Charter,* pp. 100–22; and Churchill, *Hinge of Fate,* p. 802.

26. Churchill, *Hinge of Fate,* pp. 802–03.

27. Foreign Office aide-mémoire quoted in Hilderbrand, *Dumbarton Oaks,* p. 40.

28. Russell, *History of the United Nations Charter,* p. 115.

29. Forrest Davis, "Roosevelt's World Blueprint," *Saturday Evening Post,* April 10, 1943, pp. 20–21, 109–10.

Chapter Seven
Will the Russians Participate?

1. Churchill, *Hinge of Fate*, p. 807; and Russell, *History of the United Nations Charter*, p. 108. Also see Keith Sainsbury, *Churchill and Roosevelt at War* (New York: New York University Press, 1994).

2. Schild, *Bretton Woods and Dumbarton Oaks*, pp. 22–28; and Randall Bennett Woods, "FDR and the Triumph of American Nationalism," *Presidential Studies Quarterly*, 19 (1989), pp. 567–81.

3. Russell, *History of the United Nations Charter*, pp. 110–12; and Feis, *Churchill, Roosevelt, Stalin*, pp. 208–09. A good overview of the Moscow Conference can be found in Julius W. Pratt, *Cordell Hull*, vol. II (New York: Cooper Square Publishers, 1964), pp. 620–37.

4. Welles, *Time for Decision*, pp. 371–77; Russell, *History of the United Nations Charter*, pp. 112–13.

5. Russell, *History of the United Nations Charter*, p. 115.

6. Ibid., pp. 119–22. Also Notter, *Postwar Foreign Policy Preparation*, pp. 553–54.

7. H. Bullitt Orville (ed.), *For the President: Personal and Secret* (Boston: Houghton Mifflin, 1972), pp. 503–06; Sumner Welles to FDR, November 13, 1940, Benjamin Welles Papers, Washington, D.C.; and Welles, *Seven Decisions That Shaped History*, pp. 41–43.

8. Benjamin Welles, "Sumner Welles."

9. For Bullitt's view of Welles see Will Brownell and Richard Billings, *So Close to Greatness: A Biography of William C. Bullitt* (New York: Macmillan, 1987), pp. 294–301.

10. Benjamin Welles, "Sumner Welles," chapter 19, p. 6.

11. *New York Times*, August 4, 1943; and Divine, *Second Chance*, p. 139.

12. Gellman, *Secret Affairs*, pp. 302–31; Hilderbrand, *Dumbarton Oaks*, p. 24.

13. Divine, *Second Chance*, p. 139.

14. Gellman, *Secret Affairs*, pp. 332–33. For biographical information on Stettinius see Richard L. Walker, *E. R. Stettinius, Jr.*, vol. 14 in *The American Secretaries of State and Their Diplomacy*, ed. Robert Ferrell (New York: Cooper Square Publishers, 1965), pp. 1–10.

Chapter Eight
Quebec and Moscow

1. Burns, *Roosevelt: The Soldier of Freedom*, pp. 389–99; and Gaddis Smith, *American Diplomacy during the Second World War, 1941–1945* (New York: John Wiley and Sons, 1965), pp. 72–74.

2. Russell, *History of the United Nations Charter*, pp. 122–23.

3. Sainsbury, *Churchill and Roosevelt at War*, p. 73.

4. Keith Eubank, *The Summit Conferences, 1919–1960* (Norman: University of Oklahoma Press, 1966), pp. 58–78.

5. Dallek, *Franklin D. Roosevelt and American Foreign Policy*, pp. 405–30.

6. Russell, *History of the United Nations Charter*, pp. 122–24.

7. Divine, *Second Chance*, pp. 132–33; Hull, *Memoirs*, vol. II, pp. 1258–59.

8. *New York Times*, September 22, 1943; *Newsweek*, October 4, 1943; State Department

Bulletin, 9 (September 25, 1943), pp. 207–08. All of these sources are quoted in Divine, *Second Chance,* pp. 140–44.

9. Randall Bennett Woods, *Fulbright: A Biography* (Cambridge: Cambridge University Press, 1995), p. 82. Woods offers a wonderful history of the Fulbright Resolution.

10. Connally Senate Resolution, October 14, 1943, *Congressional Record (Senate)* 1943, pp. 8293–94.

11. Russell, *History of the United Nations Charter,* pp. 128–32; John R. Deane, *The Strange Alliance: The Story of Our Efforts at Wartime Cooperation with Russia* (New York: Viking, 1947), pp. 1–10.

12. Dallek, *Franklin D. Roosevelt and American Foreign Policy,* pp. 422–23; Russell, *History of the United Nations Charter,* pp. 133–43; Winston Churchill, *The Second World War,* 6 vols. (Boston: Houghton Mifflin, 1948–53), vol. 5, *Closing the Ring* (Boston: Houghton Mifflin, 1951), pp. 284–96.

13. Hull, *Memoirs,* vol. II, p. 1299; and Divine, *Second Chance.* Also see Steven Merritt Miner, "His Master's Voice: Vyacheslav Mikhailovich Molotov as Stalin's Foreign Commissar," in Gordon A. Craig and Francis L. Loewenheim (eds.), *The Diplomats, 1939–1979* (Princeton: Princeton University Press, 1994), pp. 65–100.

14. Divine, *Second Chance,* pp. 146–50; Connally Senate Resolution, October 14, 1943, *Congressional Record (Senate).*

15. *New York Times,* November 3, 1943; *Newsweek,* November 15, 1943, pp. 42–54; and Divine, *Second Chance,* p. 150.

16. *New York Times* is quoted in Divine, *Second Chance,* p. 153.

17. Walter Lippmann to FDR, November 2, 1943, FDR Papers, PPF, 2037, FDRL.

18. Raymond Moley article in *Newsweek,* November 5, 1943, p. 112.

19. Divine, *Second Chance,* p. 154.

20. Cordell Hull, speech to Congress, November 18, 1943, State Department *Bulletin,* 9 (November 20, 1943), pp. 341–45. Also see Hull, *Memoirs,* vol. II, p. 1314.

21. Quoted in Russell, *History of the United Nations Charter.*

22. Russell, *History of the United Nations Charter,* pp. 144–45.

Chapter Nine
Cairo and Teheran

1. Dallek, *Franklin D. Roosevelt and American Foreign Policy,* pp. 418–24; and Russell, *History of the United Nations Charter,* pp. 125–46.

2. Feis, *Churchill, Roosevelt, Stalin.*

3. Burns, *Roosevelt: The Soldier of Freedom,* pp. 390–417. Keith Eubank, *Summit at Teheran* (New York: Morrow, 1985).

4. Churchill, *Closing the Ring,* pp. 314–20.

5. Sainsbury, *Churchill and Roosevelt at War,* pp. 160–78.

6. Sherwood, *Roosevelt and Hopkins,* p. 772.

7. Mountbatten quoted in Charles F. Romanus and Riley Sunderland, *Stilwell's Command Problems* (Washington, D.C.: Department of Army Historical Division, 1956), p. 65.

8. State Department *Bulletin,* 9 (December 4, 1943).

9. Sherwood, *Roosevelt and Hopkins,* p. 776.

10. Ibid., pp. 776–77.

11. *FRUS,* Teheran conference, Roosevelt-Stalin meeting, November 28, 1943, pp. 482–86. Also W. Averell Harriman and Elie Abel, *Special Envoy to Churchill and Stalin, 1941–1946* (New York: Random House, 1975), pp. 256–83.
12. Sherwood, *Roosevelt and Hopkins,* p. 781.
13. Russell, *History of the United Nations Charter,* pp. 154–55.
14. Dallek, *Franklin D. Roosevelt and American Foreign Policy,* pp. 418–41.
15. Russell, *History of the United Nations Charter,* p. 155.
16. Churchill, *Closing the Ring,* p. 363.
17. Benjamin Welles, "Sumner Welles."
18. Divine, *Second Chance,* p. 158.
19. Welles, *Seven Decisions That Shaped History,* p. 172.
20. Sherwood, *Roosevelt and Hopkins,* pp. 802–03.
21. Russell, *History of the United Nations Charter,* p. 156.
22. Quoted in Sherwood, *Roosevelt and Hopkins,* p. 790.
23. Hull, *Memoirs,* vol. II, p. 1266. The Curzon Line was the Russo-Polish border established in 1919 by the Versailles Treaty.
24. Welles, *Seven Decisions That Shaped History,* p. 136.
25. Burns, *Roosevelt: The Soldier of Freedom,* pp. 390–410; and Smith, *American Diplomacy during the Second World War,* pp. 59–79.
26. Sherwood, *Roosevelt and Hopkins,* p. 789.
27. *FRUS: Conference at Cairo and Teheran, 1943,* and the original Teheran Communiqué courtesy of FDRL (with handwritten notes from FDR).
28. Quoted in Dallek, *Franklin D. Roosevelt and American Foreign Policy,* p. 439.
29. Sherwood, *Roosevelt and Hopkins,* pp. 798–99; and Burns, *Roosevelt: The Soldier of Freedom,* pp. 410–17.
30. FDR to Sumner Welles, January 4, 1944, Sumner Welles Papers.
31. Sherwood, *Roosevelt and Hopkins,* p. 799.
32. Churchill, *Closing the Ring,* pp. 405–06.
33. Quoted in Dallek, *Franklin D. Roosevelt and American Foreign Policy,* pp. 439–40.
34. Sherwood, *Roosevelt and Hopkins,* p. 804.
35. *New York Times,* December 25, 1943; and FDR Speech, State Department *Bulletin,* 10 (January 1, 1944), pp. 3–7.
36. Divine, *Second Chance,* pp. 159–60.

Chapter Ten
High Hopes But Inherent Limits

1. Hilderbrand, *Dumbarton Oaks,* p. 105.
2. Cordell Hull to FDR, December 29, 1943 (cover letter), to "Plan for the Establishment of an International Organization for the Maintenance of International Peace and Security," December 23, 1943. Both documents can be found as Appendix F in Russell, *History of the United Nations Charter,* pp. 991–95.
3. Notter, *Postwar Foreign Policy Preparation,* p. 256; and Welles, *Where Are We Heading?* pp. 31–32.
4. Schild, *Bretton Woods and Dumbarton Oaks,* p. 59; and Notter, *Postwar Foreign Policy Preparation,* pp. 250–58.

5. For biographical information on Stettinius see Walker, *Stettinius,* and Thomas M. Campbell and George Herring (eds.), *The Diaries of Edward R. Stettinius, Jr., 1943–1946* (New York: New Viewpoints, 1975). Clinton Anderson, with Milton Viorst, *Outsider in the Senate: Senator Clinton Anderson's Memoirs* (New York: World, 1970), p. 74. Acheson's quotation is in Acheson, *Present at the Creation,* p. 88.

6. Thomas M. Campbell, *Masquerade Peace: America's U.N. Policy, 1944–1945* (Tallahassee: Florida State University Press, 1973), pp. 1–25.

7. Postwar Planning Draft Statement, March 15, 1944, State Department Postwar Planning Committee, Box 141, National Archives, Washington, D.C.

8. Hilderbrand, *Dumbarton Oaks,* pp. 5–29.

9. Schild, *Bretton Woods and Dumbarton Oaks,* pp. 49–73.

10. Hilderbrand, *Dumbarton Oaks,* pp. 6–7.

11. Russell, *History of the United Nations Charter,* pp. 271–75.

12. Hilderbrand, *Dumbarton Oaks,* p. 36.

13. Notter, *Postwar Foreign Policy Preparation,* p. 256.

14. Hilderbrand, *Dumbarton Oaks,* p. 35.

15. Ibid., pp. 32–35.

16. Russell, *History of the United Nations Charter,* pp. 273–75.

17. Ibid., pp. 234–37.

18. Hull, *Memoirs,* vol. II, p. 1596; Russell, *History of the United Nations Charter,* pp. 166–275.

19. FDR to Cordell Hull, January 24, 1944, reprinted in Russell, *History of the United Nations Charter,* p. 174.

20. Notter, *Postwar Foreign Policy Preparation,* pp. 472–83; Russell, *History of the United Nations Charter,* pp. 337–39.

21. Dallek, *Franklin D. Roosevelt and American Foreign Policy,* p. 460.

22. Henry Stimson and McGeorge Bundy, *On Active Service in Peace and War* (New York: Harper & Brothers, 1947–48), pp. 600–01.

23. Walter Millis with Eugene Duffield (eds.), *The Forrestal Diaries* (New York: Viking Press, 1951), p. 8.

24. *FRUS: The Conference at Malta and Yalta, 1945,* p. 107n.

25. Hilderbrand, *Dumbarton Oaks,* p. 37.

26. Ibid., p. 47.

27. Russell, *History of the United Nations Charter,* p. 393.

28. Notter, *Postwar Foreign Policy Preparation,* p. 278; Hilderbrand, *Dumbarton Oaks,* p. 61; and Feis, *Churchill, Roosevelt, Stalin,* p. 253.

Chapter Eleven
Domestic Politics in 1944

1. Divine, *Second Chance,* pp. 192–93.

2. Joseph H. Ball, "Your Move, Mister President," *Saturday Evening Post,* February 19, 1944, p. 19; and Divine, *Second Chance,* pp. 193–94.

3. State Department *Bulletin,* 10 (April 15, 1944), pp. 335–42; and *New York Times,* April 10, 1943.

4. Russell, *History of the United Nations Charter,* pp. 194–95.

5. Arthur H. Vandenberg, Jr. (ed.), *The Private Papers of Senator Vandenberg* (Boston: Houghton Mifflin, 1952), pp. 95–96.
6. Ibid.
7. Russell, *History of the United Nations Charter*, p. 195.
8. Hull, *Memoirs*, vol. II, pp. 1662–64.
9. Forrest Davis, "What Really Happened at Teheran," *Saturday Evening Post*, May 13, 1944, p. 13, and May 20, 1944, p. 22.
10. Divine, *Second Chance*, pp. 200–10. *Saturday Evening Post*, June 24, 1944, p. 104.
11. Divine, *Second Chance*, pp. 200–03.
12. Ibid., pp. 204–06.
13. Ibid. Also *Time*, June 26, 1944, p. 18.
14. Divine, *Second Chance*, pp. 206–08.
15. Burns, *Roosevelt: The Soldier of Freedom, 1940–1945*, pp. 513–16; and William C. Widenor, "American Planning for the United Nations: Have We Been Asking the Right Questions?" *Diplomatic History*, 6, 1982, pp. 245–65. Also see Welles, *Time for Decision*; Walter Lippmann, *U.S. War Aims*; and Reinhold Niebuhr, *Children of Light and Children of Darkness* (New York: Scribner's, 1944).
16. For information on the Dumbarton Oaks mansion see Joseph H. Alsop (with Adam Platt), *"I've Seen the Best of It": Memoirs* (New York: Norton, 1992), pp. 88–90.
17. Hull, *Memoirs*, vol. II, pp. 1671–73.
18. Russell, *History of the United Nations Charter*, pp. 392–408. Acheson, *Present at the Creation*.
19. Richardson Dougall, "The U.S. Department of State from Hull to Acheson," in Craig and Loewenheim (eds.), *The Diplomats, 1939–1979*, pp. 39–64.
20. Stettinius Diary, April 12 and 19, 1944, University of Virginia Library, Charlottesville, Virginia; Alexander Cadogan, *Diaries of Sir Alexander Cadogan, O.M., 1938–1945*, edited by David Dilks (New York: Putnam, 1972), pp. 617–18. Both quoted in Hilderbrand, *Dumbarton Oaks*, pp. 68–69.
21. Hilderbrand, *Dumbarton Oaks*, p. 69.

Chapter Twelve
The Dumbarton Oaks Conference I

1. Meisler, *United Nations: The First Fifty Years*, pp. 4–5.
2. James Reston, *Deadline* (New York: Random House, 1991), pp. 134–35.
3. Statement by the Committee of the State Department Correspondents Association, August 24, 1944, Harley Notter File, General Records of the Department of State, National Archives, Washington, D.C.
4. Divine, *Second Chance*, p. 221. *Detroit Free Press* quoted in Campbell, *Masquerade Peace*, p. 30.
5. Stettinius Conference Calendar Notes for September 5, 1944, Stettinius Papers, University of Virginia.
6. The membership rosters of the four delegations at Dumbarton Oaks can be found as an appendix in Hilderbrand, *Dumbarton Oaks*, pp. 258–60.
7. Stettinius, Dumbarton Oaks Diary, August 22, 1944, Stettinius Papers, University of Virginia. Also see Campbell, *Masquerade Peace*, p. 32.

8. McNeill, *America, Britain, and Russia,* p. 501.
9. Dallek, *Franklin D. Roosevelt and American Foreign Policy,* pp. 442–84.
10. Russell, *History of the United Nations Charter,* pp. 178–79.
11. Dwight D. Eisenhower, *Crusade in Europe* (Garden City, N.Y.: Doubleday, 1948), p. 218.
12. Warren F. Kimball, *Swords or Ploughshares? The Morgenthau Plan for Defeated Nazi Germany, 1943–1946* (Philadelphia: Lippincott, 1976); and John Morton Blum, *From the Morgenthau Diaries,* vol. 3: *Years of War, 1941–45* (Boston: Houghton Mifflin, 1967).
13. Dallek, *Franklin D. Roosevelt and American Foreign Policy,* p. 474; and Churchill, *The Second World War,* 6 vols. (Boston: Houghton Mifflin, 1948–53), vol. 6, *Triumph and Tragedy,* p. 156.
14. Quoted in Dallek, *Franklin D. Roosevelt and American Foreign Policy,* p. 477.
15. Ibid., pp. 463–84.
16. Burns, *Roosevelt: The Soldier of Freedom,* p. 535.
17. Quoted in Dallek, *Franklin D. Roosevelt and American Foreign Policy,* p. 468.
18. Quoted in Russell, *History of the United Nations Charter,* pp. 183–85.
19. Schild, *Bretton Woods and Dumbarton Oaks,* pp. 45–47; and Dallek, *Franklin D. Roosevelt and American Foreign Policy,* pp. 466–79.
20. Edward M. Bennett, *Franklin D. Roosevelt and the Search for Victory* (Wilmington, Del.: Scholarly Resources, 1990), pp. 127–44.
21. Campbell, *Masquerade Peace,* pp. 34–38.
22. *FRUS,* 1944, vol. I, p. 735; the *Zvezda* article quoted in Campbell, *Masquerade Peace,* pp. 36–37.
23. Schild, *Bretton Woods and Dumbarton Oaks,* pp. 156–66.
24. Campbell, *Masquerade Peace,* p. 37.
25. Ibid., pp. 39–45. Also Schild, *Bretton Woods and Dumbarton Oaks,* and Russell, *History of the United Nations Charter.*
26. Arthur S. Vandenberg to Cordell Hull, August 29, 1944, Stettinius Papers, University of Virginia.
27. Schild, *Bretton Woods and Dumbarton Oaks,* pp. 156–67.
28. Meisler, *United Nations: The First Fifty Years,* pp. 1–20.
29. Hilderbrand, *Dumbarton Oaks,* pp. 95–97; and Campbell, *Masquerade Peace,* p. 41.
30. Russell, *History of the United Nations Charter,* pp. 445–57.
31. Ibid.
32. Hilderbrand, *Dumbarton Oaks,* p. 96; Dallek, *Franklin D. Roosevelt and American Foreign Policy,* pp. 466–67.
33. Hilderbrand, *Dumbarton Oaks,* pp. 97–98.
34. Divine, *Second Chance,* p. 225; Dallek, *Franklin D. Roosevelt and American Foreign Policy,* p. 467; and Hilderbrand, *Dumbarton Oaks,* p. 99.

Chapter Thirteen
The Dumbarton Oaks Conference II

1. Stettinius, Dumbarton Oaks Diary, August 29, 1944, Stettinius Papers, University of Virginia.

2. Hilderbrand, *Dumbarton Oaks*, p. 217.

3. *FRUS,* 1944, vol. I, pp. 772–76.

4. *FRUS,* 1944, vol. I, pp. 784–86.

5. Feis, *Churchill, Roosevelt, Stalin,* pp. 430–33; Hull, *Memoirs,* vol. II, pp. 1678–80; and Divine, *Second Chance,* pp. 225–26.

6. Edward R. Stettinius, *Roosevelt and the Russians: The Yalta Conference,* ed. Walter Johnson (Garden City, N.Y.: Doubleday, 1949), pp. 18–22.

7. Hilderbrand, *Dumbarton Oaks,* pp. 214–17.

8. Campbell, *Masquerade Peace,* pp. 48–49; and *FRUS,* 1944, vol. I, pp. 798–804.

9. Campbell, *Masquerade Peace,* p. 49; and *FRUS,* 1944, vol. I, pp. 805–06.

10. Feis, *Churchill, Roosevelt, Stalin,* pp. 410–11.

11. Campbell, *Masquerade Peace,* pp. 52–53.

12. Hilderbrand, *Dumbarton Oaks,* p. 222.

13. Ibid., p. 211.

14. Campbell, *Masquerade Peace,* p. 53.

15. Stettinius, Dumbarton Oaks, Calendar notes, September 1944, Stettinius Papers, University of Virginia.

16. Hilderbrand, *Dumbarton Oaks,* p. 220.

17. Israel (ed.), *War Diary of Breckinridge Long,* pp. 216–20; and Hilderbrand, *Dumbarton Oaks,* p. 221.

18. Campbell, *Masquerade Peace,* pp. 55–57.

19. Ibid., p. 56.

20. Divine, *Second Chance,* p. 226.

21. Israel (ed.), *The War Diary of Breckinridge Long,* pp. 376–77. The Koo conversations took place on August 30, 1944.

22. Divine, *Second Chance,* p. 227.

23. Webster is quoted in Hilderbrand, *Dumbarton Oaks,* p. 223.

24. State Department *Bulletin,* 11 (October 8, 1944), pp. 365–74.

25. Hilderbrand, *Dumbarton Oaks,* pp. 245–57.

Chapter Fourteen
The 1944 Election

1. William D. Leahy, *I Was There* (New York: McGraw-Hill, 1950), p. 239.

2. Robert E. Gilbert, "Disability, Illness, and the Presidency: The Case of Franklin D. Roosevelt," *Politics and Life Sciences,* 7 (no. 1) (August 1988), pp. 33–49.

3. Dallek, *Franklin D. Roosevelt and American Foreign Policy,* p. 413. FDR, January 11, 1944, State of the Union, FDR speeches, Franklin Roosevelt Library, Hyde Park, N.Y.

4. Burns, *Roosevelt: The Soldier of Freedom,* p. 424.

5. Ibid., pp. 498–507.

6. Alonzo L. Hamby, *Man of the People: A Life of Harry S. Truman* (New York: Oxford University Press, 1995), pp. 278–90.

7. Gilbert, "Disability, Illness, and the Presidency," p. 40.

8. Divine, *Second Chance,* pp. 209–10.

9. *New Republic,* June 26, 1944, p. 833.

10. Divine, *Second Chance,* pp. 215–16.
11. Hoopes, *The Devil and John Foster Dulles,* p. 57; and Pruessen, *John Foster Dulles,* pp. 218–34.
12. Divine, *Second Chance,* p. 219.
13. Franklin Roosevelt, "Remarks to the Men from the U.S.S. *Baltimore,*" August 9, 1944, PPS 1820 (President's Speech File), 1522, FDRL. Also see Burns, *Roosevelt: The Soldier of Freedom,* pp. 507–09.
14. David McCullough, *Truman* (New York: Simon & Schuster, 1992), p. 672.
15. Burns, *Roosevelt: The Soldier of Freedom,* pp. 521–22.
16. Divine, *Second Chance,* pp. 236–37.
17. Neal, *Dark Horse,* pp. 293–324.
18. Divine, *Second Chance,* pp. 237–38.
19. Ibid.
20. *New York Times,* November 3, 1944.
21. Divine, *Second Chance,* pp. 238–41.
22. Burns, *Roosevelt: The Soldier of Freedom,* pp. 521–34.
23. *New York Times,* November 16, 1944.
24. *New Republic,* November 20, 1944.
25. Divine, *Second Chance,* p. 242.

Chapter Fifteen
An Unsettling Winter

1. Gellman, *Secret Affairs,* p. 359.
2. Ibid., p. 362.
3. Divine, *Second Chance,* pp. 243–44.
4. Acheson, *Present at the Creation,* p. 88.
5. Walker, *Stettinius,* pp. 1–10.
6. Divine, *Second Chance,* pp. 245–47.
7. Scott Donaldson, *Archibald MacLeish: An American Life* (Boston: Houghton Mifflin, 1992), pp. 329-95.
8. Divine, *Second Chance,* pp. 246–47.
9. Ibid., pp. 250–51.
10. Pruessen, *John Foster Dulles,* p. 236.
11. Feis, *Churchill, Roosevelt, Stalin,* pp. 551–52.
12. Hoopes and Brinkley, *Driven Patriot,* pp. 233–34.
13. Dallek, *Franklin D. Roosevelt and American Foreign Policy,* pp. 503–05.
14. Divine, *Second Chance,* p. 261.
15. Franklin Roosevelt, "State of the Union Address," January 6, 1945, PPS 1820 (speech 1568), FDRL.
16. *FRUS: Conferences at Malta and Yalta, 1945,* pp. 39–40; and Dallek, *Franklin D. Roosevelt and American Foreign Policy,* pp. 506–07.
17. Burns, *Roosevelt: The Soldier of Freedom,* pp. 557–97.
18. Stephen E. Ambrose, *Rise to Globalism: American Foreign Policy since 1938,* 7th rev. ed. (New York: Penguin, 1993), pp. 15–34; and Frank Freidel, *Franklin Roosevelt: A Rendezvous with Destiny* (Boston: Little, Brown, 1990), pp. 577–92.

19. Burns, *Roosevelt: The Soldier of Freedom*, pp. 484–95; and Ambrose, *Rise to Globalism*, pp. 35–51.
20. Burns, *Roosevelt: The Soldier of Freedom*, pp. 564–80; and Diane Shaver Clemens, *Yalta* (New York: Oxford University Press, 1970), pp. 216–43.
21. Clemens, *Yalta*, pp. 113–17.
22. Stettinius, *Roosevelt and the Russians*, pp. 114–15; Churchill, *Triumph and Tragedy*, pp. 298–99; and David Robertson, *Sly and Able: A Political Biography of James F. Byrnes* (New York: Norton, 1994), pp. 348–89.
23. Dallek, *Franklin D. Roosevelt and American Foreign Policy*, p. 510; and Divine, *Second Chance*, p. 265.
24. Clemens, *Yalta*, pp. 216–43; and Freidel, *Franklin D. Roosevelt*, pp. 585–92; and Robertson, *Sly and Able*.
25. Hoopes and Brinkley, *Driven Patriot*, p. 235.
26. Stettinius, *Roosevelt and the Russians*, pp. 190–91.
27. Ibid., pp. 280–82. Also *FRUS: Malta and Yalta*, pp. 969–73.
28. Sherwood, *Roosevelt and Hopkins*, pp. 869–70.
29. Divine, *Second Chance*, pp. 267–68.
30. *Time*, February 19, 1945.
31. *Newsweek*, February 19, 1945.
32. Divine, *Second Chance*, p. 268. Also see Clark Eichelberger, *Organizing for Peace: A Personal History of the Founding of the United Nations* (New York: Harper, 1977).
33. Burns, *Roosevelt: The Soldier of Freedom*, p. 579.
34. Dallek, *Franklin D. Roosevelt and American Foreign Policy*, p. 520; and Divine, *Second Chance*, p. 270.
35. Ibid.
36. Franklin Roosevelt, "Message to Congress Regarding the Yalta Conference," March 1, 1945, PPS 1820 (speech 1572), FDRL.
37. Berle and Jacobs (eds.), *Navigating the Rapids*, pp. 476–77; and Luard, *History of the United Nations*, vol. 1, pp. 29–36.
38. Dallek, *Franklin D. Roosevelt and American Foreign Policy*, p. 522; and Divine, *Second Chance*, pp. 270–71.
39. Vandenberg, *Private Papers of Senator Vandenberg*, pp. 156–60.
40. Dallek, *Franklin D. Roosevelt and American Foreign Policy*, pp. 522–23; and Divine, *Second Chance*, p. 274.
41. Dallek, *Franklin D. Roosevelt and American Foreign Policy*, pp. 522–23; and Divine, *Second Chance*, p. 276.
42. Vandenberg, *Private Papers of Senator Vandenberg*, pp. 159–60 (combined diary entries from March 23 and 27, 1945). Also see Burns, *Roosevelt: The Soldier of Freedom*, pp. 599–601.
43. Divine, *Second Chance*, p. 274.
44. Sherwood, *Roosevelt and Hopkins*.
45. Dallek, *Franklin D. Roosevelt and American Foreign Policy*, p. 528; and Burns, *Roosevelt: The Soldier of Freedom*, pp. 599–612.
46. *New Republic*, April 23, 1945.

Chapter Sixteen
Contention and Compromise at San Francisco

1. Harry S Truman, *Memoirs: Year of Decision,* vol. 1 (Garden City, N.Y.: Doubleday, 1955), pp. 4–23; and Divine, *Second Chance,* pp. 279–80.
2. Luard, *History of the United Nations,* vol. 1, pp. 37–68. For U.S. Ultra intelligence gathering see Steve Schlesinger, "FDR's Five Policemen," *World Policy Journal,* 9, no. 3 (Fall 1994), pp. 88–93.
3. *New York Times,* April 26, 1945; *Time,* May 7, 1945; Hamby, *Man of the People,* pp. 317–18; and Truman, *Memoirs: Years of Decision,* vol. 1, pp. 94–95.
4. Stettinius, *Roosevelt and the Russians,* pp. 301–04; Russell, *History of the United Nations Charter,* pp. 634–35; and Campbell, *Masquerade Peace,* pp. 159–61.
5. *FRUS, 1945, General: The United Nations,* pp. 384–85; and Campbell, *Masquerade Peace,* pp. 161–63.
6. Walker, *Stettinius,* pp. 75–78; Meisler, *United Nations: The First Fifty Years,* p. 33.
7. Clemens, *Yalta,* pp. 216–43.
8. Russell, *History of the United Nations Charter,* pp. 628–29; and Churchill, *Triumph and Tragedy,* pp. 431–33.
9. State Department *Bulletin,* 12 (April 22, 1945), p. 725.
10. McCullough, *Truman,* pp. 372–76.
11. Sherwood, *Roosevelt and Hopkins,* pp. 893–98; and Vandenberg, *The Private Papers of Senator Vandenberg,* p. 178.
12. Russell, *History of the United Nations Charter,* p. 636.
13. Vandenberg, *The Private Papers of Senator Vandenberg,* pp. 181–82; and Russell, *History of the United Nations Charter,* pp. 636–38.
14. Russell, *History of the United Nations Charter,* pp. 637–39.
15. Lippmann quoted in Divine, *Second Chance,* p. 291.
16. Russell, *History of the United Nations Charter,* p. 639.
17. Campbell, *Masquerade Peace,* p. 163.
18. Russell, *History of the United Nations Charter,* pp. 636–712.
19. Divine, *Second Chance,* p. 293.
20. Shotwell, *The Autobiography of James T. Shotwell,* pp. 313–14; and Divine, *Second Chance,* pp. 291–92.
21. Campbell, *Masquerade Peace,* p. 164.
22. Russell, *History of the United Nations Charter,* p. 556; and Luard, *History of the United Nations,* pp. 37–68.
23. Campbell, *Masquerade Peace,* pp. 164–67.
24. Ibid., pp. 164–75.
25. *New York Times,* March 5, 1945; and Russell, *History of the United Nations Charter,* pp. 562–66.
26. Russell, *History of the United Nations Charter,* pp. 690–92.
27. Campbell, *Masquerade Peace,* pp. 163–67.
28. Ibid., pp. 165–69.
29. Pruessen, *John Foster Dulles,* pp. 191–289.
30. Campbell, *Masquerade Peace,* pp. 167–68.
31. John Foster Dulles to Edward Stettinius, May 8, 1945, Stettinius Papers, University of Virginia, Charlottesville; and Campbell, *Masquerade Peace,* pp. 168–69.

32. Campbell, *Masquerade Peace*, p. 170.
33. *FRUS,* 1945, vol. 1, p. 547; Campbell, *Masquerade Peace*, pp. 170–71; and Stimson Diary, May 10, 1945, microfilm, Sterling Library, Yale University.
34. Russell, *History of the United Nations Charter,* pp. 697–700.
35. *FRUS,* 1945, vol. 1, pp. 672–92.
36. *FRUS,* 1945, vol. 1, p. 674. Also Campbell, *Masquerade Peace,* pp. 171–72.
37. *FRUS,* 1945, vol. 1, p. 692.
38. Russell, *History of the United Nations Charter,* pp. 1035–63.
39. Arthur Vandenberg Diary, May 13, 1945, Vandenberg Papers, Library of Congress, Washington, D.C.
40. Stettinius, San Francisco Diary, May 14, 1945, Stettinius Papers, University of Virginia.
41. Russell, *History of the United Nations Charter,* pp. 1043–44.
42. Ibid.
43. *Time,* May 14, 1945.
44. Divine, *Second Chance,* pp. 294–95; Russell, *History of the United Nations Charter,* pp. 713–49.
45. Schlesinger, "FDR's Five Policemen."
46. Campbell, *Masquerade Peace*, p. 177.
47. Russell, *History of the United Nations Charter,* pp. 720–49. Also Campbell, *Masquerade Peace,* pp. 178–82.
48. Russell, *History of the United Nations Charter,* pp. 732–35.
49. Divine, *Second Chance,* p. 295.
50. Campbell, *Masquerade Peace*, pp. 182–88.
51. Russell, *History of the United Nations Charter,* pp. 732–33; Vandenberg, *The Private Papers of Senator Vandenberg,* pp. 201–03.
52. Sherwood, *Roosevelt and Hopkins*, pp. 910–15.
53. Ibid.
54. Campbell, *Masquerade Peace*, pp. 184–90.
55. Divine, *Second Chance,* pp. 294–97.
56. Russell, *History of the United Nations Charter,* pp. 733–40.
57. Campbell, *Masquerade Peace*, pp. 188–90.
58. Hamby, *Man of the People,* p. 321. For Turner and the signing of the charter see Kathleen Teltsch, "The Early Years," in Amy Janello and Brennon Jones (eds.), *A Global Affair: An Inside Look at the United Nations* (New York: Jones and Janello, 1995), pp. 14–41.
59. Meisler, *United Nations: The First Fifty Years,* pp. 19–20.
60. Hull quoted in Divine, *Second Chance,* pp. 296–97.
61. *Time,* June 18, 1945, pp. 24–25; Gellman, *Secret Affairs,* p. 384.
62. *Nation,* June 30, 1945.

Epilogue

1. Divine, *Second Chance,* pp. 303–15.
2. Two particularly good studies of the Cold War during the Truman years are John Lewis Gaddis, *The United States and the Origins of the Cold War, 1941–1947* (New York:

Columbia University Press, 1972), and Melvyn P. Leffler, *A Preponderance of Power: National Security, the Truman Administration and the Cold War* (Stanford: Stanford University Press, 1992).

3. FDR Address to Congress, March 1, 1945, FDRL, Hyde Park, N.Y.

4. For an interesting overview of U.N. accomplishments during the Cold War see Janello and Jones (eds.), *Global Affair*, and Meisler, *United Nations: The First Fifty Years.*

5. Ibid.

6. Meisler, *United Nations: The First Fifty Years,* pp. 58–59.

7. Meisler, *United Nations: The First Fifty Years,* pp. 111–12; and Hoopes, *The Devil and John Foster Dulles,* pp. 382–88.

8. Brian Urquart, *Hammarskjöld* (New York: Knopf, 1972); and Mark W. Zacher, *Dag Hammarskjöld's United Nations* (New York: Columbia University Press, 1970).

9. Arthur M. Schlesinger, Jr., *A Thousand Days: John F. Kennedy in the White House* (Boston: Houghton Mifflin, 1965); James G. Blight and David A. Welch, *On the Brink: Americans and Soviets Reexamine the Cuban Missile Crisis* (New York: Hill & Wang, 1990); and Graham T. Allison, *The Essence of Decision: Explaining the Cuban Missile Crisis* (Boston: Little, Brown, 1971).

10. *New York Times,* September 28, 1993.

11. Statistics are from the clipping files of the United Nations Association.

12. *Time,* October 23, 1995.

13. Ibid.

14. Paul Kennedy and Bruce Russett, "Reforming the United Nations," *Foreign Affairs* 74 (September–October 1995), pp. 56–71.

15. Margaret Anstee (former U.N. Under Secretary), letter to the editor, *New York Times,* October 4, 1995.

16. Jesse Helms, "Fixing the U.N." *Foreign Affairs* 75 (September–October 1996), pp. 2–7.

17. Meisler, *United Nations: The First Fifty Years,* pp. 130–48. Also Stanley Meisler, "From Great Hope to Scapegoat," *The Washington Monthly* (July–August 1996), pp. 30–34.

18. *Washington Post,* October 19, 1995.

19. *Washington Post,* June 25, 1995.

20. The full text of the United Nations Charter is reproduced in the appendix.

Bibliography

Abramson, Rudy. *Spanning the Century: The Life of W. Averell Harriman.* New York: Morrow, 1992.

Acheson, Dean. *Present at the Creation: My Years in the State Department.* New York: Norton, 1969.

Allison, Graham T. *The Essence of Decision: Explaining the Cuban Missile Crisis.* Boston: Little, Brown, 1971.

Alsop, Joseph, with Adam Platt. *"I've Seen the Best of It": Memoirs.* New York: Norton, 1992.

Ambrose, Stephen E. *Rise to Globalism: American Foreign Policy Since 1938.* 7th rev. ed. New York: Penguin Books, 1993.

Ambrosius, Lloyd E. "Woodrow Wilson's Health and the Treaty Fight." *International History Review* 9 (February 1987), pp. 73–84.

———. *Woodrow Wilson and the American Diplomatic Tradition: The Treaty Fight in Perspective.* Cambridge: Cambridge University Press, 1987.

Anderson, Clinton, with Milton Viorst. *Outsider in the Senate: Senator Clinton Anderson's Memoirs.* New York: World, 1970.

Bagby, Wesley M. *The Road to Normalcy: The Presidential Campaign and Election of 1920.* Baltimore: Johns Hopkins University Press, 1962.

Baily, Thomas A. *Woodrow Wilson and the Great Betrayal.* New York: Macmillan, 1944.

Ball, Joseph H. "Your Move, Mister President." *Saturday Evening Post,* February, 19, 1944, 19.

Barker, Elisbeth. *Churchill and Eden at War.* New York: St. Martin's Press, 1978.

Bennett, Edward M. *Franklin D. Roosevelt and the Search for Security: American-Soviet Relations, 1939–1945.* Wilmington, Del.: Scholarly Resources, 1990.

Berle, Beatrice B., and Francis Jacobs, eds. *Navigating the Rapids, 1918–1971: From the Papers of Adolf A. Berle.* New York: Harcourt Brace Jovanovich, 1973.

Blight, James G., and David A. Welch, *On the Brink: Americans and Soviets Reexamine the Cuban Missile Crisis.* New York: Hill & Wang, 1990.

Blum, John, ed. *From the Morgenthau Diaries.* 3 vols. Boston: Houghton Mifflin, 1959–67. Vol. 3, *Years of War, 1941–1945,* 1967.

Blum, John M., ed. *The Price of Vision: The Diary of Henry A. Wallace, 1942–1946.* Boston: Houghton Mifflin, 1973.

Brinkley, Douglas, and David R. Facey-Crowther, eds. *The Atlantic Charter.* New York: St. Martin's Press, 1994.

Brownell, Will, and Richard Billings. *So Close to Greatness: A Biography of William C. Bullitt.* New York: Macmillan, 1987.

Burns, James MacGregor. *Roosevelt: The Soldier of Freedom.* New York: Harcourt Brace Jovanovich, 1970.

Byrnes, James. *All in One Lifetime.* New York: Harper & Brothers, 1958.

————. Papers. Special Collections, Robert Muldrow Cooper Library, Clemson University, Clemson, S.C.

Cadogan, Sir Alexander. *The Diaries of Sir Alexander Cadogan, O.M., 1938–1945.* Edited by David Dilks. New York: Putnam, 1972.

Campbell, Thomas M. *Masquerade Peace: America's U.N. Policy, 1944–1945.* Tallahassee: Florida State University Press, 1973.

Campbell, Thomas, and George Herring, eds. *The Diaries of Edward R. Stettinius, Jr.* New York: New Viewpoints, 1975.

Chadwin, Mark Lincoln. *The Warhawks: American Interventionists Before Pearl Harbor.* New York: Norton, 1968.

Childs, Marquis. *Witness to Power.* New York: McGraw-Hill, 1975.

Churchill, Winston. *The Second World War.* 6 vols. Boston: Houghton Mifflin, 1948–53.

Clemens, Diane Shaver. *Yalta.* New York: Oxford University Press, 1970.

Clements, Kenrick A. *Woodrow Wilson: World Statesman.* Boston: Twayne, 1987.

Craig, Gordon A., and Francis L. Loewenheim, eds. *The Diplomats, 1939–1979.* Princeton: Princeton University Press, 1994.

Dallek, Robert. *Franklin D. Roosevelt and American Foreign Policy, 1932–1945.* New York: Oxford University Press, 1979.

Davis, Forrest. "Roosevelt's World Blueprint." *Saturday Evening Post,* April 10, 1943, pp. 20–21, 109–10.

Davis, Forrest. "What Really Happened at Tehran?" *Saturday Evening Post,* part 1, May 13, 1944, pp. 12–13, 37–41; and part 2, May 20, 1944, pp. 22–23, 43–48.

Deane, John R. *The Strange Alliance: The Story of Our Efforts at Wartime Cooperation with Russia.* New York: Viking, 1947.

Dilks, David, ed. *The Diaries of Sir Alexander Cadogan, 1938–1945.* New York: Putnam, 1972.

Divine, Robert A. *Second Chance: The Triumph of Internationalism in America during World War II.* New York: Atheneum, 1967.

————. *Roosevelt and World War II.* Baltimore: Johns Hopkins University Press, 1969.

Donaldson, Scott. *Archibald MacLeish: An American Life.* Boston: Houghton Mifflin, 1992.

Donovan, Frank. *Mr. Roosevelt's Four Freedoms: The Story Behind the United Nations Charter.* New York: Dodd, Mead, 1966.

Eden, Anthony. *The Reckoning: Memoirs of Sir Anthony Eden, Earl of Avon.* Boston: Houghton Mifflin, 1965.

Eichelberger, Clark M. *Organizing for Peace: A Personal History of the Founding of the United Nations.* New York: Harper, 1977.

Eubank, Keith. *The Summit Conferences, 1919–1960.* Norman: University of Oklahoma Press, 1966.

————. *Summit at Teheran.* New York: Morrow, 1985.

Farnsworth, Beatrice. *William C. Bullitt and the Soviet Union.* Bloomington: Indiana University Press, 1967.

Feis, Herbert. *Churchill, Roosevelt, Stalin: The War They Waged and the Peace They Sought.* Princeton: Princeton University Press, 1957.

Freidel, Frank. *Franklin D. Roosevelt: The Triumph.* Boston: Little, Brown, 1956.

———. *Franklin Roosevelt: A Rendezvous with Destiny*. Boston: Little, Brown, 1990.

Gaddis, John Lewis. *The United States and the Origins of the Cold War, 1941–1947*. New York: Columbia University Press, 1972.

Gellman, Irvin F. *Secret Affairs: Franklin Roosevelt, Cordell Hull, and Sumner Welles*. Baltimore: Johns Hopkins University Press, 1995.

Gilbert, Martin. *Winston S. Churchill*. 8 vols. Boston: Houghton Mifflin, 1977–83.

Goodrich, Leland M., and Edvard Hambro. *Charter of the United Nations: Commentary and Documents*. 2nd ed. Boston: World Peace Federation, 1949.

Grayson, Cary *Woodrow Wilson: An Intimate Memoir*. New York: Holt, Rinehart, and Winston, 1960.

Grollman, Catherine. "Cordell Hull and His Concept of a World Organization." Ph.D. diss., University of North Carolina, 1965.

Hamby, Alonzo L. *Man of the People: A Life of Harry S. Truman*. New York: Oxford University Press, 1995.

Harriman, W. Averell, and Abel, Elie. *Special Envoy to Churchill and Stalin, 1941–1946*. New York: Random House, 1975.

Hassett, William. *Off the Record with FDR, 1942–1945*. New Brunswick, N.J.: Rutgers University Press, 1958.

Heinrichs, Waldo. *Threshold of War: Franklin D. Roosevelt and American Entry into World War II*. New York: Oxford University Press, 1988.

Heller, Francis, and John Gillingham, eds. *NATO and the Atlantic Alliance*. New York: St. Martin's Press, 1993.

Hilderbrand, Robert C. *Dumbarton Oaks: The Origins of the United Nations and the Search for Postwar Security*. Chapel Hill: University of North Carolina Press, 1990.

Hinton, Harold. *Cordell Hull: A Biography*. New York: Doubleday, Doran, 1942.

Hoopes, Townsend. *The Devil and John Foster Dulles*. Boston: Little, Brown, 1973.

Hoopes, Townsend, and Douglas Brinkley. *Driven Patriot: The Life and Times of James Forrestal*. New York: Knopf, 1992.

Hoover, Herbert, and Hugh Gibson. *The Problems of Lasting Peace*. Garden City, N.Y.: Doubleday, 1942.

Hull, Cordell. *The Memoirs of Cordell Hull*. 2 vols. New York: Macmillan, 1948.

———. Papers. Library of Congress, Manuscript Division, Washington, D.C.

Hurtsfield, Julian G. *America and the French Nation, 1939–1945*. Chapel Hill: University of North Carolina Press, 1986.

Iriye, Akira. *Across the Pacific: An Inner History of American-East Asian Relations*. New York: Harcourt, Brace, and World, 1967.

Israel, Fred L., ed. *The War Diary of Breckinridge Long: Selections from the Years 1939–1945*. Lincoln: University of Nebraska Press, 1966.

Janello, Amy, and Brennon Jones, eds. *A Global Affair: An Inside Look at the United Nations*. New York: Jones and Janello, 1995.

Johnson, Donald Bruce. *The Republican Party and Wendell Willkie*. Urbana: University of Illinois Press, 1960.

Kennedy, Paul, and Bruce Russett. "Reforming the United Nations." *Foreign Affairs* 74 (September–October 1995), pp. 56–71.

Kimball, Warren F. *The Most Unsordid Act: Lend-Lease, 1939–1941*. Baltimore: Johns Hopkins University Press, 1969.

————. *The Juggler: Franklin Roosevelt as Wartime Statesman.* Princeton: Princeton University Press, 1991.

Kimball, Warren F., ed. *Churchill and Roosevelt: The Complete Correspondence, 1939–1945.* 3 vols. Princeton: Princeton University Press, 1984.

————. *Franklin D. Roosevelt and the World Crisis, 1939–1941.* Lexington, Mass.: Heath, 1973.

————. *Swords or Ploughshares? The Morgenthau Plan for Defeated Nazi Germany, 1943–1946.* Philadelphia: Lippincott, 1976.

Knock, Thomas J. *To End All Wars: Woodrow Wilson and the Quest for a New World Order.* Princeton: Princeton University Press, 1992.

Langer, William L., and Everett S. Gleason. *The Undeclared War: 1939–1940.* New York: Harper & Row, 1952.

Lash, Joseph P. *Eleanor and Franklin.* New York: Norton, 1971.

————. *Roosevelt and Churchill, 1931–1941: The Partnership that Saved the West.* New York: Norton, 1976.

Leahy, William D. *I Was There.* New York: McGraw-Hill, 1950.

Leffler, Melvyn P. *A Preponderance of Power: National Security, the Truman Administration and the Cold War.* Stanford: Stanford University Press, 1992.

Lewis, Richard. *Churchill as War Leader.* New York: Carroll and Graf, 1991.

Link, Arthur. *Woodrow Wilson: Revolution, War, and Peace.* Arlington Heights, Ill.: Harlan-Davidson Press, 1979.

Lippmann, Walter. *U.S. Foreign Policy: Shield of the Republic.* Boston: Little, Brown, 1943.

————. *U.S. War Aims.* Boston: Little, Brown, 1944.

Luard, Evan. *A History of the United Nations.* Vol. 1: *The Years of Western Domination, 1945–1955.* New York: St. Martin's Press, 1982.

Luce, Henry. "The American Century." *Life*, February 17, 1941, pp. 61–65.

Macmillan, Harold. *The Blast of War, 1939–1945.* New York: Harper & Row, 1968.

McCullough, David. *Truman.* New York: Simon & Schuster, 1992.

McJimsey, George. *Harry Hopkins: Ally of the Poor and Defender of Democracy.* Cambridge, Mass.: Harvard University Press, 1987.

McNeill, William H. *America, Britain, and Russia: Their Cooperation and Conflict, 1941–1946.* New York: Oxford University Press, 1953.

Meisler, Stanley. *United Nations: The First Fifty Years.* New York: Atlantic Monthly Press, 1995.

Merli, Frank T., and Theodore Wilson, eds. *Makers of American Diplomacy.* New York: Charles Scribner's Sons, 1974.

Millis, Walter, with Eugene Duffield, eds. *The Forrestal Diaries.* New York: Viking, 1951.

Morgan, Ted. *FDR: A Biography.* New York: Simon & Schuster, 1985.

Murray, Stuart, and James McCabe, eds. *Norman Rockwell's Four Freedoms: Images that Inspire a Nation.* Stockbridge, Mass.: Berkshire House, 1993.

Neal, Steve. *Dark Horse: A Biography of Wendell Willkie.* Garden City, N.Y.: Doubleday, 1984.

Niebuhr, Reinhold. *Children of Light and Children of Darkness.* New York: Scribner's, 1944.

Notter, Harley A. *Postwar Foreign Policy Preparation, 1939–1945.* Department of State Publication 3580. Washington, D.C.: GPO, 1950.

O'Conner, Raymond G. *Diplomacy for Victory: FDR and Unconditional Surrender.* New York: Norton, 1971.

Official File. Franklin D. Roosevelt Library, Hyde Park, N.Y.

O'Neill, William. *A Democracy at War: America's Fight at Home and Abroad in World War II.* New York: Free Press, 1993.

Orville, H. Bullitt, ed. *For the President: Personal and Secret.* Boston: Houghton Mifflin, 1972.

Orwell, George. *The War Commentaries* ed. W. J. West. New York: Viking Penguin, 1985.

Pasvolsky, Leo. Papers. Library of Congress, Manuscript Division, Washington, D.C.

Pogue, Forrest C. *George C. Marshall: Ordeal and Hope, 1939–1942.* New York: Viking, 1966.

———. *George C. Marshall: Organizer of Victory, 1943–1945.* New York: Viking, 1973.

Post, Jerrold M., and Robert S. Robins. *When Illness Strikes the Leader: The Dilemma of the Captive King.* New Haven: Yale University Press, 1993.

Pratt, Julius W. *Cordell Hull.* 2 vols. New York: Cooper Square, 1964.

———. *Cordell Hull: 1933–44.* Vols. 12 and 13 in *The American Secretaries of State and Their Diplomacy,* ed. Robert Ferrell. New York: Cooper Square, 1964.

Presidential Press Conferences of Franklin D. Roosevelt. Franklin D. Roosevelt Library, Hyde Park, N.Y.

President's Personal File. Franklin D. Roosevelt Library, Hyde Park, N.Y.

President's Secretary File. Franklin D. Roosevelt Library, Hyde Park, N.Y.

Pruessen, Ronald W. *John Foster Dulles: The Road to Power.* New York: Free Press, 1982.

Range, Willard. *Franklin D. Roosevelt's World Order.* Athens: University of Georgia Press, 1959.

Reston, James. *Deadline.* New York: Random House, 1991.

Reynolds, David. *The Creation of the Anglo-American Alliance, 1937–41: A Study in Competitive Cooperation.* Chapel Hill: University of North Carolina Press, 1982.

Reynolds, David, Warren F. Kimball, and A. O. Chubarian. *Allies at War: The Soviet, American, and British Experience, 1939–1945.* New York: St. Martin's Press, 1994.

Robertson, David. *Sly and Able: A Political Biography of James F. Byrnes.* New York: Norton, 1994.

Romanus, Charles F., and Riley Sunderland. *Stilwell's Command Problems.* Washington, D.C.: Department of Army Historical Division, 1956.

Roosevelt, Eleanor. *This I Remember.* New York: Harper & Brothers, 1949.

———. *The Autobiography of Eleanor Roosevelt.* New York: Harper, 1958.

Rosenman, Samuel. *Working with Roosevelt.* New York: Da Capo, 1952, 1972.

———. Papers. Franklin D. Roosevelt Library, Hyde Park, N.Y.

Rosenman, Samuel I., ed. *The Public Papers and Addresses of Franklin D. Roosevelt.* 13 vols. New York: Macmillan, 1938–50.

Ross, Ishbel. *Power and Grace: The Life of Mrs. Woodrow Wilson.* New York: Putnam, 1975.

Russell, Ruth B. *A History of the United Nation's Charter: The Role of the United States, 1940–1945.* Washington, D.C.: Brookings Institution, 1958.

Sainsbury, Keith. *Churchill and Roosevelt at War.* New York: New York University Press, 1994.

Schild, Georg. *Bretton Woods and Dumbarton Oaks: American Economic and Political Postwar Planning in the Summer of 1944.* New York: St. Martin's Press, 1995.

———. "The Roosevelt Administration and the United Nations." *World Affairs* (Summer 1995), pp. 26–34.

Schlesinger, Arthur M., Jr. *The Age of Roosevelt.* 3 vols. Boston: Houghton Mifflin, 1957–60.

———. *A Thousand Days: John F. Kennedy in the White House.* Boston: Houghton Mifflin, 1965.

Schlesinger, Stephen. "FDR's Five Policemen." *World Policy Journal,* 11, no. 3 (Fall 1994), pp. 88–93.

Schulzinger, Robert D. *The Wise Men of Foreign Affairs: The History of the Council on Foreign Relations.* New York: Columbia University Press, 1984.

Schwarz, Jordan. *Liberal: Adolf A. Berle and the Vision of an American Era.* New York: Free Press, 1987.

Sherwood, Robert E. *Roosevelt and Hopkins: An Intimate History.* New York: Harper, 1948.

Shogan, Robert. *Hard Bargain.* New York: Scribner, 1995.

Shotwell, James T. *The Great Decision.* New York: Macmillan, 1944.

———. *The Autobiography of James T. Shotwell.* Indianapolis: Bobbs-Merrill, 1961.

———. *On the Rim of the Abyss.* New York: Macmillan, 1936; reprint, New York: Garland, 1972.

Smith, Gaddis. *American Diplomacy during the Second World War, 1941–1945.* New York: John Wiley and Sons, 1965.

Smith, Gene. *When the Cheering Stopped: The Last Years of Woodrow Wilson.* New York: Time, 1964.

Spykman, Nicholas J. *America's Strategy in World Politics.* New York: Harcourt Brace, 1942.

Steel, Ronald. *Walter Lippmann and the American Century.* Boston: Little, Brown, 1980.

Steigerwald, David. *Wilsonian Idealism.* Ithaca: Cornell University Press, 1994.

Stettinius, Edward R., Jr. *Lend-Lease: Weapon for Victory.* New York: Macmillan, 1944.

———. *Roosevelt and the Russians: The Yalta Conference,* ed. Walter Johnson. Garden City, N.Y.: Doubleday, 1949.

———. Papers. University of Virginia, Manuscript Department, Alderman Library, Charlottesville, Va.

Stimson, Henry, and McGeorge Bundy. *On Active Service in Peace and War.* New York: Harper & Brothers, 1947–48.

Streit, Clarence. *Union Now.* New York: Harper & Brothers, 1939.

Thomas, Hugh. *The Spanish Civil War.* New York: Viking Press, 1961.

Tompkins, C. David. *Senator Arthur H. Vandenberg: The Evolution of a Modern Republican, 1884–1945.* Lansing: Michigan State University Press, 1970.

Truman, Harry S. *Memoirs: Year of Decision.* Garden City, N.Y.: Doubleday, 1955.

Tuchman, Barbara. *Stilwell and the American Experience in China, 1911–1945.* New York: Macmillan, 1971.

Tumulty, J. *Woodrow Wilson As I Knew Him.* New York: Doubleday, Page, 1921.

U.S. Department of State. *Bulletin.*

———. *Papers Relating to the Foreign Relations of the United States. The Conferences at Washington, 1941–1942, and Casablanca, 1943.* Washington, D.C.: GPO, 1970.

———. *The Conferences at Washington and Quebec, 1943.* Washington, D.C.: GPO, 1970.

———. *The Conferences at Cairo and Teheran, 1943.* Washington, D.C.: GPO, 1961.

———. *Annual Volumes, 1941–1946,* Washington, D.C.: GPO, 1958–70.

————. *The Conference of Quebec, 1944.* 2 vols. Washington, D.C.: GPO, 1960.

————. *The Conferences of Malta and Yalta, 1945.* Washington, D.C.: GPO, 1955.

————. *The United Nations Conference on International Organization, San Francisco, April 25 to June 26, 1945. Selected Documents.* Washington, D.C.: GPO, 1946.

Urquart, Brian. *Hammarskjöld.* New York: Knopf, 1972.

Utley, Jonathan. *Going to War with Japan, 1937–1941.* Knoxville: University of Tennessee Press, 1985.

Vandenberg, Arthur H., Jr., ed. *The Private Papers of Senator Vandenberg.* Boston: Houghton Mifflin, 1952.

Walker, J. Samuel. *Henry A. Wallace and American Foreign Policy.* Westport, Conn.: Greenwood, 1976.

Walker, Richard L. *E. R. Stettinius, Jr.* Vol. 14 in *The American Secretaries of State and Their Diplomacy,* ed. Robert Ferrell. New York: Cooper Square, 1965.

Walton, Richard J. *Henry Wallace, Harry Truman and the Cold War.* New York: Viking Press, 1976.

Ward, Geoffrey C. *A First-Class Temperament: The Emergence of Franklin Roosevelt.* New York: Harper & Row, 1989.

Watson, Edward. Papers. University of Virginia, Manuscript Department, Alderman Library, Charlottesville, Va.

Welles, Benjamin. Private Papers. Washington, D.C.

Welles, Benjamin. "Sumner Welles." Unpublished manuscript.

Welles, Sumner. *The World of the Four Freedoms.* New York: Harper & Brothers, 1943.

————. *The Time for Decision.* New York: Harper & Brothers, 1944.

————. *Where Are We Heading?* New York: Harper & Brothers, 1946.

————. *We Need Not Fail.* Boston: Houghton Mifflin, 1948.

————. *Seven Decisions That Shaped History.* New York: Harper & Brothers, 1951.

————. "The Shaping of Our Future." *Reader's Digest* 44 (July 1944), pp. 41–44.

————. File. War Branch History, Record Group 59, National Archives, Washington, D.C.

Widenor, William C. *Henry Cabot Lodge and the Search for an American Foreign Policy.* Berkeley: University of California Press, 1979.

————. "American Planning for the United Nations: Have We Been Asking the Right Questions?" *Diplomatic History* 6 (1982), pp. 245–65.

Willkie, Wendell L. *One World.* In Wendell Willkie et al., *Prefaces to Peace.* New York: Simon & Schuster, 1943.

Wilson, Edith Bolling Galt. *My Memoir.* Indianapolis: Bobbs-Merrill, 1938.

Wilson, Theodore A. *The First Summit: Roosevelt and Churchill at Placentia Bay, 1941.* Rev. ed. Lawrence: University Press of Kansas, 1991.

Woods, Randall Bennett. *Fulbright: A Biography.* Cambridge: Cambridge University Press, 1995.

————. "FDR and the Triumph of American Nationalism." *Presidential Studies Quarterly* 19 (1989), pp. 567–81.

————. *A Changing of the Guard: Multilateralism and Internationalism in Anglo-American Relations, 1941–1946.* Chapel Hill: University of North Carolina Press, 1990.

Zacher, Mark W. *Dag Hammarskjöld's United Nations.* New York: Columbia University Press, 1970.

Index